WIN
YOUR CASE

WIN
YOUR CASE

How to Present, Persuade, Prevail—
Every Place, Every Time

GERRY SPENCE

St. Martin's Press ❧ New York

www.stmartins.com

Library of Congress Cataloging-in-Publication Data

Spence, Gerry.
 Win your case : how to present, persuade, and prevail—every place, every time / Gerry Spence—1st ed.
    p. cm.
  ISBN 0-312-33881-3
  EAN 978-0-312-33881-7
  1. Persuasion (Psychology) I. Title.

  BF637.P4S67 2005
  153.8'52—dc22   2005040704

First Edition: June 2005

10 9 8 7 6 5 4 3 2 1

This book is dedicated to our grandchildren:

Tara Spence
Lana Spence
Margana Suendermann
Dawa P. Doma Sherpa
Charlie Hawks
Rio Suendermann
Ariella Spence
Cade Hawks
Henry Hawks
Dylan Spence
Emma Hawks
Ulises Spence
Senia Spence

and

To my great and loyal partner, Edward Moriarity, who with skill and wisdom fought side by side with me in many a winning courtroom war.

Contents

CONTENTS

WIN
YOUR CASE

WHO NEEDS THIS BOOK?

ARE YOU A TRIAL LAWYER **and losing too often?** Consider the possibility that it's not the jury system, or a bad judge, or a witness that turned on you. Maybe you need to take a new look at what you're doing both in and out of the courtroom. Isn't there a better way to deal with jurors, with judges, and yes, with yourself? What you've been doing may have worked once, but it's not working now. There might be something in these pages that will help. This book may save your bacon.

Going to court? You should give your lawyer this book. Is your lawyer representing you before a jury or a judge at his full, exploding capacity? Or is your lawyer making his presentation in the old, ineffective ways of most trial lawyers—his brittle, intellectual, nonfeeling, unemotional, passionless, stiff enunciations burdened with those big words? Is he conducting a distant, hostile examination of jurors and witnesses that make him look good but leave him distrusted by the jury? Worse, is he putting on a show that even you know doesn't come from his heart? Your lawyer should read this book.

Are you preparing to make a presentment to the board or your boss? You'd better read this book. A principle theme of this work is that the techniques of a trial in court are as much a part of the presentation of your case before boards and bosses as the genes of the primates are a part of us. The means and methods and mental sets I teach in presenting a case in court are often parallel to those that should be employed in presenting a case to a board, a boss, a commission, or a customer. I've discovered in over fifty years in the courtroom that the most effective presentments out of court take on the format of a winning trial in the courtroom. You don't have to be a trial lawyer to learn these methods. But you do need to acquire a winning state of mind, an approach that opens up both you and the decision maker to your presentation. If it's time for you to present your cause to a *power person*, the decision maker, this book will show you how.

WHERE I'M COMING FROM

IT'S WAR OUT THERE—plain and simple war. In times past the species battled for their territory with axes and spears. The same genes are at work today. The trial lawyer in the courtroom is a warrior. The executive battling in the trenches of business is at war. The salesman approaching the reluctant customer must conquer. The teacher, the worker, the administrator, the citizen before the city counsel, all seeking something, perhaps wanting change, perhaps simply seeking recognition, are engaged in a war.

It's a war over ideas. Ideas are the territory possessed by the *power person*—the decision maker. Ideas have power. In the courtroom the idea of the prosecutor is to put the accused behind bars—even to execute him. The civil trial lawyer has the idea that money and justice are equivalents, and to compensate his client's injury he wants money. Jurors are the *power persons*—the decision makers. The executive has an idea that will forward the profit of his company. The *power person* may be a governmental regulatory agency, a board of directors, or the stockholders at large. The teacher or worker or citizen may seek change, but the *power person*—the school principal, the boss, or the city council—always stands in the way. Their position, their viewpoint, their possession of whatever is sought from them is their territory. And this war is over that turf, the turf the *power person* possesses. This book is about how to win that war.

The history of man is the history of war. In the first trials, trial by duel, the winner supposedly occupied the side of right since the winner was said to have been chosen by divine powers. Such trials by physical combat were a means to settle disputes between the king's subjects short of war. And the place where these domestic conflicts were settled was a room set aside by the king in the king's court called a courtroom.

In the courtroom of old the contestants fought to submission or death. Each side engaged a champion to fight for them. The king or his lords were able to field the most fearsome mercenaries of all, and those who contested these *power persons* rarely prevailed. As civilization advanced, the warriors in the king's court were replaced by advocates for each side. Today they are known as trial lawyers. But the same historical paradigm is still in place. Trial lawyers fight to submission with words, not swords. And in and out of business lay persons fight a never-ending battle for the territory of ideas, for whether it's a sale one seeks to close or a promotion one longs for, whether it's a contest at the school board or a fight before a board of directors, all are wars in which the territory to be conquered is one of ideas—ideas that win.

Trial lawyers and lay persons have much in common. The methods of trial work are so similar to the best and most successful out-of-court presentations that I ask you to read and take in the whole of this book as if you were a trial lawyer yourself. If you can begin to master what I am teaching here for trial lawyers you will have absorbed the necessary stuff for winning, not only in your out-of-court endeavors, but perhaps in life itself.

For more than fifty years I've fought these many wars for both the powerful and the poor in the courtrooms of this country. Although there are many skillful advocates at work in the law, I am convinced that most lawyers don't know how to try a case. They were never taught in law school. They were never taught because their teachers, for the most part, have been those academic drones who've never experienced a client clinging to him like a drowning person in deep water whose life depends upon the lawyer's skill to convince a jury.

For over ten years I've conducted the nonprofit, pro bono Trial Lawyer's College that I established at my ranch near Dubois, Wyoming, a school devoted to the training of lawyers for the people. We've conducted many sessions and seminars throughout the nation. We count thousands of graduates across the land who've learned our methods, methods which have magically transformed ordinary, yeoman, struggling trial lawyers, men and women who were afraid of the courtroom and who lost more than they won, into powerful advocates with skills they never dreamed they could possess.

At Trial Lawyer's College we teach a presentation that begins with the self, with a knowledge of who we are and an understanding that we are unique, incomparable, and therefore, in that way, perfect. The humble, frightened, shy men and women, young and old, accepting themselves and understanding their uniqueness, learn the power of being genuine, including the power of their fear, their inexperience, their less-than-fashion-magazine appearance, and their ordinary, nontheatrical voices. They learn to imitate no one. We find ourselves at the cutting edge of trial technique. We've broken free of the standard approach to the trial of cases, which is most often stultifying, false, unmoving, bereft of honest human emotion, too full of tricks and technique, and too often a waste of the court's and litigants' time and resources.

The approach we teach is so simple it is sometimes difficult for lawyers, locked in their left brain lobes, to understand. Our method begins with the self. It demands that we tell the truth, even when it is painful. The method is based on the story and the storyteller. It shuns the deadly intellectual, artificial and pretentious. It focuses instead on the spontaneous, and on crawling inside the hide of our adversaries so that we understand them as well as we understand ourselves. It emphasizes the inimitable power of caring and deemphasizes the use of force and intimidation as a means of persuasion.

Almost without exception, our students, trial lawyers of all ages, with varying abilities and experience, have discovered a magical new power that has brought them unimagined victories in the courtroom. It is this new approach to winning in the courtroom that I explain and teach in this book, not only to trial lawyers, but to the out-of-court presenters who will discover that they can make their case and win every time—in the courtroom, the boardroom, the marketplace, and the workplace, indeed, every place.

Gerry Spence
Jackson Hole, Wyoming

Part One

GATHERING THE POWER TO WIN

(Preparing Ourselves for War)

1. THE POWER OF DISCOVERING THE SELF

THE WISDOM OF UNCLE SLIM. Uncle Slim, my father's oldest brother, was a cowboy. Grandpa Spence said he was the smartest of his three sons. Uncle Slim was the kind of a man who thought that if it couldn't be done from the back of a horse it wasn't worth doing at all. He had those thin bowed legs that looked like they'd been molded around a barrel, and he wore an old Stetson that came together with four finger creases at the peak. A leather tong that extended from the hat's crown, down to the back of his head, and up again on the other side, held his hat against the wind—not that string dudes wear tied around their chins. His face below the hat line was ruddy and his hide tough, and above his hat line his skin was white and his hair thin. Both summer and winter he wore long cotton underwear buttoned up high. Claimed he wore it in the winter against the cold and in the summer as insulation against the heat. The one thing he valued most of all was a good horse.

One day I was standing at the corral with Uncle Slim. He was leaning on the top rail and laughing his high-pitched laugh that sounded like the end note of a bull elk's bugle.

"Look at that dude over there trying ta saddle his horse. And look at that saddle. It's one of them thousand-dollar kind." It was a pretty thing—shiny black leather with silver spangles and silver braid around the cantle. "And look at that nag he's tryin' ta put it on." Then he turned to me and, almost serious, he said, "Ya can't get nowhere with a thousand-dollar saddle on a ten-dollar horse."

Our thousand-dollar saddles. Back then I was a young lawyer living in the town of Riverton, Wyoming, population probably five thousand isolated souls. I'd tried quite a few jury cases—if a case is worth trying it ought to be tried before twelve good citizens—and I thought I knew a lot. I'd been to law school and I'd been the prosecuting attorney in Fremont County for eight years, a county that covered endless prairies and towering mountains, and that included the Wind River Indian Reservation with its tribes of Shoshone and Arapaho Native Americans. The county was nearly as large as some eastern states, with the small cow town of Shoshoni at one end and another small cow town called Dubois at the other. The people were spread out as sparsely as the land itself. You could probably match the county's population in a single block in Chicago or New York. And although I thought I knew how to try a case, what Uncle Slim said got me to thinking. We lawyers were like that dude with the fancy saddle and the old nag. We thought that the saddle was more important than the horse we put it on.

Our education, our experience, and the endless tricks and techniques we've been taught in order to make our sale to the jury, the board, the customer, or the boss have become our saddles. And they are heavy. We attend motivational seminars put on by gurus, training sessions about how to speak, how to organize our presentations, how to supplement them with graphics—and, especially, how to be like the guru. We put the fancy spangles on our saddles by learning the tricks of others, the big boys, the famous ones with those towering reputations who, in the process of telling us how to do it, line their pockets. But after decades of applying these so-called tricks of the trade, we still don't win—not often enough. Something is wrong and we suspect it's something wrong with us, something at the core, something we don't want to look at, think about, or admit. If we could only find the right role model to follow perhaps we too could become a winner.

So we attend more seminars, read more how-to books, and at last, having imitated the best of them, we still come up short. Sometimes the tricks we've learned work. But not often enough. Life's entire potpourri of tricks, techniques, procedures, and processes have become the saddle we've been taught to mount in order to win. That saddle is expensive and covered with glittery stuff. But in the end it doesn't seem to do much good.

But what about the horse? We've never been taught the wisdom of Uncle Slim—*"Ya can't get nowhere with a thousand-dollar saddle on a ten-dollar horse."* Let us call ourselves the presenters, those who face the jury, the board, the boss, and the customer, and try to win our cases. We presenters can absorb all the law the professors can pound into us. We can learn all the courtroom techniques and nifty tricks the big-time lawyers teach; we can be the most intelligent, the cutest, the cleverest, intellectually ambidextrous swashbucklers ever to swagger into a courtroom or a city council meeting, but what if we know nothing about becoming a person? We're the ten-dollar horse.

After fifty years making my presentations in and out of the courtroom I've learned one thing for certain: *It all begins with the person, with who each of us is.* If we have no knowledge of who we are, if we have no insight into the self, if we have never heeded the admonition of the sages—"Know thyself"—we walk before the *power persons* (the jury, the board, the boss, the administrator) as a stranger to the self. And all of the participants at the presentation will remain as strangers to us as well.

If the lawyer is blind to the composition of the self, how can he know anything of the persons who compose the jury? If the executive knows nothing of herself, how can she know anything of her governing board? How can the lawyer know what compels the witnesses' testimony or the judge's rulings? How can the worker know what goes on in the mind of the boss if he has entered that place of war—the boss's office—as only the ten-dollar horse? As Atticus Finch, the fictional lawyer in *To Kill a Mockingbird,* said to his young daughter who had a penchant to do battle with her fists, "You never really understand a person until you consider things from his point of view . . . until you climb into his skin and walk around in it." We cannot understand human conduct without understanding others, and we cannot understand others without first becoming acquainted with ourselves.

Life in the chicken house. It is easier for me to think and teach with metaphors. Uncle Slim's ten-dollar horse is one. Let me engage another—life in the chicken house. Most of us assume we know ourselves. Haven't we lived intimately with this person for all of these years? But we live inside our own self-

11

constructed chicken house, and we've locked the door against our fear of some mythical, marauding coyote that will surely do us in if we throw open the door and venture out. As a consequence we trudge though our lives within those four bleak walls, and over and over bounce against the walls until we have grown used to our self-imposed boundaries.

It's taken a lifetime to build our chicken house. The walls are composed of images of who we are, or the equally inaccurate visuals of ourselves imposed on us by our parents, teachers, and peers. The walls are the defenses we impose against our fear of experiencing the self. We've constructed the walls against the pains of childhood from various forms of injury—the parent who physically or psychologically abused us, or spawned feelings of rejection or abandonment, the teacher who told us we are stupid, that we couldn't draw a tree that looked like a tree, or a bullying brother or the beautiful sister who got all of the attention. Whatever the pain, that tender organism known as the *self* takes on such defenses as are available—denial of the self, a mythological reconstruction of the self, shallow rationalizations that excuse the self, a closure against feeling—and once the walls are constructed we live our lives within them believing we are safely ensconced against harm.

Within the four walls of the chicken house most of us have become walking, talking conglomerations of habits, a monumental psychic pile composed of habitual thoughts and feelings, the same old ideas and beliefs, predictable responses and brittle attitudes, so that if we are encountered once, either by ourselves or others, we need not be experienced again. To know us once is to know us forever. When we say we know ourselves, all we really know are the few square feet of the chicken house and nothing of the endless expanse of the landscape beyond. Yet, I say it is more dangerous to live within those walls than to live free, for the risk of living in the chicken house is that one may never have lived at all.

Escaping the chicken house. Discovering the self. Erich Fromm, the great psychoanalyst, said, "Man's main task in life is to give birth to himself, to become who he potentially is." So how do we discover the self?

The discovery of the self is a lifetime adventure. It begins when we recognize how frightened we are to venture beyond the door. This lifelong business of self-discovery can take many forms. I've experienced counseling and gone the route of the once stylish "encounter sessions." I've been trained as a leader in "sensitivity groups," trained lawyers in the psychodramatic technique, and like a starving child at a smorgasbord, I've read voraciously. I've spent years discussing my loves, my pains, my fears, my guilt, my agonies, and my hang-ups with friends who would listen, especially with my wife, Imaging. I've painted, written poetry, and become a professional photographer because these art forms are roads to secret places in the self that cannot otherwise be visited. I've authored fifteen books, including two novels, mostly to discover what I know and how I feel, and, in the end, to help me identify the self to myself. I've traveled in distant, primitive cultures and talked to every man, woman, child, dog, tree, and posy I thought might possess any insight into this journey called life. I've visited the happy homeless wretches on the streets, the old boy who lives under the bridge, and the recluse who hides out in a hut in the wilderness of Wyoming. Perfectly endowed, we possess all the knowledge necessary to complete this journey. Such knowledge does not come from the guru in the cave, but from the guru within. We are psychic archeologists engaged in an archeological dig of the self.

At Trial Lawyer's College, where we teach lawyers how to win for the ordinary person against mammoth odds—against gigantic government and monstrous corporations—the first days are spent in assisting lawyers to become better acquainted with themselves. They experience themselves in exercises known as psychodrama, a group process that has been described as a play created spontaneously, with neither script nor rehearsal, for the purpose of gaining an understanding of the self that can be achieved only through action. *Psycho-drama*

To know oneself empowers the presenter to crawl inside the hide of the participants in the trial, and such self-knowledge becomes the foundation of his conduct and strategy in every phase of the war he will engage in. If he knows himself, he will best be able to acquire that critical knowledge of those he encounters in the trial or presentation.

What is true for the training of successful trial lawyers is also true for the winning presenter. We all carry with us certain issues that hang us up like old laundry on a sagging clothes line. Some is deep, furtive stuff that we've so thoroughly tromped down that we've transformed ourselves into disadvantaged persons with crippled psyches, no longer free to run and jump and dance and create.

We can begin breaking out of the chicken house in many ways. At Trial

Lawyer's College we require the participants to get up one morning before sunrise. They're instructed to go out into the wilderness that surrounds the ranch where we conduct the school and to find a place in sight of no one, a place that becomes their place. Then in their solitude, as they await the sun to come bursting over the mountain, they are to ask themselves two simple questions: "Who am I, and what am I going to do with the rest of my life?" Several hours later they come down for breakfast, but they remain silent until they meet in the barn and share with each other what they've discovered about themselves.

The silence and aloneness, the total focus on the self, is the magic. And it's available to all of us, whether we're driving to work in our cars or sitting in an afternoon under a fir tree in the park. How can we hear the quiet inner voice of the self over the blare of TV, the mindless jabbering of the car radio, the beat and blast of the workplace, and the shouting demons of fear and frustration that howl constantly at our eardrums?

When one asks the self, "Who am I?" something powerful and lasting will be revealed as if the mirror of the universe is at work. One woman said her experience was like taking off a hard-boiled eggshell. "I never knew the softness inside." Another said, "I'm screwed up. But if I weren't, I wouldn't be able to feel the pain of others. My scars are beautiful." Still another said, "I met someone I'd never known before and I think I'm going to like him, namely me." Strange, I thought, how such simple life-giving experiences are denied us—by us.

The opportunity to discover the self—to experience life while we are alive, as opposed to dying before we are dead—includes every aspect of discovery and creativity. To the casual observer it must seem patently ridiculous for lawyers at a trial lawyer's college to be painting—something they have not done since grade school. Equally unrelated to the image of the powerful courtroom advocate is the lawyer standing on a table before his fellow students, embarrassed, not carrying a tune very well, but singing a solo, his favorite song, from the heart. Grizzled veteran lawyers find themselves writing poetry and sharing it unabashedly with their fellow students. Such exercises are available to all of us. No patent or copyright protects their use. By learning to listen to ourselves, to fearlessly experience ourselves, we learn to listen to and discover others.

The scope of this book is not to teach us how to know ourselves. Such is not a teachable skill. There are no "How to Know Thyself" courses offered in college. Self-knowledge always remains a work in progress, a different one for each of us, one that reveals a changing landscape as we travel through our lives.

To grab another metaphor: I think of my life as a trip down the river in a canoe. I am on the river. I can't get off. I must take each day's trip one day at a time. There can be no plan, for how can one plan when there is no map and the river is always changing? My furious paddling in the river seems foolish. It doesn't alter the course of the river. Yet paddling is my work. I am engaged with the river. The river and I are together in this thing, whatever it is, and, in that way, the river and I are the same, for neither of us can stop the flow. At last, I do not wish to stop it. I wish only to take the trip with a sharp awareness, with a deep gratitude, and a raw joy that I have the chance.

My own struggle to discover the self. Because I have preached to you about self-discovery I should not present myself as above the fray. As I will later argue, credibility is the key to winning. One cannot be credible without first being honest about the self. If I ask you to accept my teachings, it seems appropriate that you know something of the teacher, and that the teacher is willing to be as open with you as he will ask you to be with others when you present your case.

I was born of an extremely religious mother who found God in church and a father who found God at the end of a fishing rod or a hunting rifle. I grew up in the mountains of Wyoming and was in all ways exposed to the church God, as my mother saw him, and to the nature God as my father saw him. In the depression era I enjoyed a poor but protected childhood. As I grew into adolescence I was a pimple-faced kid who wanted badly to be accepted by his peers and who always tried too hard. I had little going for me—no great looks, no family with a social position, no money, no car, no sports letter to wear on my sweater, and I wasn't a particularly brainy child either. When I entered college I longed to join a fraternity, because in those unenlightened days, any boy who was anything at all pledged to a fraternity. I was never so much as invited for a look by a single house on campus. And how, pray tell, could I ever make it with a girl if I didn't have a frat pin to pin on her pretty sweater? Besides, I was working on the railroad to put myself though school and I often came to class covered with soot from the old coal-burning engines and looked more like a black-faced minstrel than a potential frat boy who would bring honor and glory to the brotherhood. In short, I was a nothing. Today those feelings still squirm around at my core like worms in the soul, and they frequently come popping out in ways that cause me to be shy in groups, or sometimes to annoyingly overplay my hand.

As a young person the overriding question for me was how could a nobody ever become a somebody? I didn't do particularly well in high school, nor did I in my first years in college. Then, at nineteen, I got married—after a startling, bedazzling revelation, that someone could actually *love me*.

At twenty, in my first year in law school, my angel mother killed herself.

My uncle found her body in a shallow ditch in my grandfather's orchard, the barrel of my father's hunting rifle in her mouth. As a staunch Christian woman, she was devastated by my behavior as I entered adolescence and early manhood. A boy who drank and smoked and cursed and fornicated was destined for hell. And I thought that this angel mother, who never spoke unkindly about anyone and who had promised her first son, me, to God, must have killed herself out of her agony over my sins, which were plentiful and which I had made little effort to hide.

My resulting guilt was consuming. The pain of it was so devastating I found it difficult to cope in any reasonable fashion, and it took me thirty years of self-torture, of striking out in impotent rage at the world, at all who lived and died, and against all of my mother's teachings, before I could begin to manage my anger, my guilt, my pain, and, at last, my utter confusion about who I was.

Yet her suicide became a strange sort of gift to me. She had always given me all that she was able to give. But her death compelled me to begin untangling the hidden psychic mess I had tried so valiantly to ignore. I had no choice. I had to discover who this person I called Gerry Spence was—and to understand who my mother was. I have written and spoken of this agony many times and wept from the pain of it on countless occasions. I have been tormented endlessly over her death and over my resulting guilt. I have incessantly asked that question: Who am I? And as soon as I found the answers—or thought I had—I forgot them, only to endure the pain-racked learning process all over again.

But one day I was able to step into the shoes of my mother and learn that her death had something to do with who *she* was. I learned that my guilt emerged from an infantile belief that the worlds—hers, mine, and everyone else's—were somehow attached at their centers to me. She killed herself because of her own issues, real or misperceived by her, and she dealt with them in response to the psychic demons that haunted her and frightened her and pained her—to death. As I learned to stand in the shoes of my mother I learned much about her that I had never realized before. She had her own life, her own set of horrors, her own dread, her own guilt, and her own pain. She was who she was. I had to love her, understand her pain, and accept her for who she was. And most of all, I had to learn to live my life on my own terms without carrying the unmanageable burden of blame for her death, which at last I realized did not belong to me.

The gift that my mother gave me was to force me out of the chicken house, to dig into my own reservoir, and to begin a lifetime journey toward self-discovery. Her gift permitted me, although imperfectly, and certainly with many relapses, to live a life both in and out of the courtroom that has been much richer, much more fulfilling and insightful, a life that has been mostly responsible for whatever successes I have enjoyed in the trial of cases on behalf of those who have been injured more than I.

Her gift gave me a better ability to crawl into the hide of others, my clients, the witnesses, the jurors, the judge, and to try to understand them. It gave me a power in the courtroom that I would not have enjoyed but for her gift. I have often told my lawyer students and all others who will listen, that we do not grow much from joy and pleasure, and we do not learn much from winning. We grow and bloom from our pain and from the lessons of the self that we learn from our pain.

I don't mean to say, of course, that before you can become a successful presenter you must suffer the suicide of a parent or some other such psychic wreckage. But most of us have experienced personal pain of one kind or another. We have felt rejected, unloved, put aside, or dominated. We have had parents who have been distant and cold, or cruel and abusive. We have encountered our own problems with drugs or alcohol, or we have suffered physical injury. Whatever the pain, we have defended against it—often in inappropriate ways.

Humans, like the simplest organism, take whatever steps that may be available to avoid pain. Sometimes we deny its existence, bury it. The purpose here is not to set out some easy panacea for mental health. I am merely suggesting that to become aware, to become open to ourselves is the first step toward becoming a person and learning how, in the end, to become open to others. It is that magic that begins to build the powerful horse we need to win.

As important as it is to understand ourselves, ought we not learn something of the person who has been at the other end of our pain? We have not become this person we call the *self* in a vacuum. If we could better understand the abuse of a drunken father—not excuse him but understand him—if we could see that he fought his own psychic devils that took the form, say, of his own abusive parent, would we not be better able to realize that the pain we suffered as a child at his hands had little to do with us and much to do with him? Might we not grow more from such understanding than from our anger, from even our hatred that may have become a part of our functional personality? The mirror is always at work. By understanding the other we will, in the end, better understand ourselves, and by understanding ourselves we will be able to more accurately understand those we encounter in this world of war.

2. THE INDOMITABLE POWER OF OUR UNIQUENESS

J OINING THE GREAT CHURCH OF UNIFORMITY. I've tried to impress on the unimpressionable that the power of each individual is in his or her uniqueness. When our uniqueness is fully discovered and launched, we are indomitable. But we have no ears for simple truths. Instead we worship in the Church of Uniformity into which, from our earliest days, we were herded by our parents and peers. Over a lifetime we've become indoctrinated with the idea that sameness is blessed. We aspire to become like the role models dangled before us—Barbie dolls for little girls and, after they travel beyond puberty, the anorexic models of the glamor magazines. The Ralph Lauren Polo emblem adorns our jockey shorts, and we must lug Louis Vuitton luggage, even though its design is as artistically defunct as gravel.

Ours is a society that demands sameness. We are transformed into uniform products that consume uniform products; our craving for sameness is essential to keep the social machine running. In high school and college we are educated in order to convert our unique beauty into spare parts for the system—the massive machine out there needs administrators, engineers, accountants, designers, computer experts, workers, and lawyers. Like all spare parts we must be uniform in order to fit smoothly into the machine without any disruption when an old part gives out.

Television tells us what makes us happy and what our goals in life should

American Psycho

be—especially how we should spend our money. This voice, the voice of power, tells us who we should hate and for what causes our children should die. In passing, we lose even a vague suspicion of our own uniqueness. Most people I know (although they vehemently deny it) want to be like others—to fit in. They want to talk the current lingo, walk in hip shoes, belong to the right clubs, play golf, and drive a BMW. They want to know the up-there people, say the smart things at those deadly stand-up cocktail parties, smile when they should, and say nothing that could possibly be interpreted as antisocial, and, God forbid, mutter not a word that contradicts conventional wisdom. They want to be politically correct and socially acceptable, despite the fact that to do so they may trade that which is right for that which is convenient, painless, and mindless. In short, too many of us have given up the perfect self to become a phony imitation of others.

Conformity in our looks (our fifty-dollar haircuts and two-hundred-dollar sunglasses), our dress (the latest designer "worn out" jeans), our thought (patriotism is supporting our nation's latest war), and our values (money above all others) have become the standards set for us by those in power. We demand to be like others and discount ourselves when we fail. If we are seen as different we become alarmed and our viscera begin to cramp. Will we be rejected as "strange" or "weird"? Being different is an abysmal appellation, so some pierce their tongues, their navels, their ears, and whatever else, in order to become the same in their difference. We wish the protection of our kind just as zebras appear safer within the herd because they all wear the same black-and-white stripes.

There are innumerable ways to murder a person, but the most subtle and pernicious of these is to mutilate the soul of the innocent by denying or downgrading their uniqueness and their beauty. That crime was long ago committed against most of us when we were too young to defend ourselves against the cruel assaults leveled against us in the name of the proper rearing of children.

From the beginning we've been compared to each other. We compete for grades, for places on the football team, or for a part in the school play. We are tested throughout our school experience and rated against national averages in order to enter college. Law schools administer the LSAT, and if we do not measure up we are cast out.

As taught by tyrannical political correctness, we strive to disavow our prejudices, even though they cast their murky shadows on our souls. In accordance with its commands we wave the flag along with the mob of flag wavers, despite the fact that we're not sure the actions of our country are just. The plague of sameness has stricken us all so that we dare not walk out our front doors without checking to see that we will be accepted into the bleating herd.

The lesson of the thumbs. I say look at your thumbs. Do you see that they have a print, one that is different from any other thumbprint in the world, different from any print of any human being who has ever walked the face of this earth and distinct from any print of any who will ever grace this earth again? Your thumbprint is utterly individual to you. Why, then, can't we understand that our very essence as persons, let us say our souls, is also unique among all other living human beings and among all those who shall ever in the future take a breath?

One of my great joys is to discover the differences I see in myself as well as the differences I observe in every other human being I encounter. Although we are the same in countless ways, we are, nevertheless, as different from one another as diamonds from rubies, which makes each stone unique, beautiful, and valuable. Since we are not the same, since each of us is different from all others, we cannot be compared, and therefore each of us is perfect.

We can become the person of our dreams only when we recognize that our uniqueness is the most powerful asset we can envision and that the dream must be of our perfect selves. Our blessed differences come popping out of our DNA crying to be recognized and appreciated. Our uniqueness is the greatest gift of our creation. But by the time we are ready to assert ourselves on the world, our beauty has been mostly drowned in the baptismal waters into which the Church of Uniformity has immersed us. *What happens when is it w/ clients?*

I am saddened when I see lawyers try to imitate other lawyers. To try to be like someone else is like taking a perfect pearl to a pawn broker with the thought of trading it for a phony replica of the Hope Diamond. This is the very motive behind celebrity endorsements of today's widely advertised products. When Michael Jordan embraces Nike shoes, Nike is saying, "Maybe you can be a little bit like Michael Jordan if you will plunk down a couple of bills to buy our shoes." I have tried to avoid joining the masses of the walking dead who, attempting to be alive, imitate each other and in the process give up their own lives.

A person's power in the courtroom or the boardroom, and a salesperson's ability to make the sale, emerges from his or her uniqueness. The storming orator can be vanquished easily by one who stands before the decision maker and is wholly himself. The other day I sat observing a lawyer in court. He was smallish, with a potbelly and a bald head, that little rim of hair around the sides cut so short that his large ears looked like saucers. His feet pointed out like a duck's. He wore glasses that balanced precariously on a bulbous nose. He blinked a lot when he talked, and his voice was diminutive and scratchy. Yet there was a power in his presence. Despite the fact that he seemed timid and stiff, he also seemed satisfied with who he was and unaware of what most would consider his glaring deficits. One soon forgot that he didn't look like he'd just jumped out of *GQ*. His clothes were ill-fitting and cheap. But the lawyer's presence and style threatened no one on the jury or in the courtroom, and he was obviously and genuinely intransigent in his belief that his cause was just.

I began to admire this little man's courage. Once in a while a small amount of humor, mostly a distant chuckle at himself, would slip out. His vulnerability was palpable. I began to like him very much, to pull for him; and I saw how unique he was, this man with the big heart and the unself-conscious smile and an attractiveness that no movie star could have matched. Of course, he won his case.

After the trial I talked with him. He was representing a parent who had wrongfully been accused of child abuse, and as he talked the tears returned to his eyes. He fought them back.

"The worst thing that can happen to a father is to be charged with hurting his child when he's innocent. Innocent!" he said again. The tears returned. He was talking to me, not the jury.

"You have a lot of power," I said.

He looked at me, surprised. "Power?" He seemed so fragile.

"Yes," I said. "It comes out of caring. Caring is contagious," as I have said so often. "And it comes out of something else. I think you appreciate who you are."

He gave me a quizzical look. Then he nodded and said, "I'm all I got. And it's enough." He couldn't have asked for more.

Vision, the magical door. If I could give one gift to each of you, it would be a vision of what you might become if only your unique self could be fully discovered and appreciated. I was given that gift by my parents and by certain sainted teachers. But the vision can be destroyed, smashed by one careless statement. Our psyches are fragile things and need to be cared for with great tenderness. I remember Velma Linford, my speech teacher in high school, telling me I had a beautiful voice, when she must have been observing her own vision of what that screechy, adolescent voice might one day become. But I adopted her vision, and later took voice lessons and considered the possibility of becoming an opera singer.

Judge Franklin B. Sheldon, who used to skin me alive from the bench when I was a beginning lawyer, once took me into chambers and said, "Someday you'll become a great trial lawyer." He had his own vision of how this fumbling, frightened beginner might develop, and he shared it with me.

I also remember a certain judge who, during his critique of my law school mock trial, told me, "You'll never become a trial lawyer, Mr. Spence. You just as well give that up right now and look for something more attuned to your talents—examining real estate abstracts or something like that." For a long time his cruel assessment haunted me, for, young or old, we are prone to cultivate as our own the visions that others plant in us.

But the visions my parents shared with me as a child survived, and later so did those of my wife, Imaging. I could do anything that I set my mind to. I'd decided to become a successful trial lawyer. Later, my literary agent, Peter Lampack, shared his vision with me concerning my writing. He thought that down the line I might become a successful author. I have been blessed with the kindness and vision of caring people. And as for that crusty old judge who cast me into the gloomy pits—I knew him. He had never been of much account in the courtroom himself and was eager to withhold the possibility of success from anyone else. Those kind often sit in high authority, but sodden in low self-esteem, and are secretly elated when those around them fail.

I think of the woman who had a three-year-old child named Betsy. The child was born blind. The woman was of a well-known religious order. She said, "You know, children are born with original sin. They don't know the difference between right and wrong. I have a belt in the closet I use on Betsy for that purpose." The mother, not the child, was blind. And the original sin was not Betsy's. That kind of parent is a danger to the human race. They're destroyers of visions. Visions, especially a child's vision, have the power to magically change the child, to pull up the blinds and throw open the door to the wonderful possibilities that life offers each of us.

Whether or not we've been gifted with splendid visions from others, we are, at last, caretakers of our own visions. One day I heard a lawyer say, "I am annoyed when I look at myself." After he had spent some days at Trial Lawyer's College, I heard the same lawyer speak of a new hope. "I'm a coward," he said. "But I'm finding the courage to be myself." To throw off old, wrongly transplanted ideas of the self and begin to search for the unique, perfect self does require courage. But it's a courage we all possess.

In my case, I knew no lawyers to emulate, not in the small, wayside town of Riverton, Wyoming, a hundred miles from nowhere. I had to manufacture my own vision of what a lawyer should be. I thought for a while he should talk like Franklin D. Roosevelt, but that didn't work very well in Wyoming. Somehow, over the years I've learned that the perfect vision of the self *is* the self, an ever-changing vision as I grew, one that I've been struggling to achieve for more than these seven and a half decades. And I suggest to you that your best vision, too, is the incomparable, inimitable, genuine you.

So, we are about to enter the courtroom or the office of, say, the customer. We will take into that place the most powerful person there. This person has no great, spreading-oak-tree biceps, nor the glamor of the current ga-ga girl of films. We will bring in the real person—the one with whom we've become acquainted—the one with all the warts, the fears, the humbleness of a genuine person, the caring person emitting the shining light of credibility. We will bring in a person who tells the truth even when the truth seems hurtful. We, the genuine person who has shaken off all of the pretenses, all the efforts to become like someone else, who has begun the long road to self-discovery, will be unconquerable because the power *is* in our uniqueness. Such a person is believed because, at last, a genuine person is believable.

3. THE MAGICAL POWER OF FEELING

OST OF US WALK INTO the battlefield pushing a huge wheelbarrow in front of us that bears a gigantic talking head—ours. Our feelings are crushed beneath the load of a noisy brain. As has become pathological in these times, our ability to feel has been supplanted by that tyrant called the intellect. We think. We do not feel. From the time we were children our left brain has become so completely dominant and our native feelings so rejected that we can no longer call upon them to reveal the truth, for the truth is most often a feeling.

Murdering the self. We were born with a complete set of perfect feelings. Instinctively we knew how to cry when we were hurt, to shout when we were angry, to run when we were afraid, to jump with joy, and to feel love. By the time we entered the war zone of adulthood we lost our greatest of all gifts, the ability to feel. Along the road of life we've been shamed about our feelings and taught to bind them up like the feet of the little Chinese girls of old so that, as fully functional human beings, we end up as crippled as they. We've been taught that feelings are for the weak; that real men shouldn't cry; that feelings are something to be carefully avoided lest we be cast into some tear-filled pit where we can no longer make rational decisions, a place where one loses control and one's personal demons come suddenly screaming out; that the "touchy-feely" person is to be regarded as someone maudlin and mushy; that crying is for the simpering sentimental, and those who yield to it are certainly not to be trusted, that fear is for cowards, and that the expression of true anger is for the uncool.

We are the products of a system that shuns feelings like we avoid a crazy cousin in church. Many of us have lost track of our feelings. Even our attempt at credibility is based on intellectual offerings of one kind or another. We've become so accustomed to thinking, to the abstract, to the intellectual expression of every experience, that we cannot connect with what once made us attractive, credible persons—our feelings. Dostoyevsky, the great Russian writer, said, "The opposite of hate is not love—it is the relentless pursuit of the rational mind." In the end, to murder one's feelings is to murder the self.

Take a child as our role model—as we should. Children say things like, "I'm scared," or "I don't like this," or "I'm tired," or they cry when they see a dead bird on the pavement, or jump up and down with joy at the thought of going to the zoo. They come leaping up on our laps and hug us in spontaneous expressions of love. We say they are innocent. I say they are honest. And they are credible. We believe them and respect them because they are innocent, which is another way of saying they have not yet learned that their feelings are to be disregarded, distrusted, and disdained.

Not long ago I was conducting a trial lawyer's seminar in which the issue of racism came up, as it often does and should. I asked the lawyer to reverse roles with the African American in the exercise, to become the black defendant charged with a murder in an all-white court. "How does it feel to be in his shoes?" I asked.

The lawyer was silent for a long time as if to sort through a tangled spaghetti of thoughts. Finally he said, "I think that they might be prejudiced."

"Thinking is not a feeling," I said. "How does it *feel* to be in his shoes?"

He thought some more. "Well, I think I might not be able to trust them."

"Perhaps not," I said. "But how does it *feel* for you to be in his shoes?"

"I told you," he said.

"Thinking is not *feeling*," I said again.

He looked at me as if he were confounded. What was I asking of him? He had gone to the storeroom of his mind and brought up everything he could *think* of.

"Do you *feel* afraid?" I asked.

He was silent.

"Do you *feel* angry at such a jury—at these white folks who, because you are black, perhaps won't be fair, and who, because you are black, may even hate you, even if you're innocent?"

"I suppose so," he said.

"Maybe you want to run because you *feel* fear?"

"I don't know," he said. "If I ran I think they'd believe I was guilty."

"Yes, that's what you *think,* all right. But if you could *feel* your fear, perhaps then you could explain to the jury how it is for your client to sit there alone, the only black person in the courtroom where his life is at stake."

He didn't answer.

I was asking him to enter into a strange world of feeling, where his only refuge was the thinking mind. I say that learning to feel again is more powerful than all of the body building the strong men of our culture can accomplish.

The most powerful person in the courtroom is the vulnerable person, the lawyer who is aware of his feelings and can share them honestly with the jurors. By learning that it's all right to feel love, to be afraid, to feel helpless and alone, we also learn that these feelings abound in those around us. In the courtroom or the boardroom, in council chambers or the boss's office we begin to understand that *power persons,* too, have feelings the same as we. And we realize that if we cannot feel, if we know little of ourselves, we have a minimal credibility to offer anyone else.

Feelings and trust. So, how do I get you to trust me? The answer is simple: I have to be trustworthy. I cannot be a clever sneak. I cannot be a word shark. I cannot lie to you. I cannot hide. I cannot evade. I must be open. I must tell you who I am. I have to pull open the chest cavity and let you see the pounding heart. I have to let you see the source of my tears. I have to let you see the joy and the frustration. I have to let you see my fears. I have to let you see who I am if I expect you to trust me. To be trustworthy is to be real.

Feelings and justice. Think what we lawyers learned in our respective schools—those dreary places populated with hairy-browed old drones who ceaselessly blew their dry, pedantic winds on us until we withered like pansies in the desert. How many times we were admonished to never get emotionally involved over our clients' cases, that we must hold back, yes, smother, trounce, destroy, deny, obliterate, shred, stamp down, and dispose of our feelings lest we perish in their fire. What a colossal imbecility! So goes the call of the pedagogical sirens. "Do not bring your whole self into the courtroom or the boardroom or any other room. Leave yourself behind. Come in armed with leaden logic devoted to empty intellectualisms. And by all means, do not be who you are."

Experiencing injustice is an emotion. Ask anyone who's been to court as a litigant and lost. Ask the mother whose children have been ripped from her or the worker who's been wrongfully fired from his job and cannot feed his family whether being denied justice is an emotion. Ask the innocent citizen who's been accused of a crime or the worker whose retirement was stolen by a fraudulent CEO.

Then one day a jury, with its verdict, or a boss or a board embraces the litigant with a just decision. Isn't justice an emotion? The feelings of defeat or of winning are not intellectual processes. A judge looks down on us and says, "There is no room for emotion in this courtroom." He might as well have said there is no room for justice in a court of justice.

Logic is but a shifty product of the brain. We arrive at a just decision through our feelings. We *feel* what is right. Look up at those nine, old, black-robed deacons on the United States Supreme Court. Each is a peerless example of the intellectual athlete. Each is the big-brained virtuoso whose decisions are logic-laden products of the mind. As they sit there on high, look at their faces staring blankly down, their infallible wisdom marinated in thought and fried to a crisp in reason. Do we see any hint of the human there? Are any of these judges a member of the species? Do they weep? Do they writhe over the misery and pain their decision may bring to millions? Do they even speak to us in language that is meaningful as we trudge through our own lives?

If logic and reason, the hard, cold products of the mind, can be relied upon to deliver justice or produce the truth, how is it that these brain-heavy judges rarely agree? Five-to-four decisions are the rule, not the exception. Nearly half of the court must be unjust and wrong nearly half of the time. Each decision, whether the majority or minority, exudes logic and reason like the obfuscating ink from a jellyfish, and in language as opaque. The minority could have as easily become the decision of the court. At once we realize that logic, no matter how pretty and neat, that reason, no matter how seemingly profound and deep, does not necessarily produce truth, much less justice. Logic and reason often become but tools used by those in power to deliver their load of injustice to the people. And ultimate truth, if, indeed, it exists, is rarely recognizable in the endless rows of long words that crowd page after page of most judicial regurgitations.

I have no quarrel with scholarship, indeed, I embrace it if it leads to useful discovery. But too often, particularly where the fodder of the courts is decayed precedent, I see judges acting like cattle that lie in the shade and endlessly chew the same cud over and over. I think of what Nietzsche said: "I have left the house of the scholars and I have slammed the door behind me. Too long I sat hungry at their table."

Lawyers, as well as most other professionals who have been excreted from the universities, have been taught that stylish, intellectual facility is the key to winning. The pedagogues in the universities form young people in their own image. Intelligence, as we understand its common meaning—the ability of the mind to acquire and apply knowledge, the power to think and to reason—is nothing more than one of the myriad functions of the brain, perhaps a lesser one. But it is given great weight because we have devised certain debatable tests by which we claim we can measure it.

J. P. Gilford, the analytical psychologist, theorized there are more than one hundred and fifty abilities that constitute intelligence. To me, measurable intelligence is like salt in the oatmeal. You need enough of it to make the porridge palatable, but if the mix is mostly salt with only a pinch of oats the whole dish has to be thrown out. I say that if intelligence is viewed as something useful and empowering, which of course it is, then the person who is intelligent enough to have acquired a working knowledge of the self is among the most intelligent of all.

As we remember, the college graduate's ability to perform certain intellectual functions is tested and retested until the graduate moves out into the real world. A narrow aspect of the would-be attorney's mind is tested with the Law School Admissions Test (LSAT), a computer-driven monstrosity that measures whether the candidate for law school can play certain word games well, which test is not predictive of his success in or out of law school. Then the graduating student takes the bar exam, another computer-driven test that measures none of the important traits of a lawyer such as honesty, devotion to justice, bravery, caring—not even the ability to communicate effectively.

I've stood before judges with those freakish, one-dimensional heads, and with souls that must look like dried-up prunes, who condemn witnesses who showed their feelings. And I've had them demand that their attorney hide his feelings as well. "This is no place for emotions, Mr. Spence," I've heard such judges say, who, if the truth were known, were terrified of their own raw feelings.

Yet a person without feeling is little better than an automaton. And such an individual, whether a judge or a CEO, can possess no real credibility, for we can manufacture a talking dummy that will espouse whatever the dummy is programmed to say, but no one can manufacture something that feels and can honestly relate such feelings to other humans. Facts have no meaning absent their emotional content.

Feelings—the ultimate decision maker. I have said I have no quarrel with the intellect. These words were born of it. I simply do not wish the head to rule every aspect of the human experience, nor feelings to be reduced to some unsavory attachment to the person, something akin to original sin. Moreover, I am not a fan of flabby sentimentality that by its excessiveness mocks honest feeling. But be assured—despite all their protests to the contrary—the decisions of most *power persons* are rooted in the very feelings they deny. A simple and universal process is at work. *We feel first, then decide accordingly*. Our decision may be wrong. It can even be spiteful or evil, and we will announce our decision only after we have smeared it with the stuff of the left lobe—with brain-laden, unemotional, cold, linear reasoning. The feeling came first and it was at the feeling level that the decision was made.

Big words hide. Jurors complain that the fancy talk of lawyers and experts flies over their heads. "Those big words," they complain. "Why don't they talk to us like human beings?" The truth is that those who make their presentations with words as long as an eighteen-wheeler are hiding something. Often big words hide incompetence. They also hide the presenter's fear. But jurors and other decision makers feel put down, minimized by this flouting of a massive technical vocabulary that's empty of caring and conviction. Big words often hide small minds.

Despite the presenter's opposite intent, his choice of uppity words portrays a demeanor that will likely separate him from the decision maker and thereby destroy his credibility. But let the same person tell the decision maker,

Alienation / lack of
confidence

the jury, the board, how he feels, let such a person show his fear, his caring, even his appropriate anger as his feelings come seeping through ordinary words, and the decision makers will embrace him because they can relate to him as a person.

Our invisible truth-seeking tentacles. Because most members of the species have the ability to lie to one another, sometimes convincingly, and since by such guile they possess the ability to hurt us, so, too, have we acquired a protective, biological advantage—the innate ability to recognize those who cannot be trusted.

I envision the ordinary person surrounded with countless invisible, highly sensitive psychic feelers that look and look, and listen, and feel, trying to identify any danger that may lurk behind that seemingly honest face, behind that mask of credibility. I tell lawyers that none of us is clever enough to choose the right words, the right vocal intonation, the right rhythms in our speech, the right facial expression, the right hand and body movements, and to choose them simultaneously, word after word, sentence after sentence, unless we are telling the truth as we perceive it, yes, as we feel it.

When we are less than candid the listener will likely pick up something that seems incongruent. Some word, some sound, some idea doesn't match up. Ask the listener what has alerted him and he may tell us he doesn't know. All he can say is, "There's something about that guy I don't trust." Was it an inappropriate facial expression, a slightly incongruent sound in the voice, a hand gesture that seemed fake? We don't need to know what raised our suspicions. A psychic feeler picked up something that didn't fit. Something told us that the presenter didn't believe what he was saying—and if he didn't believe it why should we? To trot around fooling ourselves that we can consistently fool the decision maker is to permit our naked arrogance to squander our chance at winning.

Give me a frightened young woman standing with shaking knees before the jury, one who cares to the core for her client, one who will show who she is—honest, afraid, involved, and caring—and I'll give you a lawyer who will win against the best heads and the quickest wits. Although her saddle may be very plain, that young woman rides a better horse. That woman is credible and the jury feels it and trusts her.

If we are business persons, no matter how inept, no matter how intimidated by the boss or the board, we will win if out of our unfolding hearts comes the truth of our presentation. That truth includes the revelation of our feelings. Yes, we care. Yes, we're afraid. We may be inexperienced. We're taking risks—risks that we may be rejected, even cast out. But we are open and honest about who we are and what we feel. In the end, our candor and caring cast a dazzling, if humble light on our presentation that leaves all of our shortcomings in forgotten shadows.

Owning our feelings. When we stand before a jury or any other decision maker without owning our feelings we hide the most important part of us. One of the decision maker's invisible tentacles has detected that something is held back. What is it? And how can we trust someone who is hiding something?

Often we don't have to identify our feelings for the jury—to say, "I feel angry," or "I feel afraid," or "I feel lonely" or sad, or confused, or lost. But when we are in touch with our feelings they'll show through. Our outrage at the injustice will come roaring out in the sound of our voices and the choice of our words. Our love of justice will be observed in our energy. Some call it charisma. I call it an opening up of the self.

To move others we must first be moved. To persuade others, we must first be credible. To be credible we must tell the truth, and the truth always begins with our feelings.

Acting and credibility. Although an actor in a movie may be convincing, some more so than others, he is taught to *become* the character he portrays. One sweet summer day in the mountains at Trial Lawyer's College we gathered in the old barn's loft, the whole class of lawyers, some old hands and some neophytes along with our staff, about seventy men and women representing a variety of ethnic origins and from nearly every state in the union. The gathering was being led by the great Josh Carton, the magical man who teaches actors. On this occasion he was teaching trial lawyers how to simply be themselves—be as little children, as it were, to permit their lifes' energies to explode. A favorite at the school, Josh was in the midst of his lecture-demonstration when we heard the ominous sound of a helicopter beating its way onto the pasture just outside the barn.

I ran out and was surprised to find my friend Harrison Ford emerging from the cockpit as if he were, indeed, Indiana Jones. He'd decided to fly in and just say hello. I led him up to the barn where the whole class was waiting to see whether the police or the marines had landed. When Harrison walked in they couldn't believe the whole serendipitous event. For sure, I'd planned it—this most famous of all movie stars walking into the barn just as they were learning about the business of acting.

With some urging by me, Harrison finally sat on the edge of a table in front of the gathering and reluctantly began answering questions.

"What is the most important thing an actor needs to know?" someone asked.

"He needs to be *real,*" Harrison said, as if the words had come from me. Some of the students looked at me suspiciously.

"But he is only acting. How can he be real?" another asked.

"The actor has to *become* the person, feel the person—be who he is. He has to honestly portray who the person is he's become." Then as if I had prompted him, and without any knowledge of what I had been preaching, Harrison said, "If you're not honest, no one will believe the character you've become."

The class was still suspicious that I'd set this up with Harrison. But his own credibility soon showed through. "Acting is simply telling the truth about the character one portrays," he said again.

That, of course, is my message here. One may perform, put on airs, or try to be like Clarence Darrow or Jack Welsh of General Electric fame, but to be credible, one must tell the truth, not only about one's self, but about his client, his case, or his cause. It is such a simple proposition—one that no one is ever taught in any law school or at Harvard Business School. The rule is so easy to say: *To be perceived as credible, one must be credible.*

4. THE POWER OF LISTENING

LISTENING TO THE SELF. Perhaps the greatest listeners are not those who listen to other people, but who are expert at listening to themselves. Listening is a skill that trumps all others. The words may flow from our mouths like the great Euphrates river and our style may be as dramatic as the best of Euripides, but unless we have mastered the skill of listening we will be reduced to little more than the playback system on a recording device. Since we have already learned (and always knew) that communication is a two-way street, it is not enough to learn what we are going to say, or practice how we are going to say it. We must first be able to listen and to *hear* (they are different) what is being said both by ourselves to ourselves and by the *power person* to us and to others.

Earplugs against the third voice. If we listen to ourselves we will hear voices. Don't be alarmed. It isn't like somebody comes blustering onto our stage and hollers, "Now hear this!" Nor is it the voice of ghosts, goblins, or the inner raging of the insane. They're not very loud voices. The voices, of course, are silent, except in our minds where they are heard. Some call them ideas. The actual words that form our ideas are not always clear, but the ideas come, and they can be heard behind the cacophony of what the outer ears are hearing.

If we listen to ourselves, even as we speak, it's a quiet suggestion that we should follow this path or that, that we should add this marvelous metaphor, slow down the presentation, or pause so our listeners will be able to absorb what we are saying. If we listen to ourselves as we speak we will hear the rhythms we should employ—the beat of the drums of our presentation. If we listen we will know when the voice should rise to put sound italics over a thought, a phrase. If we listen we will know when we are reaching the climax of our presentation that will be underscored with the excitement and power of our voice. And if we listen we will know when to end it.

I must say that most people who speak, either to a friend, jury, or board, do not listen to themselves. They are tied to the habit of old ideas and are stuck in the ruts of their predictable thoughts. They fail to listen to determine if a new image, some spontaneous concept, may be tapping timidly at the door, pleading to enter. They go through life with earplugs smashed into the deepest recesses of their mind's ear—the *third ear*—and nothing is permitted to enter the mind or escape the lips that has not been thoroughly thought out, read, or memorized. Their public speaking is like feeding guests leftover pizza from last month's office party.

I see speech makers reading their speeches—and most can't read very well. More often I hear speakers lashed to the post of their notes. Struggle as they may to be convincing, they fail to penetrate the third ear of their audience, for it's the third ear that hears best that which was first heard in the third ear of the speaker. *Spontaneity* is the key that unlocks the door of the listener, because that which is spontaneous is honest and is heard as honest. And if it is honest it convinces. If it is honest it moves the other to our side, to our way of thinking. If it is honest it wins. In the end, the product of spontaneity wins.

I'm not arguing that one cannot write an honest, thoughtful line that can later be read aloud. Indeed, I am trying to write honest lines here. But honesty is not only in the words. As we have seen, honesty is exposed in the texture of the sounds and rhythms of the voice. If we listen to someone say as the roof caves in, "My God, George, watch out! The roof is caving in!" or you hear the person read, "As the roof caved in he hollered to George to watch out," it is immediately apparent which carries the better truth.

When we're tied to our notes, or worse, when we're frozen in the words of a memorized script, the sounds, the language, the whole dramatic movement is lost. Listen to the anchor persons on the evening news—the placid smiles pasted on their otherwise dead faces, their lips forming the words, their eyes glued to the teleprompters. They tell us in their singsong voices about murders and rapes and unspeakable horrors of every description, and even, occasionally, of joy. We are unmoved. We hear about thousands killed or maimed in bombings across the world. Nothing happens. We go on eating our popcorn. The flow of blood may turn the rivers scarlet and the dead bodies may well lie bloating in the sun, but as they read, the anchor persons provide us nothing more than the deadened sound of the written word.

But put the reporter on the scene, the microphone in her hand. Let her look at the devastation and speak outside of the script and we begin to respond in kind. Television has learned to put the grieving mother and the irate citizen who was robbed or cheated before the cameras. The shocked passersby who have just witnessed a horror do not read from a script or speak a memorized line. Such persons broadcast a vivid, moving message. That which moves us is the inner voice that people hear in themselves and pass on to us.

The other day I was called on to speak at a peace rally at the conclusion of a peace march though town. I had no time to gather up any sort of organizational thought concerning what I might say. Moreover, a crowd of thousands of eager listeners, all expecting me to say something remotely intelligent, is somewhat intimidating. My heart was racing as I walked up to the speaker's podium. The microphone was staring at me along with thousands of eyes. The crowd suddenly quieted. Even dogs, anticipating something, stopped barking and the children ceased their crying. There was that horrible moment of silence as the crowd waited.

My mind was blank. White. I looked out over the crowd. I could feel the butterflies flying in sync with the beating of my heart. Then I consciously removed the earplugs against my inner voice. As soon as I began to listen, that small, quiet voice said, "This is what people look like in a free nation." And I began my speech with what I heard. I said, "I see you looking at me, wondering what I will say, hoping I will say something worth your while to hear. I want to tell you how you look to me. You are what people look like in a free nation." The inner voice directed the words. "What I see are thousands of beautiful people of every description. I see the young who will carry on this fight for us after we are gone. I see workers and businesspersons and mothers and babies. I see old men—none as old as I. And you are beautiful. And what I want to say into your beautiful faces is, 'We will win this fight.'

"Hatred cannot destroy such beauty. War, which is the ultimate terror, the blood of the slain innocent filling the gutters, the babies lying rotting in the streets, the charred corpses of their mothers gathering flies, cannot bring peace and cannot stop terror. We cannot stop terror by terrorizing. We cannot stop hate by hating. We cannot stop killing by killing. We cannot bring peace by waging war. The bursting of bombs that fragment the villages of innocent people and blow their arms and legs from their bodies are not missiles of love and of peace." They were words not from a written script but words that escaped the lips when the earplugs of the third ear were pulled out.

The speech went on for another ten minutes. As I listened, the third ear told me when the climax was near. It also told me to stop. To let silence settle in once more. To bring the people into my focus and me into theirs by the power of utter silence. Then I heard the question in my third ear. "How many children must we murder in our attempt to extinguish one evil man? Let us count them, and when I have reached enough, let me know. One? Two? Forty? Seven hundred? Ten thousand?" The inner voice told me to continue until I was stopped. Suddenly someone in the crowd yelled, "None! None! None!" And the crowd began to chant, "None, none, none."

Then came the inner voice saying, "It's time to end this. Better to be brief than sorry." And the question was, of course, what shall I say to bring this speech to a powerful end? The question and the answer in response took less than a second. "Peace comes when we realize that their babies are as precious to them as ours are to us." I saw a child below me in its mother's arms. A good listener is one who not only hears his inner voice, but who takes the risk of doing what the voice suggests. I motioned to the mother to come up to the podium with her child and took the child by its hand. Then I said, "Let us save them all."

I say listen to yourself. We hear our inner voices constantly, but most of us are not expert in listening to them. We silently talk to ourselves and hear ourselves during nearly every waking moment of the day. The words I write on this page were first spoken in my mind and heard in my third ear only seconds before my fingers began putting them on the page. As if by some black and evil magic when we speak to the *power person,* the juror, the boss, we insert earplugs into our third ears and speak like deafened mannequins capable only of reciting what is prompted by the well-rehearsed notes we drag to the speaker's platform.

Behind the words I'm speaking I hear a small prompting from my third ear. Sometimes I get two or three such promptings that come along in rapid succession. I must do something so as not to forget these cues. I've learned to tuck in my little finger (as if one is making a fist with only that digit). This slightly uncomfortable cramping of the little finger is to remind me to give this example or offer that metaphor, or it may simply remind me where I am in the talk so I can return from short side trips and pick up the theme—a marker that keeps me from becoming lost.

Editing the inner voice. Having heard the inner voice with our third ear, are we at liberty to always express aloud whatever we've heard? I have preached the imperative of truth telling. Every civilized society abhors assaults, either physical or verbal, and as members of that society we are bound by its rules the same as we are bound by its laws. If we expressed every thought we have heard from the inner voice we would find ourselves in a world of trouble. "I ought to kill the sonofabitch," or "He'd probably steal milk from babies if he were smart enough to sell it," or "His breath would offend a skunk." The unedited inner voice would cause us to lose the friends we need and create a host of enemies we do not.

But the inner voice is also equipped with an automatic editing device. The editor hovers above the action like a member of the security police in a helicopter. It contains the ear within the third ear. We experience the ear's editor every day. If we are listening we not only hear the spontaneous product of the mind, but we sort through that product in order to recite only that which may be expressed without injury. It is not only important to listen to the voice but also to respect the editor. Without hearing the inner voice we will create nothing, say little of interest, and say it as if we were speaking from the bottom of a tub of mud. But if we listen to the inner voice and do not also listen to its editor we may find ourselves sentenced to the outhouse or some other house not of our choosing.

I say the editor is nearly always trustworthy. Yet we are timid creatures. "Do I dare say that? What will they think of me? How will it sound to this audience?" The questions that a cautious editor raises often stifle us to the point that we'd just as well have ignored the third ear in the first place. Those edits that are obviously deleterious need to be heeded. But we must ignore edits that seek to eliminate new thoughts, new ideas, new ways of saying something, unfamiliar physical movements such as my invitation to the mother to bring her child to the podium. These risks of doing something in the moment are the risks we should take. The discomfort we feel is not because what we are about to do or say is dangerous. It's that it's new and different and creative—all the things that make a presentation powerful.

In court during the final argument I asked the jury what a witness would have said had the prosecution had the courage to call him. "Where was Mr. Bernstein? Where is he hiding? Ask the prosecutor who sits over there with a smile on his face. What would he say if Bernstein were here? The prosecutor knows."

Suddenly the inner voice says, "Go over and become the witness, Bernstein, and take the stand yourself."

I hear my editor reply, "That's a little risky." Then I ask myself, "What will the prosecutor do? What will the judge say? Will I be embarrassed in front of the jury?" The questions are posed in a fleeting second, but some force urges me on. I walk to the witness chair and sit down. I look over at the jury, and I begin, "My name is Orville Bernstein. I live in—well, the prosecutor knows where I live. It's a big secret. But I'm here, and here is what I have to say: I was there when Mr. Hammil was shot. It isn't the way prosecutor said it at all. . . ." The prosecutor objects, and the objection is sustained. What the witness would have said remains a mystery to the jurors, and my listening to the inner voice may have won the case.

In a civil case I made a plea for justice that was bursting with compassion for the victim of a corporation's negligence. I heard an inner voice say, "Bring the plaintiff up to the jury so he is standing beside you as you talk about him." Again, it was risky business. I had never seen it done in court before. But it is one thing to see a human being as a mere occupier of a seat next to counsel across the room, to see him sit silently there day after day, and it's quite another thing to bring the person up close to the jury so that they see every pain-induced wrinkle in his face and the shadows of agony behind his eyes.

Learning to hear with the third ear. How does one become an expert in listening to the inner voice and hearing it with the third ear? It takes practice, in the same way that one becomes proficient at playing the guitar. If we have never strummed a cord we cannot play the simplest tune.

Begin talking out loud to yourself when you're alone. Don't be alarmed. It's no sign that the psyche is splitting. As you drive down the road begin listening to your thoughts and speaking them aloud. Don't be afraid of the old saw, "You don't need to worry about talking to yourself until you begin answering yourself." Become the editor—hear what the editor says. Is your hesitancy to take the risk well founded, or are you only afraid to be different? If in doubt, take the risk. Better to be scorned than to bore. Better to be slightly outrageous than to join the walking dead.

If you do this for a month as you drive to work each day you'll be able to hear the inner voice, to become aware of its sounds, its rhythms, its wisdom, its creativity, and yes, its beauty. And when you present your case you'll be able to hear the inner voice speaking clearly to you so that what you say and do is no longer the dreary, warmed-over stuff one slogs through from the written text.

Listening to the other. Daily we practice the art of nonhearing. We have become advanced in the skill of turning off the world so that, in important ways, we have become deaf mutes neither capable of hearing what is happening around us nor responding to what we hear in a sensitive, effective way. We hear words, but only their sounds. Truth is, most of us have not had the experience of being listened to closely. Hence we have developed little skill in listening closely.

How could it be otherwise? We get up in the morning and the first thing we encounter is rarely a discourse with the self. We have a relationship with the *Today* show or turn on some talk show host and listen to his blaring, obnoxious inanities we confuse with intelligent observations. We say little if anything to our house spouse: "How did you sleep? Did you let the dog out? What's going on in your day today? Don't forget the grocery list. We're out of coffee and cereal."

In our car on our way to work we listen to the news, which is mostly the yappings of some hysterical voice screaming about Toby's Almost-New-Car Lot, or we turn on the jump and jive that exposes our ears to a variety of shattering discords accompanied by utterly meaningless words. We have lunch with someone from our office in a restaurant that is so noisy a hundred-megaton bomb could be exploded across the street and we would go right on yelling at the top of our voices.

We are being trained not to hear anything but what the voice of Big Brother (the corporate overlord) wants us to hear. We are being trained not to tune in to ourselves but to tune ourselves out and tune in the programs that Madison Avenue prepares for us, so that we, the New Indians, as it were, will voluntarily give up whatever we have in exchange for the trinkets and beads and booze that the corporate overlord wishes to sell us from the company store. In short, we have become deaf mutes of a kind. Woah . . .

Learning to tune out, not in. We should become experts in tuning out that which is the intrusive noise called television, the vacuous conversations of the attendees at a cocktail party, and the jarring, empty hullabaloo that surrounds us every day. I am often accused of not listening to what is going on around me when, indeed, I am listening to what is going on within me. My wife, Imaging, claims I enjoy what she calls "a rich inner life," one that seems unaware of the outside world. But we do not need to know most of the overflow of information we are exposed to.

You could listen intently to every word that is spoken at the average dinner party, and the next morning, when called upon to give a short summary of what was said, nothing, purely nothing, would come to mind. Five couples talked incessantly, usually over each other, for three hours, but little of interest was said and nothing of import was heard. Although I offered my own startling inanities at the dinner and attempted to be as lithe as any with my comebacks and humor, still, at last, what I offered will likely be as memorable as the bagatelles I endured from the other guests. The next morning I, too, for the life of me couldn't tell you what I said. And this is okay . . . really.

Whether we are being bombarded by the media, the masses, the "music," or the otherwise miserable, we need the ability to tune out the noise and tune in ourselves. I am not suggesting we should live our lives isolated from the world around us. I am simply saying that, if for no better reason than self-defense, we ought to develop the skill of tuning out that omnipresent noise pollution in favor of what is often the more interesting world within. Although we wish to develop the skill of hearing others around us, we must also be able to tune them out when they provide only noise pollution. A listening device, which in part is what we are, is of little

41

value if the on–off button is not functional. In the end we must tune out and then tune in.

The inimitable power of the third ear. If we desire the magic that will empower us to win, we must learn how to hear what has *not* been said. The *power person* speaks. The witness on the stand gives his answer. The judge comments on an objection or makes a hasty decision. Yes, our loved one says she didn't really care that we got home after midnight. Have we heard them? Have we listened to what was actually said but not said?

A skilled listener will have heard the other person with such sensitivity, with such a sympathetic, tuned-in third ear, that the listener hears not only what the other has said, but has felt the feelings behind the words. Indeed, the skillful listener may well hear what the other meant but never heard himself.

At Trial Lawyer's College we do an exercise in listening that is intended to develop this magic. It works in the following way: A person selected in advance has a story to tell about something important in that person's life, and that person takes the stage. Let us call the storyteller Marge. An expert listener who we will call Henry accompanies the storyteller. Both are seated, Henry seated slightly behind the storyteller, Marge, so that he can see her body language as she tells her story and at the same time be out of Marge's direct line of vision. She begins her story. She is nervous at first because she is on stage. Moreover, she is not speaking directly to Henry, but to the audience.

Henry is instructed not only to listen to the words Marge is speaking, but to listen intently with his third ear to what Marge is *not* saying. Often what we say aloud to others is akin to an iceberg—more of it floats under water than above. It is this unsaid part of the story that Henry is instructed to hear and to speak out loud as he hears it. If the unspoken thought that Henry hears with his third ear and reports to Marge rings true to Marge she will nod her head in the affirmative and continue on with her story. If, on the other hand, what Henry reports does not fit, Marge will reject it with a negative shake of her head and continue on. The process might go like this:

As Marge begins her story she folds her arms across her chest and crosses her legs, a stance that typifies someone under stress from the anxiety of the moment. Henry, the listener, doubles Marge's body language and crosses his own arms and legs, in this manner aiding himself in understanding the feeling that Marge is experiencing.

42

Marge: Before I start this story I want you to know that it is true.

Henry: But I am afraid to tell all of it. (Marge nods yes.) → *should she agree?*

Marge: I love my husband very much. (Her arms are still crossed and there is no conviction in her voice.)

Henry: But there are some things about our relationship that bother me. (Marge nods yes.) *Caramel.*

Marge: We have a good relationship and we are both devoted to each other.

Henry: But sometimes I think he isn't as understanding as he should be. (Marge nods yes.)

Marge: He works very hard.

Henry: But so do I. (Marge nods yes.)

Marge: And we are trying to save our money to buy a home of our own. (She has begun to lean forward as if to attack. Henry doubles her.)

Henry: A home of our own is a dream I have always had, and I think it is worth working for. (Marge nods yes.)

Marge: I think that if we work hard enough and save our money that that dream is within reach. (Her voice changes, as if giving a lecture to her husband.)

Henry: But I don't think that my husband wants a home of our own as badly as I do. (Marge nods yes.) *I guess knowing there's more?*

At this point in the exercise, if we were not listening with a third ear, Marge would have said simply: "Before I start this story I want you to know that it is true and that I love my husband very much. We have a good relationship and we are both devoted to each other. My husband works very hard and we are trying to save our money to buy a home of our own. I think that if we work hard enough and save our money that that dream is within reach."

But the skilled listener has heard and seen a good deal more. He has heard that Marge is afraid to tell all of her story, that their relationship is not as good as she wishes it were, that her dream for a home of their own is not happening because her husband is merely giving lip service to it.

Marge's story goes on:

Marge: I am not against owning a new car. Lord knows, the one we have is nearly ten years old. (Again, the sound of her voice is as if she were arguing with her husband.)

Henry: But we can get by with the old one. (Marge shakes her head in dis-agreement. The listened-to says no when the listener goes astray.)

Marge: We need a different car. Our old car has broken down several times and I'm afraid it will quit on me sometime on the freeway at night, and I would be very afraid if that happened. So I think we need a different car all right. But the car my husband wants to buy is a sports car, one of those sleek-looking things, you know the kind I mean.

Henry: Yes, the kind that cost a lot of money. (Marge nods yes.)

Marge: And I just don't think we can afford it given our goal to own a home of our own. Besides, who needs a sports car to go to work every day?

Henry: Yes, and I wonder who he is trying to impress? (Marge nods yes.)

Marge: All we need is cheap but reliable transportation. One of those small economy cars would work just fine. We could buy a secondhand, low-mileage model for half the price of the sports car he wants. (Marge looks pained and frustrated. Henry doubles even her facial expressions and the sound of her voice.)

Henry: And really, who *is* he trying to impress with a new sports car? I wonder if he has an agenda that I am not aware of. (Marge nods yes.)

Marge: And yes, I will have to say that he has been getting home a little late lately and often has the smell of alcohol on his breath. But I am not the jealous type and I would not, under any circumstances, doubt his loyalty. And I do not.

Henry: Yet, I can't be sure. He wants this car. He would probably be ashamed to take another woman out in the old car we own.

Marge begins to cry. She turns to Henry and says, "I have never let myself think that. That is not part of my story. My story is about not being able to get a home of our own, and it is not a story about a cheating husband. And I don't believe he is."

Now they revert back to their respective roles:

Marge: I guess I'm not all that opposed to a sports car. They can be fun.

Henry: I hope he is being true to me. I would gladly agree to a sports car if I could be sure there was nothing going on. (Marge nods yes.)

Marge: Yes.

44

And that's the end of a story that otherwise would have sounded quite benign—a simple conflict between a married couple on how to spend their money. The listening skill is best experienced when the listener tunes in to the feelings created by the words, more than to the simple words themselves. In our example, Marge's words seem to be about how money should be spent, but the feeling that the words impart is one of a woman who is worried that her marriage is failing.

When we are cross-examining a witness or listening to the boss's position on a raise, or, indeed, listening to our loved ones discuss an issue that is important to them, we usually hear only that which the speaker feels safe to tell us. Listen to the corporate head make his presentation on the company's condition, or the president as he delivers his state of the union speech. The other side of the story will be left out as surely as the thief forgets to tell us that he was stealing the blind man's wallet when he helped him across the street.

Practicing with the third ear. One need not take the stage to perform the listening exercise of Marge and Henry in order to become better skilled in the art of listening with the third ear. The exercise is easy to do, and the reward of achieving a greater listening skill is great. Instead of slogging along at another boring cocktail party, why not set up your own listening exercise? Unbeknownst to our storyteller at the party (everyone wants to tell something about themselves) we can begin to perform the function of Henry by injecting our understanding of the deeper statements that the storyteller is making. If we are right, he will likely nod or say yes and continue. He has discovered something important about us—that we are good listeners—which encourages him to share his story with us more intimately. We can become Henry on any occasion, at any place. Let's be Henry when we talk to our spouses, our children, the boss, the judge, the jury, and the witness. You'll have more fun talking

Over the years I have been a guest on a number of nationally televised talk shows. I remember many years ago when I was asked to be on the show of a now-famous late-night host who then was just beginning. When the camera was on me he would ask a question, and when I turned to answer him he was nowhere to be found, buried as he was in his notes, as he got ready to ask me the next question or to make the next quip.

It is almost impossible to talk to the back of someone's head, and from his standpoint, because he was not listening but was tied to his notes, his questions were shallow, sometimes silly. The interview was a catastrophe. On the other hand, I have been a guest on *The Larry King Show* many times. No one is better at the interview than Larry, who listens intently to your answer, nods his acceptance of your answer, or asks the next question based on what you have just said. He creates a relationship that encourages the guest to feel secure, to tell the whole story. Yes, he does not often ask the hard question. But hard questions often send those being interviewed scurrying into hiding.

In the same way as the late-night show host who was tied to his notes, I see lawyers in the courtroom tied to theirs. They have not heard a single answer of the witness. They have not heard any of the unspoken words of the witness. They have not been listening with either their own, two exterior ears and surely not with their third ear. As a consequence, the lawyer bumbles along and the examination usually goes nowhere. The witness is left in control, because the lawyer is controlled by his notes—filling the room with the sound of his voice that, as it were, signifies nothing. — American Psycho/Macbeth

We need to employ our deeper listening to what is being said *as it is being said* and see how far this method of listening will take us, not only in understanding the real story but in creating a stronger bond between ourselves and the storytellers. We must show the other that we are willing to hear. We all need to be heard, and heard deeply. It feels good to be heard. In the end, the right to be heard and understood is the cornerstone of justice.

Life is often a lonely affair—even for those surrounded by others every day. The stuff of friendship is understanding. The power of persuasion is understanding those we attempt to convince. And, as we have discovered, understanding the other can best be achieved by listening deeply with our third ear. Therein lies the magic. Therein lies the power of listening.

5. THE POWER OF FEAR—OURS AND THEIRS

S ETTING THE MIND FOR WAR. Preparing ourselves for our individual battles is like a nation preparing itself for war. The requirements for winning are many, the most important of which is the state of mind we take into the battlefield. We hear our leaders claiming our cause is just. The enemy is an abominable beast and the safety of the nation, yes, the world, rests upon our victory. Both sides make mirrored claims. We are not afraid—Roosevelt pronouncing from noble heights, "We have nothing to fear but fear itself." God is on our side—God and justice and reason and honor and human rights and dignity—all are on our side. No honest arguments can be made by our opponent. We will win because we are right and power is on the side of right.

But we're afraid. It's dangerous to launch ourselves into any war—wars in the world, at home, at work, or in the courtroom—because all wars seek to alter the status quo and power will fight us down to its toenails. In the civil courts it's risky to attempt an extraction of money from a corporation for its negligence—to challenge the power of billions of dollars and thousands of employees, its army of lawyers and its corps of experts. We could lose, and the cost of such a war is immense in time, money, and the expenditure of human resources. But more than the costs, if we lose the battle, our reputations, our dearest asset, may be irrevocably damaged and our client's life will be left broken with disappointment and perhaps with a devastating, unfulfilled need.

If we are employed by a corporation it's risky to face management for whatever reason. Management is not people-friendly. It is money-friendly. Management has no beating red heart. Its heart is dead, green from the stain of dollars. The people who make up management are also afraid—afraid of their loss of power in intramural wars. Justice is only a word. Fairness is only another word. Workers are but digits that can be replaced with other digits. Those who have power feel it down to their gonads. It's the stuff that runs businesses and conquers competitors in and out of the organization. Power pushes one up the ladder to the top (where one is eventually toppled). In short, power is beautiful, lush, and wonderful (and a great aphrodisiac), and those in power do not wish to lose it—not any of it—nor to share it—not any of it—nor to risk it—not any of it.

But power is also fragile. It can be conquered by dangerous ideas—for example, that the organization should care more about people than about money, that it should be driven by what's good for society, not profit alone, that the condition of workers is more important than figures on the profit and loss statement. Such ideas can cost profit, and since in this society money is seen as the ultimate power, and since justice is often equated in dollars, power's panicked grip on money will never be loosened except in the rarest of circumstances—most likely where a little money will eventually save the organization a lot of money.

Beseeching the power structure for money, for any change in policy that requires money, for recognition that might encourage the further expenditure of money, yes, for fairness or justice that is expressed in terms of money, is risky because those who support such a change will be seen as a threat to power, and those who threaten are seen as the enemy and are put at risk. They risk their jobs, their acceptance by the power structure, and their reputations as worthy members of the organization (not to mention their promised invitation into the local country club). In the end, we are always afraid in various degrees of confronting power.

What about approaching politicians for help, for change? That too is dangerous. Politicians are constantly looking over their shoulders at their human constituency while they slip their hands into the pockets of their nonhuman constituency, their corporate sponsors. Politicians have power, but it has been bought with false promises to the people, and much of it has been paid for with corporate money. Politicians are at once in conflict, since the interest of the people is often antithetical to the interest of the corporation that subsidizes the politician.

"Write your congressman" is the unremitting cry of the impotent. The politician will not change his vote, no matter how many letters, if his underlying power—money—is diminished a dime. The letter writer keeps the U.S. Postal Service in business and provides employment to bored congressional assistants who send out thousands of form letters in response. *Dew'd*

The conflicts of power are endemic in the system. We go to war for oil and corporate profit, not liberty. We destroy the people's pristine forests so that the corporation may sell old-growth redwoods to Japan. We desecrate our wilderness, the precious property of the people, to line the pockets of business. We pollute our rivers, lakes, and oceans—the people's jewels—for corporate enrichment. We poison our air to secure the right of the corporation to make money. We injure workers to save dollars for the corporation. We die in hospitals from the neglect of hospital managers whose first concern is paying dividends to the shareholders. The conflict between the people who elect the politician and the corporations who buy such elections is configured in the system in such a way that money wins.

It is dangerous to stand up against an illegal, immoral war, to call one's country to task for its wrongdoing. The danger is that we'll be seen as unpatriotic. Those who have the courage to speak out, to lay down their bodies to save the environment, to march and to protest, are seen as kooks and fools and some are held up as dangerous and put in jail. When we fight to save our rivers and our lakes and our air we are often confronted by workers whose jobs are threatened if the pollution of the corporations is shut down. When we sue large corporations they sometimes countersue and put our personal assets at risk. When we take on the negligent doctor who has injured us, we face legislators, controlled by the insurance industry, who put caps on our ability to get justice. But no caps are put on the profit that negligent caregivers can make and none are put on the insurance industry to curb its greed. Every attempt to get justice, to change the status quo, to make the slightest indent in the armor of power is dangerous. We are afraid of taking on wars we may lose. Futile endeavors may deliver ulcers and heart attacks and the pounding of creditors at our doors, and we envision ourselves standing in the unemployment lines questioning our worth.

As I walk into the courtroom I feel the urgency of a spastic bladder that demands emptying in response to ancient genes that are preparing me for physical combat. I sweat in that air-conditioned room. What if I lose? What if I must watch them drag my innocent client off to some damnable hole called a penitentiary? What if, in a civil case, my client will endure the rest of her life without medical help, strapped to a wheelchair, a helpless victim of not only the negligent company that I am suing, but also of my own failure as a lawyer?

In the case of the presenter who wants something from the company, a raise, better conditions, shorter hours, a different system—or in the case of the citizen who forwards a just cause or a salesperson whose product must be sold or he'll be chucked as excess corporate baggage—what if he fails? What if the person confronting power loses his job or is seen as one of those wackos who stands only one rung above the idiot preaching on the street corner? What if he brings shame on his family, or is humiliated in front of his peers? What if none of the above occurs and his rejection confirms what he has always suspected—that he is not worth a tinker's damn to anyone, not to himself, his boss, or even his family. For the person undertaking these small wars, wars that are all-consuming to him, the stakes are exceedingly high.

Understanding their fear. So we're afraid? Well, so are they. The mirror is still at work. In every war the powermonger is afraid. It knows the fear it causes in the other nation, which will cause that nation to also become aggressive and dangerous in its defense. Both sides are soaked in fear and both sides proclaim how unafraid they are. So it is in every battle. Again we hear the battle cries, "The enemy will be destroyed. We cannot be beaten. We are right. God is on our side." But behind it all is a mutual fear.

How do we measure the fear of our opponent in the courtroom or elsewhere? We begin by measuring our own. If we can simply be in the moment, put aside all of the racket from both inside and outside, and in that moment of turning inward feel our fear, we will begin to understand the fear that is powering the enemy. He may not show it. He may look calm. He may laugh and joke. He may threaten. He may puff up like a challenged dog or raise his tail like a cornered skunk, but he is afraid. And we can measure his fear by our own. We both risk the same stakes. A loss on our side that results in damage to our position, our reputation, our financial health, or our emotional well-being reflects the same urgent feelings of our opponent. If we increase the intensity of our attack we only increase the fear level of our opponent and raise the level of his response.

We had hoped he would run. We had hoped he would pay, or give in. We had hoped he would lie down on his back like a whipped pup with his feet in the air. But humans, and particularly groups of humans in the form of government or corporate clusters, do not typically react to their fear by appeasement or surrender. I have never seen a corporation equipped with feet with which to flee nor any government entity with legs with which to retreat.

But the persons manipulating these organizations are afraid. Despite their power, what if they are beaten? What if they win but lose stature? What if the public is turned against them? What if they are criticized for judgments that prove harmful to the organization and they lose some or all of their power? What if they lose the most precious of all things—that lovely green?

How we deal with our fear is the only concern. How the opponent deals with his is his problem—one that he will likely not handle as well as we handle ours. He will likely use more force, expend more money, threaten us more, attempt to injure our standing in the courtroom or elsewhere, which only further motivates us. The more our opponent becomes frightened, the harder our task of winning will become. I say never intentionally set out to frighten an opponent. If we can hold our opponent's fear to a minimum it will be that much easier to defeat him.

Dealing with our fear. I've always been afraid. From the time I was a little boy I was afraid. I thought I was a coward and I felt like one. My father was a brave man, a gentle man, but to me he seemed fearless. I knew I could never be totally loved by him because I wasn't brave like he was. How could a brave father love a son who was such a sissy at heart? Even after all these years, when I go into a courtroom I still feel fear. People's lives and my career are in my hands. I'm afraid I'm going to fail. Indeed, now as an old man I am completing the circle of fear. I am as afraid as I was when I was a young man trying my first case. I am only better at admitting it. And the question for me has always been, how do I deal with that fear?

To me, fear is one of the most painful of human experiences. It is an ugly, raw emotional ulcer that stains everything I think and do. I cannot run from it. I cannot shed its prickly shroud. I cannot expel the feeling of dread. My chest is tight and my belly is in spasm. I would rather smash my thumb in the car door than go around all day suffocating in fear.

Yet over the years I've found that my fear can be a powerful gift. First, I've never known a dead man who was afraid. Fear reminds me I'm quite alive. I've never known anybody who cared, who was facing something difficult, who wasn't afraid—afraid of failure. If we aren't afraid it means we don't care. Fear leads us to the better parts of us.

Although I'd rather suffer most physical pain than the pain of fear, I need to feel it—to take it into myself. Fear is like a pack of dogs—it chases us, and if we try to run or hide from it the dogs will continue their chase until finally, exhausted, we fall and are devoured. But if we turn on the dogs, turn on the fear, concentrate on it and feel it, we're taken into a different world. Something happens to the dogs when we face the dogs. They begin to slink away. Embracing fear we leave fear powerless. *Fear becomes afraid of us.*

When we're afraid and do not own it as a legitimate, useful tool, when we hide from it, fear tends to put on different masks. My own response to unattended fear is to attack, to become aggressive and hostile. Afraid, the lion attacks. Like the rabbit that runs to its hole, some people evade. The frightened killdeer hops along crying, acting as if it has a broken wing so that we may follow it away from its nest. It misleads. We distrust people who evade or mislead, and we reject them. We see witnesses who react to their fear in much the same ways—as do we. The only appropriate method to deal with fear is *to own it.*

When it came time for me to make my closing argument in the defense of Randy Weaver in the Ruby Ridge murder case the judge peered down at me and said, "Mr. Spence, you may begin your argument." My heart was pounding. The jury was watching, waiting to finally judge me, my client, and our defense. Could I answer the United States attorney? His argument had been powerful. To listen to the D.A., Randy Weaver was this vicious skinhead, this murderer who had conspired to kill a United States marshal. Would they believe what I knew was true—that the government, not Randy Weaver, was the murderer? My throat felt tight. My mind was blank. The juices of the fear drowned out all wisdom and clouded the eyes. I was afraid and I reverted to the animal. I wanted to attack the opponent. Damn the fear!

I looked down at my feet and tried to locate exactly where my fear lay. There it was, where I could always find it—high up along the ribs in my chest.

I felt it, all of it that I could take into myself. Then I looked up at the jury.

"Ladies and gentlemen of the jury," I began. "I wish I weren't so afraid." I could hear my own words as if I were listening to another person in the court-room. "I wish, after all of these years in the courtroom I didn't feel this way. You'd think I could get over it."

I thought some of the jurors looked surprised. Here was this lawyer who had taken the United States government head on, who'd cross-examined more than fifty mostly hostile government witnesses—the FBI, the marshals, the government experts—and he was now confessing his fear?

"I'm afraid I won't be able to make the kind of argument to you that Randy Weaver deserves," I said. "After nearly three months of trial, I'm afraid I won't measure up. I wish I were a better lawyer." Every word I said was true. And I knew that the jurors themselves were afraid—the *mirror*. After confessing my fear I spoke to them about their fear. They, too, must be afraid. What if they convicted an innocent man? What if they missed important clues in the evidence? What if, at last, they failed to render justice?

The jurors and I connected. I could feel it—the symbiotic relationship that we shared—and my fear began to melt away. I saw the jurors' faces relax, their arms and legs begin to unfold. Soon my argument took on its own life, one gilded with my feelings. And because I was in touch with my feelings I could be both angry and humorous. The jury was invested in my argument and lis-tened intently to it despite its flaws—the false starts, the errors in syntax, the trails that wandered off and finally came back again. They listened to my argu-ment because it was real and because I was real, and the jury acquitted Randy Weaver, who was indeed an innocent man.

Some would say it was because of the oratory. Cicero was the great teacher of oratory and argument. His view was that to speak from the heart was a fool-ishness not befitting a public speaker. He approached his argument by first identifying his goal. Then he asked himself, what does my audience want for themselves? His next question was, how can I manipulate their minds and their psyches to believe as I wish them to believe, to act as I wish them to act? How do I hide my weak arguments and bedazzle them with my language and its music?

But in a world in which value is placed on justice above oratory, on truth above rhetoric, the Ciceronian is soon discovered. He is too skillful, too unmoved by the soul, too pretty and distant, too clever and beguiling. Who would trust a dangerous rascal who could argue either side of the case with equal skill but without an honest commitment of his own?

In the Randy Weaver case my oratory, as it were, was of a different sort—one that arose from the heart, the head merely its guide. Besides, the jurors had lived with me and I with them all of those months. They'd seen me in every possible situation. They'd seen me say I didn't know, when I didn't. They'd seen me admit that I was confused when I was, that I was wrong when I'd been wrong. They saw that I cared for Randy Weaver, and that I was outraged when the prosecutors attempted to unfairly demonize him by attacking his religious beliefs—beliefs I didn't share. By the time of the final argument I'd long ago established credibility with the jury, both by telling the truth about my case and about myself. Had Cicero made his arguments before a modern jury, I take it he would have been greatly admired for his skill, but the jurors' psychic tentacles that seek out the pretender would likely have revealed him along the way, no matter how sharply his skill had been honed.

In the Weaver case my quest for credibility began early on—with my consciously feeling the pain of fear and dealing with it. The fighter in the ring is marinated in his fear and energized by it. He enters the ring sweating, his heart pounding. He tries to look confident. He waves at the crowd and attempts to stare down his opponent. He is bursting with power he never dreamed of. His reactions are quicker. His instincts take over. In the same way, the fighter in the courtroom absorbs fear into himself, and out of that painful cauldron his creative juices come boiling out and cause him to react intuitively and powerfully. The adrenaline that urges us to fight or flee nourishes our energy and empowers us, and it is the principal ingredient that makes up the winning stuff of courtroom drama.

In the same way, when we face the boss—that powerful overlord who can write the pink slip as fast as the slaughtermaster cuts the throat of the lamb—a fever of fear takes over. "My God! What am I doing here? I really could do without the promotion. He's going to put me in the troublemaker file, and when the next cuts come, I go. I need to feed the kids." But up the line, the vice president is feeling the same way. The top guy topples. The board, the president, they are all vulnerable and can be dumped by the turn of some unforeseen event that's lying there like a land mine in their path. Management dances on a slippery floor.

It is all right to be afraid. One cannot be brave without fear. Those young fools who love danger and feel no fear are only fools. Courage comes when we recognize our fear, face it, and hurl ourselves into the battle. I think of Captain Ahab, in *Moby Dick,* who said he wanted no men on his ship who were not afraid of the whale—which means that he didn't want any fools around him. The line between courage and foolhardiness is narrow.

At last we see fear as our friend. It warns us, protects us, and prepares us for battle. The sages were never afraid of fear. They embraced it, learned from it, grew from it, and survived to become old sages.

As we already know, the risks we face are great. *But the greatest risk of all is doing nothing when something needs doing.* The organism that does nothing soon dies. I see it everywhere, every day, men and women who have lived their lives inside their own locked closets of fear. Like plants in the dark, they wither, turn yellow, and die. Is it not better that we should have lived fully, bravely, and died in the sun?

Withholding permission to be beaten. There are those few who can never be beaten. We call them champions. We see them as superheroes—like Muhammad Ali, who, although decisions went against him both in and out of the ring, was never beaten. Something different, something shiny, vibrant, heroic, creates an aura around this kind. Something unconquerable. *I say we cannot be beaten without giving our permission to be beaten.*

We can deal with the prospect of defeat in several ways. We can accept our defeat, make excuses for it, and call upon the astounding ability of the human mind to rationalize it. We can run and become encased in a different kind of pain, the throbbing realization of cowardice, which is more painful than the pain of having fought and lost. Or we can simply refuse to give our opponent permission to defeat us.

I remember how painful my first loss in the courtroom was—watching a mother walk out of the courtroom with her young crippled son on crutches at her side. The jury had given nothing and had found in favor of the negligent railroad. Found against justice. Found that the boy could never be awarded the funds necessary to pay the medical bills for the operations he would need for many years. I wept. The weeping did no good. I was angry. I turned the anger inward and I hated myself, loathed my incompetence, and felt the ugly sting of guilt.

Other defeats followed, four others in a row. I would never become a trial lawyer. I would never win. I remembered as a child how I was afraid of the bully on the school grounds who chased me home. Breathless, I ran to the safety of the house only to meet my father who had a different idea about bullies. "They can only win if you let them," my father said matter of factly.

"He's bigger'n me," I said. "He's tougher'n me."

"Well, when he knocks you down, just get up again," my father said, as if the solution were as plain as anything. "And then when he knocks you down again, get up again. Pretty soon he'll understand that he can't beat you. Just keep getting up and he'll finally give up." I didn't think that was a very good approach. Getting beaten up didn't appeal to me, and I continued to run and cower. But over the years the pain of secretly acknowledging my cowardice proved to be far worse than the beating I might have taken.

As a young lawyer there came a time when the lessons of my father came seeping up through my wretchedness. Did I need this pain of defeat? I had stood up in the courtroom and been knocked down. I had gotten up again, only to be knocked down again and again. Was the pain of defeat a necessary part of my life? For the hungry hawk there must be a prey. It is our choice: We can continue to play the role of prey or refuse that role.

Once I understood that simple shift in paradigm from one who gives his permission to be defeated to one who withholds it, everything about me began to change—my voice, my posture, my self-esteem, my confidence, even my walk. One is either prey, victim, sufferer, wounded, loser, and casualty, and is devoured, or one is unconquerable.

So one becomes full of the self? Yes. The perfect, indomitable self that can feel fear and love as well. My opponent may win the case, but he has not defeated me. My appeals will follow. The gift of surrender will not come. The submission as prey will not come. The prophet can be hung, the saint executed, the true believer jailed, the leader assassinated, but they are not defeated. A life's sentence in prison against Nelson Mandela, the South African statesman and first black president of South Africa did not defeat him. The murder of Martin Luther King Jr. did not defeat him. And the crucifixion of Christ only insured his immortality. None of these men have been defeated to this moment.

Changing one's vision of the self gives birth to a new person. The question is no longer why am I being defeated? No question is asked. The indomitable self radiates from the person and beams out in a sort of invisible halo of power. It is more than charisma. It is awesome to behold, like a roaring river. It need not take on the thunder of the orator. It is often quiet and easy, but the power is there—a sense that to conquer the person one would have to kill him with an ax.

Things change in the presence of such a person. Doors open. Respect is given as automatically as a smile returns a smile. Possessing such power, the person can be humble, and gentle, and loving, because refusing to give permission to be defeated, a simple, transforming state of mind, no longer requires the false accouterments of power—bravado, arrogance, and conceit. This power which is achieved by retaining what has belonged to us all along—our refusal to give our permission to be defeated—is complete and perfect in itself.

Yet we also give ourselves permission to lose a battle to win the war. Often I meet people who are intransigent concerning some minor issue in their lives. When, as it were, their ship has taken a broadside hit we find them fussing over a leaky faucet. We must choose our battles and where we will fight them and when. I do not preach against losing every battle. I only say we shall never deliver our permission to be beaten in the war.

Preparing the witness against fear. If we are afraid, how then does our client feel? How does the witness feel who must take an oath to tell the truth but who also knows he will be attacked by the opposing counsel in order to display him as a liar? One may encounter nearly every danger in the courtroom, but few are as potentially destructive as the witness's reaction to his own fear.

We have already seen that when we're afraid, we tend to revert to our animal state in defense of our fear. We attack or run or hide or evade, and we have seen that none of these reactions to fear are acceptable to the jury. We do not trust a witness who is hostile, or one who will not be open with us, who hides. We are leery of the witness who fudges and hedges. So, if the witness is left to deal with his fear according to his natural instincts, we will likely present a witness who will disappoint us.

As we have already seen, there is no way for either us or our witness to deal with fear effectively except to face it head on. But how? I sit down with the witness, even the veteran witness, and lay the issue out on the table. I begin by saying something like this: "You know, being a witness is not an easy task. It's hard because we know that we are being tested, that the jury might not believe us, that the other side will attack us. Lots of things to be afraid of." But remembering that we can never ask another to own his fear if we do not own ours, I might then say what is true for me. "I know what it is to be afraid. I never go into a courtroom without feeling fear. And when I put you on the stand I will be anxious. I'll think, I wonder if I can ask the right questions and whether my questions will be objected to by the other side and their objections sustained? Maybe the judge doesn't like me. Maybe he will hold against me and embarrass me in front of the jury. I'm afraid I won't be able to think fast enough, that my mind will stall. It's just the same old stuff I always feel in a courtroom—its common name is fear. And it's all right. It hones me. Actually it's my friend."

Then, and only after I have owned my own fear, do I begin to talk about the witness's fear. To a lay witness my conversation might continue as follows: "Robert, when you get on the stand you will feel the same thing. Remember, it's all right to feel fear. Because by feeling it we are going to be able to deal with it in a way that will work for us instead of against us." I have the witness's attention.

I might continue, "And when you take the stand I'm going to ask you about your fear. I want you to feel it first, and then to be totally honest with me about it." I may rehearse what I will ask him about his fear, so that the questions do not frighten him. I may take him to the courtroom at a time when it is vacant and put him on the stand. I will show him where the various members of the court will sit so that he can see the scene before he's suddenly faced with it for the first time as a witness.

When Robert is called to the stand at trial here is what the examination might sound like: "Robert, how are you feeling right now?" I have instructed him that when I ask such a question that he take the time, yes, all the time he needs to actually zoom in on his feelings. Now his answer will truthfully be, "Afraid, I guess."

"I want you to tell me everything that you're afraid of." The judge is leaning over the bench. Opposing counsel is about to object, but he isn't quite sure that his objection will be well received by the jury who wants to know why the witness is afraid.

Robert may say, "I'm afraid of them." He points to the jury.

"The jurors?"

"Yeah."

"Why are you afraid of them?"

"I'm afraid they won't believe me. I'm afraid they'll think I'm lyin'." Robert is telling the absolute truth. Nearly every witness who takes the stand takes it with a small ghostlike voice inside that whispers, *Will they believe me? What do I have to do, what do I have to say, and how do I have to say it to make them believe me?"*

We might continue with our questions about fear. "Well, Robert, is there anyone else you're afraid of here?"

"Yes." He points at the judge.

"Why are you afraid of him?"

"I don' know."

"Try to answer my question."

Then, to my surprise, he replies: "You told me you were afraid of him, too."

A small, guilty smile is all I can give. "Who else are you afraid of, Robert?"

He points to the prosecutor.

"Why are you afraid of him?"

"He's gonna ask me a lot of questions and he is smarter than me."

"Anyone else you are afraid of here?"

"Yes, I guess so."

"Who?"

"You."

"Why would you be afraid of me? I care about you. I'm here to defend you. Why would you be afraid of me?"

"I never had anybody else in charge of me before." He looks helpless.

It makes little difference how we deal with fear in the courtroom or any other room. Once it is dredged up from the murky, roiling depths and spread out in the sunshine it changes. It becomes something that can be dealt with because we have given ourselves permission to face it, and magically it loses its power. Once we understand that to be afraid is not synonymous with being a coward we can put its power to work for us. It will explode into action, into spontaneity, into emotional muscle, and into the caring and commitment we gather to win.

6. THE DANGEROUS POWER OF ANGER

WARS ARE WARS. We prepare ourselves for our wars in the same way that a nation prepares for battle. The nation begins by marinating the minds of the people with a fervor for war. We are shown the injustices and atrocities of the opponent and heated into rage at the enemy's cruelty. We are deluged with visions of his barbaric acts, and the enemy's danger to us. We grow to fear the opponent as well as to hate him, and our anger begins to replace our fear. Anger has its function in the human organism. It is an important antidote to fear.

I own a lot of anger. It tags along with me wherever I go, which is not to say that I am an angry person, but that I have a fund of anger that is available to me when I need it. Its source came from a series of experiences along my life's way, which, although painful, proved to be gifts to me. I wouldn't be spared my anger. Like steam, it is the stuff that powers the locomotive—it can power me when I call on it. But if anger is not properly contained and released with a certain discipline it can blow things to hell.

I have admonished that we must feel—that without feeling we are the walking dead and as effective as mumbling mannequins. Must we not feel our anger as well? I say yes. But note: The word *anger* is included in the word *danger*. Nothing is more dangerous than a lawyer hurling his volley of anger at a jury or a protestor jumping up at a community meeting assaulting the governing council with a barrage of hollering. The danger is not to the recipient of such wrath, but to the angry person himself who will be defeated by his own anger—dismissed as irresponsible, shunned as unreasonable, indeed, as someone to be avoided like the mumps.

Before we can decide what to do with our anger let's first understand it. What is it? What is its function? Anger arrives on the scene, all red and blistery, and usually in response to hurt. When we are hurt by the words or actions of others we are more likely to be angry than to cry. The insult hurts. We respond in anger. Betrayal brings pain. We reply in anger. When we feel helpless, the pain of it is compensated in anger. Cornered, anger is the natural antidote. Lay a nasty name on me in anger and I immediately attack back in anger with my own insult.

If we understand that anger is most often the product of injury, then don't we also understand that anger is a *secondary emotion*—that the hurt, the pain came first, after which anger rushed in to take its place? Indeed, the anger will not diminish until we have relieved ourselves of the hurt. Sometimes this process takes generations. Holy wars never end. The conflict originates in pain—the threat of domination that brought on fear, the killing, the sorrow, the retaliation, and more killing—the circle of pain never ceasing.

If we understand that anger has been seeded by hurt, is it not more useful to deal with the hurt than with the anger? Our hurt is not threatening to the person who hurt us. But our anger is. Anger begets anger. The mirror is always at work. When I am angry at you, you are most likely to return my anger with anger of your own. And the war is on. But if I say to you, "That hurt me," the response of the other is more likely to be, "I didn't mean to hurt you, or I wish I hadn't," and the war may come to an end. When I am attacked with anger, is it not better to understand that it has come out of the other's hurt? Instead of responding with my own anger, is it not better to say, "You must be hurt. How did I hurt you?" and the war, again, has a chance to end.

The danger of anger is that it threatens. When I am threatened, the fear of it, the pain, creates my own anger and the war erupts. We have already discovered that to threaten the other is to threaten the self. And as we know, retained, unexpressed anger is a danger to ourselves and to others. If I can quietly, yes, kindly communicate to the other that I am angry and why, the positive product may be peace. If I retain it, the stuff grows like noxious weeds and can take over the landscape. William Blake, the nineteenth-century English poet, wrote:

> *I was angry with my friend:*
> *I told my wrath, my wrath did end.*
> *I was angry with my foe:*
> *I told it not, my wrath did grow.*

But the nature of the telling is as critical as the telling itself. If I speak of my anger angrily I've dug my pit and fallen in it.

Injustice brings on anger. We see it all the time. The child who acts out in school, who attacks his classmates and becomes a disciplinary problem is most often the child who has been mistreated. Nothing more surely instills an unremitting, deadly anger than injustice imposed on the innocent. We see it in the helpless who storm on endlessly and are devoured by their own impotent rage. We see it in the projects, the people striking out with violence. They were born as innocent children. Having committed no crime, they were nevertheless punished with poverty, hatred, filth, and rejection, indeed, with violence—their punishment for the crime of having been born. The fact that 25 percent of all African-American males are in prison or under probation of one kind or another is shameful proof that to punish the innocent funds an enduring anger that is acted out against the system, even against the poor themselves.

When I am asked how I can defend those who have been charged with monstrous crimes I often reply that I seldom see a crime by a single individual that is as evil as the crimes the system imposes year by year on the many. And when the black prisoner from the ghettos is finally released we know the war will still be on, because injustice upon injustice breeds an unrequited anger the product of which is crime. And to the same extent that society stands as a threat to its abandoned members, so too do they stand as a threat to an enlightened society. Such chaos is called a revolution.

We have been taught from the beginning that we must not be angry. "Don't you dare be angry" is the angry warning that was dumped on us and that we, in turn, unload on our children. From the time of our innocence, our little psyches have been programmed against anger, both ours and theirs. Still, if we withhold our anger and have no healthy way to release it we may become neurotic, suffer a variety of actual physical illnesses, or we may turn our anger inward and become depressed, even suicidal.

Something is lacking in a person who cannot feel anger. Most often it's that the person does not care. When we are injured or threatened anger comes rushing in to prepare us for the fight, to survive. But it is *our* anger. It belongs to us in the same way that all our passions belong to us. They are not to be spilled carelessly on the moment's canvass. Such a painting would be a mess. But the paint of emotion, first recognized and then deftly and honestly applied, can create a masterpiece. The painting requires all shades from black to white and all colors relevant to the presentation. I am not speaking of moderation. I am addressing the skill of applying our emotions faithfully with the grace and skill of a fine painter.

In the courtroom my anger against injustice motivates me to take on the opponent—usually the large corporation or the state that prosecutes a citizen unfairly. I am glad for my anger. But for its energy I might be sitting in a back office of a large law firm drawing deadly boring business contracts or melting into the stacks of books that stare out blankly from their dusty shelves. Still, early in my career my anger defeated me more than once. I have said what we all know—we do not like angry people. But in the same way, we do not trust people who should be angry and who are not. What would we think of a man who watched his wife being physically assaulted and who stood by popping his bubble gum? What would we think of a person who was repeatedly insulted but who did not have the courage to stand up for his rights? Appropriate anger is acceptable to most of us.

In court we confront witnesses who we know are paid, champion liars. I have seen experts take the stand with all of their wrappings of authority, their gold-plated curricula vitae. As if their words descended from heaven, I have watched as they deposit loads of pure excreta on the jurors. It is not that they lie to the jury and thereby earn their monstrous fees for doing so, but that they take advantage of the innocent decision makers who look up to them because these experts have held positions of honor in the scientific world. These are professional witnesses who have learned to look over at the jurors with kind and loving eyes, who can fool even the most discerning for the relatively short time they are on the stand. Even their well-disguised speciousness would be discovered by the jurors if they testified for any extended time—by our truth-seeking psychic tentacles. But for the few hours they occupy the stand they can deceive, and they do.

I see many deserving people deprived of justice because of these well-paid frauds—the horribly crippled children negligently injured in childbirth who can never walk or speak an intelligible word, the woman who will never see again because of an incompetent surgeon asleep at the switch, the hordes of injured who lose their right to justice because insurance companies have embraced these charlatans who, case after case, spread their malignant lies on innocent jurors. Their haughty pretenses and their venomous testimony (which they know is false) always angers me, sometimes to the precipitous edge.

But if we angrily attack these petty prevaricators before their lies have been clearly demonstrated we will lose, because, although we know the truth, the jurors do not. While we are justly angered by the witness's testimony and see him as a cheat, the jurors see him as a man of enlightened authority, and our attack will appear to be generated by one who has taken a strike in the heart and, without the character to accept it gracefully, releases his anger as does the poor loser.

Until the testimony itself creates anger in the hearts of the listeners, we must redirect the energy of our anger. We do not deny it to ourselves. We feel it. But we rechannel it into a precise, thoughtful, solid cross-examination. Only when the liar is at last exposed is it time for appropriate anger. I say, don't attack the witness until the jury wants him attacked. Then we had better do our work efficiently and cleanly, and with style.

Aristotle once said, "We praise a man who feels angry on the right grounds and against the right persons and also in the right manner at the right moment and for the right length of time." That says it all.

So how do we channel our anger that ought not be dumped whenever we feel it? We are in the moment. We feel it. If we do not feel it we cannot deal with it. I speak to my anger. To myself I may say, "Hello there, anger. I feel you, I respect you, and if you will be patient, I will either let you escape at an appropriate time or I will convert your energy into something useful, perhaps, even something grand. Be patient." It is a way to become aware of the power of anger, that it's an emotion to cherish but respect. Without it I would have no moral indignation that urges me to seek justice. My anger tells me I care. It is a weapon in my arsenal, but like any dangerous weapon, one must be aware that one can kill oneself with it.

7. UNDERSTANDING POWER

I N WAR, THE MOST POWERFUL ARMY does not always win. I think of the American Revolution, the British soldiers, prettily uniformed, well trained, fully armed, the British controlling the seas and the ports, the rebels a rag-tag army of poorly trained recruits who shot at the enemy from behind trees and refused to take on the British regulars according to the then-existing rules of engagement. Power is often useless.

The United States had superior power in Vietnam but did not win the war, and our current wars call into question the power of power. How often I have walked into a courtroom where the opposing corporation was represented by a host of lawyers and assistants who dragged in imposing boxes of evidence and the most modern demonstrative equipment. They put on a show and overwhelmed the judge with endless motions, all of which were thickly briefed. But they did not win.

Endemic in power are its own limitations. Power tends to become bureaucratized. Often the right hand of power is a stranger to its left. Bureaucrats have their own power structure to struggle against, and they have each other to kick around and blame. Often they cannot make timely decisions, and those they make are sometimes made without a full understanding of the issues. Frequently a light brigade—special forces, as it were—can move in and take over while the main army is still trying to figure out what to do.

In a large personal injury case we see how the decisions come down from the insurance company that must finally pay the judgment. The case will be monitored by a member of the legal staff in the home office who in turn has no authority on his own and who must go to his supervisor. Often in large cases, the supervisor himself must get authority from higher-ups. And the lawyer representing the insurance company must make decisions based on the authority that is handed down from those bureaucratic sources. In his own firm, the same lawyer is burdened with the advice of a whole cadre of sycophants who may or may not be able to provide him with a full grasp of the case. Power often gets in the way of itself.

But in the courtroom there is no mob to fight. Only one lawyer at a time is permitted to speak. So, too, in the public meeting, in the boardroom, or the boss's office. The overwhelming power the opponent brings against us is suddenly reduced to a one-on-one engagement, and we, who no longer give our permission to be defeated, can win.

Besides, power is often without a human heart. In the courtroom the lack of simple compassion is routinely reflected in the decisions that the corporate attorneys make. One sees an overlay of cold calculation despite the corporation's attempt at feigning compassion. One cannot long pretend caring. And it is impossible to make a jury or anyone else care when we do not care. We remember: Caring is contagious.

We also remember that the American juror usually favors the underdog. A gross display of power on one side attracts a leveling attitude on the part of the jurors. Many times, and for obvious reasons, I have gone to court alone to face a bevy of powerhouse lawyers on the other side. If I have a choice between putting together a team, one consisting of a half-dozen lawyers with all of their specialties and expertise on the one hand, or just me (*and the jury*)— in the end I may be on the winning team.

Humanizing the *power person*. We are ants, all worker ants, until we need a queen. Then we feed the poor bug some special queen concoction and behold—a queen is born to whom we all bow and scrape and quake in the face of her power. We see a haberdasher or the owner of a baseball team and we put the cloak of the presidency on him, and we give him the power to destroy whole cities and conquer entire nations and we bow and curtsy and struggle for a glimpse of the great man. We take a simple carpenter and call him the son of God, and with such power he changes history. We take an ordinary lawyer, slip a black robe on him and call him your honor and catch our breath as we argue before him, this man of all wisdom who could barely find his way to the courthouse before his ascension.

We see the glorious fool who has inherited millions and we adore him, find him beautiful, wise, and even funny, because he has been anointed to a high place on account of his money and the power of it. Yet he is still but a fool—albeit a rich one. Movie stars are adored, even worshipped, especially if they die young. Although it is true that men can rise to the occasion and become great, by and large our modernday deities, major and minor, take their high places only because we put them there. *haha It's a game*

On the other hand, the greatest examples of the species may remain anonymous. I am rarely impressed with the so-called greats, the politicians, the judges, the movie stars. The truly great people of this world are rarely recognized—the mother who raises seven children by herself and sees to their education, the teacher who through her inspiration and love creates many contributing members of our society, or the poet who refuses to climb the commercial ladder and writes great poems which few will read. If we ponder who we make into our heroes we'll soon realize we are in sore need of genuine heroes. If we look carefully at those we respect, we will often find that our respect is poorly placed. Why do we respect many of the rich whose principal trait is greed? Why do we respect the movie star who has had a half dozen wives and whose narcissism has transformed him into a self-anointed fop? Why do we worship those whose power was purchased at the polls with corporate dollars? Why do we bow to judges who wear the robe of justice that covers unjust hearts?

When I walk into the courtroom and see his honor take the stand I am stricken with awe. He takes his high place on the bench and looks down on us. He has more power over me and my client than the president of the United States. He can make rulings that will forever change lives. In the courtroom he is omnipotent. I cannot strike out at him if he is a tyrant. I cannot criticize him if he is a buffoon. Yet, yesterday he may have been a lawyer with little talent and an empty fund of wisdom, but who contributed to the right political party. Why am I stricken with such awe and fear of this person?

When we invade the sacred premises of any who have power over us, the boss, the school board members, the county commissioners, all former ordinary citizens, why are we suddenly afraid to speak out? When we go before the city council why do we sometimes find ourselves nearly speechless?

The answer, of course, is that those who hold positions of power hold them because we, like the ants creating their own queen, have given them *our* power. If we begin to realize that their greatness is only *our* state of mind we will have taken the first large leap toward overcoming our fear of the *power person*.

All *power persons* are mere mortals, many of whom are dreadfully afraid of us. Some are marginally bright enough to recognize that we are the source of their power, that we can retract their power as quickly as it has been given. The politician fears us. The corporate executive fears us. We may expose him and dethrone him. The judge knows that his power is ephemeral—that the voters can cast him out into the horrors of becoming a regular citizen again, one who must once more crane his neck looking up to some other judge.

Those judges who have been appointed for life are the new kings in a democracy, and some are the worst of tyrants. But other than the fact that most of them live approximately forever, thriving, as they must, on the misery they decree on the hapless, they are still human. They fight traffic to and from work, their wives complain that they snore, they harbor their own set of neurotic quirks, and, as we, they fight protruding bellies, grow old, die, and are soon forgotten.

To those who suffer little caring for the human species, power is attractive, compelling. Bullies want power. Dictators and tyrants, the lowest form of the species, are addicted to power. I know men (and women) who, if given the power, would change the color of the moon to match their evening wear. And those who love power, who love it to the marrow, are those to whom power should never be entrusted. The ancient Chinese held that men who seek power should be denied it because they are dangerous to themselves and to others (which is the current measure by which we incarcerate people as mentally ill). Power is a devilish drug and should be outlawed for all except those who refuse to exercise it. But as we have seen, the power that others wield over us is only the power we have given them. They hold power over us and become *power persons* only because we have given them *our* power.

In the hands of politicians power is usually a desperate clutching to office.

In the hands of the cruel judge power becomes a self-christened, deistic vision of himself, one touched by heaven to bring down the wrath of God upon the miserable creatures who appear before him and their evil representatives, their lawyers. Some people experience power as a sort of psychic aphrodisiac. They are usually the weakest, the most afraid, the cowards who become spunkless milksops the moment they are divested of power. The most powerful of all are those who refuse to use it. Love is, in fact, the ultimate power and the only legitimate power. All other manifestations of power are without legitimacy.

When I walk into a courtroom I see the judge for who he is—an ordinary man with extraordinary power. But he is my judge and he belongs to me—to serve my case, my cause, with sound and just rulings. I give him the presumption of decency. But should he stray from this role and become one of those tyrants who sits up there like a maddened emperor, I may disrobe him. Without his clothing he is a disgusting sort. His skin is usually too white, bleached like a daisy that has been smothered under the manure pile. He will wear funny little pink pajamas tonight at bedtime, with patterns of little jumping teddy bears, and he'll make some excuse to his wife for his bedtime failure, who, if the truth were known, is only too pleased that he has consigned himself to his own side of the bed. I do not create such a vision of the man out of disrespect for his office. But I have no intention of respecting an office held by a man who disrespects justice. Seeing him as he most likely is permits me to keep my power. It belongs to me and I do not intend to deliver it to him, which does not mean that I will disobey his orders, display my contempt, or otherwise misconduct myself. There is a profound difference between respecting a judge's just rulings and enduring the unjust ones, as may be necessary to accomplish our goals in the case.

All I mean to say is that we must put those in power in their proper places. If they earn our respect it should be honestly given. Several judges have been my heroes. I dedicated one of my books to a judge. I have been befriended by those in power and given a boost along the way—particularly by parents and teachers who had power over me but who exercised it with love. I have known rich men who were truly great men. The exceptions are not what I've been talking about. If we must always get entangled in exceptions we can go nowhere with the overlying truth of any argument.

What I have said here can be simply put: Those in power retain their power because we give it to them or fail to reclaim it. Most in power hold on to it because they need it, indeed, because they are weak without it. Many who possess great power are ill or ill advised. That we should give them our power by becoming intimidated by theirs is to wrongly waste the power we have. For us, power, theirs and ours, belongs to us. We can give it or withhold it.

The battleground belongs to us. When we walk into a place of battle it is seldom one we know intimately. We do not wage these battles in our homes. We wage our battles in a strange environment—the courtroom, the boss's office, the boardroom, or the chambers of some hearing examiner. These are places that are most often hard and stark, or by contrast, imposingly lavish. If we are in the lushly furnished boardroom, with its long walnut table and its cushy swivel chairs, we are also intimidated by the opulence that reminds all in attendance that we visit it only at the invitation of power.

When we walk into a courtroom we are immediately thrown into a hostile environment. I have never been in a courtroom that was furnished in such a way as to create a sense of comfort and safety. The bench, of course—the throne—sits up high so that power looks down on us. Behind power is usually the flag of the nation and state reminding us that the occupant of the throne is the duly appointed agent of the ultimate earthly power. The seats in the courtroom are often those hard pews that are little better than uncomfortable benches. Perhaps from the hallway outside the courtroom we hear weeping. Nothing alive grows in the courtroom. We see no plants, no goldfish in bowls, no dogs with wagging tails. We see instead the deputy sheriffs or marshals, their shiny badges of authority glittering in the bright lights, their guns seemingly ready to kill or maim at the slightest provocation. Our client may be brought in shackles. The lawyers whisper to each other in this frightening place, even before the judge enters and the court is called to order.

These are the premises of power. They are constructed to surround us with emotional high fences with psychic barbed wire around the top. Their function is to strip us of our power before the battle begins, because no one can exercise their own power from within the confines of a psychic penitentiary— not freely, not effectively. We realize we are not out in the gentle woods sitting on a log under a lovely spring sky. Instead we have been captured and imprisoned in this hostile place by the system from which we cannot escape unless we understand the false accouterments of power.

Is it false because it is constructed?

71

All battles should be conducted out of doors. Court should be held in the middle of a pretty pasture surrounded by old pine trees and a clear stream running through it. The arguments before the city council should be in the city park or on the beach. If we should suggest such a place for these wars we would be dismissed out of hand as one qualified for a house of jibberers. But we can at will go where we choose simply by willing it so.

Every courtroom I enter belongs to me. The judge and the opposing lawyers, indeed, the hostile witnesses, are my guests. I welcome them here. I cannot do battle without an opponent, and the battle cannot be fairly fought without a referee. Since the courtroom is mine I can furnish it as I wish. All of this may be only child's play, but the power of the mind can either free us or imprison us. We will always fight a better fight if we refuse to be dragged into the dungeons of power. As the poet mused, "Stone walls do not a prison make, nor iron bars a cage." In the end, the most anxious man in prison is the warden.

W E, THE PEOPLE—OUR CRY for justice. The cost of trials is exorbitant in time, human energy, and money. Those who suffer injustices but have cases in which their money damages are too small to pay the large fees that lawyers must earn to keep their practices alive and to pay the costs incurred in such trials go without representation or are required to settle their cases on the cheap. That there is "liberty and justice" for all is the great myth in America.

In a single week I will receive scores of requests for representation— mostly from ordinary citizens who have just cases with small money damages, or complex cases that are too time consuming and costly to bring. Here are examples of only a few:

- an impoverished woman is in prison who, through ignorance, signed a plea bargain even though she was innocent—she had a learning disability and will be in prison for many years to come;
- a relative seeks help for a child, fourteen, who from the time she was an infant was abused, battered, and abandoned, and who then committed a murder and was tried as an adult, found guilty, and sentenced to life imprisonment;
- a woman in a homeless shelter is assaulted daily at the shelter and hit on for sexual favors by members of the staff;

• a man who had worked for a carrier service for eighteen years who suffered occupational arthritis in both knees, instead of being supplied proper medical care, was terminated;

• a woman whose husband died as a result of a complicated medical malpractice, but the law firm that took the case decided the cost of advancing it was too great, and she can find no other lawyer to continue the suit;

• a woman who testified honestly in a case on behalf of another employee who lost her job because of it;

• a citizen whose home was raided by government agents searching for evidence against him, whose computers were confiscated, and as a result he is out of business;

• a woman who years previously suffered from the horrors of a well-known drug that has been taken off the market and who is now afraid her daughter will suffer the same horrors;

• a young lawyer who says she is being set up by the state bar to lift her license to practice because she is "rocking the boat" of the local establishment;

• a loyal, longtime employee who criticized his corporate employer for its unlawful acts and was fired on false grounds;

• a truck driver who was dismissed because of a drunk driving conviction who had, in fact, never been convicted of anything, ever.

As is clear at a glance, most injustices result from the abuse of power.

Here is an actual letter I received that is typical of the grievances of those who have been injured and seek justice in this system.

Dear Mr. Gerry Spence,

I am writing this letter because I cannot understand why after eight years I can get no helpful responses to my situation. I have written my state senators and congressmen, also my representatives, even President Bush, but with no helpful response.

I also have sent letters to various newspapers and different media news, people like you. Still I get no helpful response.

I see on TV and in the newspaper every day articles about peoples' rights being violated. It seems all the media writes or puts on TV is if it has to do with a murder, race discrimination, or sex discrimination. They just say that they are discriminated against and the media is on it.

I was dragged 70 feet by a rail car we were moving in 1994. The doctors said I was lucky to even be alive because of my damage and blood loss. The rail car had a faulty hand brake, which my attorney proved. But because we couldn't prove what made it fail, the judge wouldn't even let my case go to trial.

We even appealed it, but they gave summary judgment to the railroad. The justice system just turned its back on me. I even lost $85,000 in legal fees, which would of paid my house off which would of helped me a lot.

I drove a semi for twenty-six years and made a very good income. Now, being amputated above my left knee, that income is gone. I just about make it on my disability check. This is so wrong after working so hard all my life. Now I am stepped on by our justice system, which I have lost all faith in.

Where are my constitutional rights to a trial in front of my peers? Terrorists even get more rights than I have received from our system. I was born in the USA in 1947, and I love my country, but it seems to me they do more for political reasons than what is right.

Sincerely,

[I have withheld the author's name.]

The other day the parents of a child who was born nearly deaf took their child to an audiologist for the child's current hearing examination and for a new hearing aid. The fee for the examination was three hundred dollars, which the family's medical insurance company refused to pay, claiming that the child's need for her latest examination was "age related." The parents were properly outraged. But the cost of taking the insurance company to court to force payment was not practical. Billions of dollars are stolen from our citizens because the justice system cannot respond to their needs. As a matter of fact, it has become widespread corporate policy to refuse to pay just bills when the amounts are too small to warrant the cost of collection and when the person to whom the money is owed is not of sufficient stature that the company wishes to retain their good will. From my experience in the courts for over fifty years I can say that when we buy an insurance policy on our car or home, what we have really purchased is the right to sue the company for its failure to pay. The company involved will nearly always pay less than what is justly due, knowing full well that the shortfall is too small to warrant a suit against them.

At Trial Lawyer's College one of our students, a fifty-five-year-old woman who looked more like a grinning little elf who'd just jumped out from under a toadstool, took as her first case one on behalf of a woman who had been sexually harassed in the workplace and who had suffered unconscionable sexual verbal assaults until she was so emotionally traumatized that she could no longer perform her duties. Then she was fired. A dozen seasoned lawyers had turned the case down. Our little elf of a woman took the case because she believed in her client, felt for her, became her, and walked into the courtroom afraid but prepared.

She stood her full five feet tall where others would have withered. She faced an unfriendly judge. She was outshown, outmaneuvered, yes, outsmarted by the company lawyers. But a jury gave her $1.3 million for her client's injuries—a remarkable testimony for the proposition that presenting one's self honestly and openly is at last the greatest power. The company appealed, and, of course, the fully expected but outrageous result occurred: The appeals court, populated by appointees of the corporate power structure, reversed the decision and our little elf's client got nothing. She has not given up.

I frequently receive letters from clients of other lawyers complaining that their lawyers do not or will not represent them fully. The list of horrors goes on, day after day, and these citizens, guaranteed justice under the constitution, cannot find competent, dedicated lawyers to represent them; nor, too often, are there fair-minded judges to hear their cases. But the system continues providing the myth of justice—what judges like to call "the appearance of justice."

Still, there are bright spots that shine through the dim and dismal. The system is much like a casino where a lot of noise is made when someone hits a jackpot—the lights flash and the chimes chime and someone comes running in with a wheelbarrow to haul off a load of quarters. But the losers slink off quietly into the night. In this country the winners in the justice system are broadcast across the headlines. On the other hand, the multitudes who never see justice are mostly silent, believing, as many do, that there must be something wrong with them, or, in this land where all are created equal, they would surely have been rendered justice.

But, as in Las Vegas, there are winners, and winners exist in the justice system as well. I have represented many of them, and good trial lawyers across the land have represented untold thousands who enjoy some level of justice. Under the right circumstances, with properly trained lawyers and in the right judicial climate, the system can be forced to deliver justice to the few who have large enough money claims to warrant the expense of time and dollars. Still, the masses in this country go without much justice, and even now the insurance industry is exercising its power with lawmakers across the land to cap damages so that justice in this country will at last become truly a myth.

But the failure of the system is nothing new. It has existed from the beginning. Our legal system is based on precedent—that is, governing the present by the past, which is nothing more or less than a means by which to keep past power in power. The purpose of this book, then, becomes even more apparent, and its need more urgent—to help lawyers better represent their clients so that justice can be wrested from the hands of power, and to aid ordinary citizens to better present their cases in this hard and complex world.

Training ourselves to win. Presumably we lawyers learned how to try a case in law school—so believes most of the public. What we really experienced in law school was a lobotomy of sorts, one that anesthetizes the law student against his emotions and attempts to reduce law to some sort of science, which, of course, is a bizarre notion, since, as we've seen, even the high court can't agree on a single proposition of law, and justice is, at last, something felt, so that what is justice for one is unjust for another. What if doctors couldn't agree on the most simple medical proposition—five saying we are merely suffering from hayfever while four say we are dying from pneumonia. Medicine is an art, but it is one based on science. Lawyering is an art, but it is based on philosophy, on values, on the ideas we harbor concerning justice.

The truth is that a young lawyer fresh out of law school who has just passed the bar and hung his gilt-edged diploma on freshly painted walls is about as ready to try a case as a surgeon who has never had a scalpel in this hand is ready to perform his first operation. In the real world of the law, the training of trial lawyers is delayed until the young lawyer has passed the bar. Then his training begins, case after case, loss after loss. I sometimes equate such losses to the stacks of corpses that doctors would pile up outside their offices if doctors had no better training in medical school than we.

Scores of trials are required before a young lawyer becomes even marginally competent in the courtroom. This fact gives the large law firm with experienced trial lawyers who represent the rich and powerful the edge. Most would-be trial lawyers attend weekend seminars, or short summer sessions.

They read books, watch tapes, and go on trying their cases, too often at the expense of their clients. Some become public defenders or work in the prosecutor's office and gradually acquire some competence in the courtroom. But most cases these days, both civil and criminal, are settled without a trial, so that the trial lawyer is becoming an endangered species. Less than two percent of the cases filed in our federal courts go to trial.

In response to what I call this "educational fraud" foisted on both lawyers and the public we have established the Trial Lawyer's College with a pro bono faculty of trial lawyers we have trained. It's our attempt to give lawyers for the people—and only lawyers for the people—insights and strategies in trial practice that will prepare them in ways that many veteran lawyers will never experience in a lifetime. Because our training is done in small groups and our facilities limited, our program is available to only a miniscule part of the total profession.

Representing the self. Many people have taken to representing themselves in court and a few have had success. Today I received the following e-mail:

> *After meeting with two lawyers today who practice at one of the top 300 law firms in the country, I made the decision the best one to defend me is me. I'll do my own research and file my own papers. Legal leg to stand on or not, I have to try. Worst case: the judge throws it out or they countersue and drive off with my 1997 Buick while I make the plates for it.*
>
> [I have withheld the name.]

In the end, it may be better for some who have suffered injustice to take on the battle *pro se* (for themselves), even if they lose. As the citizen above understood, it is better to lose fighting than to give up because one cannot get proper representation. To lie down in the battle is not only to lose the battle but to lose the self. Remember, the courts cannot prevent us from representing ourselves. We may have difficulty. We will probably get entangled in the procedural ropes. We may not know how to question a witness or how to find and present an expert. We may not know how to conduct ourselves before a jury, if, indeed, we ever get that far. The judge may get impatient and strongly suggest we get counsel. He may throw our case out because it is not legally viable, or because it has not been properly pled, or because we have failed to follow some arcane rule. Indeed, representing ourselves may simply be foolish.

But sometimes we may have advantages: I've seen judges lean over backwards to help a *pro se* plaintiff. And at trial, the person representing himself can get away with things that a seasoned trial lawyer could not. For example, the *pro se* plaintiff can innocently blurt out inadmissible facts or make improper observations that would not be tolerated from a lawyer who has a license at stake. I remember seeing a *pro se* plaintiff stand up in court and say, "I don't have any money and I can't afford one of those big shot lawyers like they're hiring over there"—pointing to the defense table. On another occasion I heard a *pro se* defendant in a criminal case say, "They offered me to plea guilty to manslaughter and they know I didn't kill nobody. The prosecutor"—pointing to the D.A. sitting at his table—"even admitted to me I didn't do anything."

Some of the better lawyers will give free advice and direction to you if they understand you are in need, that you are sincere, and that your case is just. Jurors can be sympathetic.

None of the foregoing is intended to encourage one to go to court without a competent lawyer. I have great respect for the bar as a whole and especially for those who represent the ordinary citizen, often at little profit to themselves. The justice system, such as it is, is supported almost entirely by the unsung, unknown small practitioners who, despite their inadequate training and the enormous odds against them, lay it all down for their clients and sometimes win—big time.

The small claims courts of this country are underused by the people, mostly because the public is not acquainted with their procedures. Often the jurisdiction of small claims courts go up to five thousand dollars, sometimes as high as ten thousand, so that the ordinary citizen can go into these courtrooms and sue the corporation that has refused a just payment or tries to shortchange him in the settlement. The procedures there are summary in form, and often justice can be achieved in these smaller cases.

Yet these small cases may be large in principle. Insurance companies hate small claims courts, and suing them creates an irritation like the incessant fleas on the back of the hound. They hate the itching and will often give in if it will only stop. (Cost is always the issue. Sometimes it costs them more to defend these small claims than it does to pay them.)

The problem still remains: When we sue a corporation we teach it nothing, because a corporation can learn nothing, feels nothing, and suffers nothing. If we want to sue because it is just, let us sue for our need. For the corporation, the justice we receive will be only an entry in some obscure account, probably in an office a thousand of miles away, the entry made by a bored employee without a name. But it is our justice and it belongs to us.

The odds for justice are different outside the courtroom. There the employee who approaches a board, or a citizen who presents his case before a city council will usually present his case to *power persons* who are no better trained than he. Still, training is in order. One does not run a marathon without getting into shape with many days of sweat.

Practicing. The old saw is, practice makes perfect: A lawyer is not born— he is born of practice. We rightly call lawyering the *practice* of law, because no matter what lawyers are taught, no matter how sterling their education, we become proficient only from having practiced the trial of cases over and over. So it is with surgeons who are engaged in the *practice* of medicine, which brings on the all too obvious admonition—don't practice on me.

Even to this day, and after years of speaking in court and elsewhere, I find myself practicing—walking alone along a trail somewhere trying to tell the story of my case in the most precise and vivid way. At night, as I fall asleep, I may hear the argument in my mind's ear and awaken with a better version. I ceaselessly talk the case to my wife and friends, always trying to find a better way to tell the story, to discover the verbs, especially the verbs, that will provide power and action to the story. I don't say, "He called 911." I say, "He dived at the phone, nearly jerked the phone from the wall, and beat out the numbers, 911."

What visual aids can we provide that will illustrate our case? We are provided many technical devices for in-court graphics. But a simple flip chart of blank paper on which we can sketch a picture or write important words or phrases is often as effective.

What precedents are out there? What statistics? What studies? What other stories? Who else has dealt with this problem, and how? What experts have written about such a case as ours? The Internet deprives us of any excuse for appearing before the *power person* without being fully armed with facts, studies, and statistics that support our story.

I have no doubt about the direct correlation between the number of hours

I spend in the preparation of a case and the results I achieve. Preparation is ongoing with me. Rarely am I without a small notebook on which I scribble ideas that come to me during the day. Sometimes I will hear a friend, my wife, or a child—especially a child—say something that seems well-argued and true and I make a note of it. I keep a notebook handy at the bed. Often thoughts come to me just as I am dropping off to sleep, the "hypnagogic state" as psychologists like to call it, or more often, a clarity comes bursting through like the rising sun just at the point of awakening. And the shower—ah, the shower! Something there is about warm water engulfing the body that opens the mind—a return perhaps to the embryonic fluid in which all peace and ultimate wisdom resides.

Please, may I use notes? I have already commented on the use of notes. For every hour I spend in court I spend ten hours out of court preparing. I write down every word I expect to say in the trial. The testimony of every witness is written out, question by question. The arguments are all written. It is not that they will ever be read to the jury. But the computer of the mind is being programmed. And in trial, as in war, we are continuously under siege. Opposing attorneys have one job—to defeat us. Many see interrupting our arguments or our examinations as their job, to so break up our presentation that what we're trying to say will make no sense to the jury. These are the attorneys who barrage the courtroom with volley after volley of objections, who continuously ask the judge to stop the flow of the testimony so they may trot up to the bench and make whatever objections they've concocted. Judges, too, will often join in the melee, piling on, as it were, with their rulings and admonitions, so that if we become momentarily set back we have our notes to bring us back.

I rarely refer to notes in the courtroom. They are distracting and leave the appearance of someone who doesn't know his case. When the president makes his speech he is aided with unseen teleprompters from which he reads his carefully prepared address. But the appearance is that he is speaking without notes and from the heart.

I say that it is better to speak from the heart, even given the false starts and sometimes the mistakes or omissions. When we speak from notes we proceed from the eyes, to the brain, to the vocal cords, to the audience. That part of the brain that houses our deepest feelings is skipped. At best we usually sound like the anchor man reading his script on the evening news—and even he uses a teleprompter. But when we speak from the heart without notes a different part of the brain takes over. And the magic begins.

True, it is frightening to stand up there barren of any notes. It feels naked. But if we will only begin, begin anywhere, soon, along the way, the creative, spontaneous part of the brain will take over and that which we have programmed in comes out properly gilded with appropriate emotion. As we approach the climax, the little voice we have already met tells us we are there, and the excitement, the power, flows in like flooding waters into the void. New images are created, new metaphors and stories come to mind. Our case is made, and as we approach the ending, the same little voice that has listened to us so carefully and that has magically guided us along now tells us that what we have just said makes a powerful ending note. Or, suddenly, out of the blue comes a set of phrases that trumpet across the room or whisper into the ears of our audience, and we know that we have reached a perfect ending.

Part Two

WINNING

(Waging the War—Presenting the Winning Case)

9. DISCOVERING THE STORY

EVERYTHING IN LIFE IS A STORY. Everything. We are born—which is a story—and we die, the end of that story and perhaps the beginning of another. Our life in between was a story, a book, in fact, every day a page of the story. The question is whether anyone would want to read that book. More to the point, would we want anyone to read it?

Is it a boring, empty story, one we've lived devoted to distractions, like the bear in the cage at the zoo who walks endlessly back and forth across the full length of his small pen, and at the conclusion of his life has traveled thousands of miles leading nowhere? At the end of our book of life, what is written on the last page? What if, after having filled the book with the pages of our story, there is written but two words: "So what?"

I think of the single mother I met the other day who raised seven children by herself. Her husband had abandoned her many years before. All of her children were educated and are contributing members of society. The last page of her story would not read, "So what?"

We view most of our lives in terms of story. We are fascinated by movies because of their stories in which we inhabit the life of those on the screen. Most advertisements we suffer on television are in story form. Even the nightly news is conveyed as story. *The Wall Street Journal* and *The New York Times* most often begin a feature with the story of an individual caught up in it. Elizabeth Ellis said, "Storytelling is the grandmother of all our knowledge."

"What's the story?" is the universal question. Our kids come home from school with a note from the teacher and we want to know the story. In short, almost every human action is experienced in the context of a broader story. The father going to work is engaged in the story of the office, the conflicts, the power struggles—and when he comes home at night he tells the story to his wife. The mother may be working too. Hers is likely a different story—one of sacrifice and frustration, one in which she needs to fulfill her nurturing role of mother and yet maintain her independence as an equally respected member of society.

That we see our lives and all of their chapters as stories is genetic. If we were to retreat in time to that moment when man became a member of a language-speaking species we would discover that all of his history, all of his religion, his belief systems, his culture is told and handed down in story. Consequently man became a great storyteller. The wise old members of the tribe maintained their positions of respect based on stories they passed on and the learning their stories engendered. The stories of great hunts and terrible battles were passed from generation to generation and became the history of the tribe. History, itself, is the connection of the present to the past by story.

How we perceive history depends on who is telling the story. Do we know our history from the story of the wealthy who founded this country—Washington, the richest man in the colonies, and Jefferson and all of the other slave owners who were men of wealth and position, or do we know the revolution from the standpoint of the small farmer who joined Washington's militia in order to earn a promised day's pay when pay was short? These are different stories, and the history of our country depends on which story is being told, and by whom.

The Bible is based on the stories that were handed down over the generations. But because they were the stories of our biblical ancestors they become revered, indeed holy, so that those stories are not only connected to the living, but to the dead, not only to the here and now, but, as it were, to eternity.

If we are to be successful in presenting our case we must not only discover its story, we must become good storytellers as well. Every trial, every presentation, every plea for change, every argument for justice is a story.

How to discover the story. What is the story of our case? It's not just a trial about "the plaintiff" who was injured in a car accident and suffered damages.

It's not just a story about a complaining employee who has been discharged because he's too old. Nor is it a diatribe about the evils of polluting the environment. Such issues may be of interest to a select audience, but nothing happens to heat the blood when we read the abstract language in the above sentences.

A prospective client, Danny Patterson, comes in. I ask him to take a chair and I pull one up. Nothing between us—no desk that sets up a psychological Berlin Wall that says that on my side of the desk resides all power and wisdom and that on his side of the desk is a frightened man who feels self-conscious and afraid.

Danny is a slight, serious-appearing man of about forty-five. If we ask simply what his case is about, here's what we will likely hear:

"Well, the cops came to our house—two big, burly guys and they searched our house, tore things up, and then arrested me and my wife, Judy, and took us in cuffs to jail. We were charged with possession of an illegal substance—marijuana—and with resisting arrest and assault on an officer with a deadly weapon. Our bail was set at $100,000 cash, which we couldn't make. While we were waiting for our preliminary hearing the D.A. dismissed the cases against us because the stuff they took out of our house wasn't marijuana but some alfalfa leaves we kept in a plastic envelope to feed our guinea pig. We want to sue the police and the city for false arrest."

Obviously that's not the whole story. Most people can't explain the horror they've experienced, and most interviewers can't hear or feel what that experience must have been like. As Danny tells us his story let's *become* Danny. Let's try to *feel* what he and his wife felt and experienced.

Lawyer: Danny, take me to that morning when they arrested you. Let's actually be there, right now. What are you doing?

Danny: Well, I'd just let the dog out.

Lawyer: No, you are *letting* the dog out.

Danny: Right. (He picks up on the idea that we want to be in the present.) It's cold, and fresh snow is on the ground, and the dog starts raising hell, barking at something around the side of the house. I see some tracks in the snow and I step off the porch and follow the tracks and then I see 'em—a couple of toughs looking into our bedroom window.

(As the story proceeds we continue absorbing the experience, still attempting to *become* Danny Patterson. I often rely on a phrase that lets the protagonist know I understand him and that helps me experience his feelings. The phrase is, "It must have been . . ." or "You must be . . .")

Example:

Lawyer: So you must be startled and suddenly afraid. So, what are you doing?

(Note: The present tense brings the event to the here and now instead of a memory.)

Danny: I holler at 'em. "What the hell you doin' there?" And they come charging at me, the big one in the front. He's a real mean-looking guy in a rumpled suit. About six-two. The other one, a shorter one, sorta fat, is in a suit and tie, right behind them. If they hadn't been in suits they'd a looked like a couple of bums.

Lawyer: If I were you I'd be running back into the house, slamming the door and locking it. (We project ourselves into Danny's experience, trying to think and feel as he did at that moment.)

Danny: That's just what I'm doing.

Lawyer: What happens next?

Danny: I call the police.

Lawyer: What are you saying to them?

Danny: I say, "This is Danny Patterson at 24 Melrose Lane and there's a couple of thugs trying to break into my house. And before I can get their answer the thugs are beating at my front door.

Lawyer: What are you doing now?

Danny: I'm so scared I drop the phone. I'm not about to open that door. I run to the closet and get my shotgun. I hunt birds. I pump in a shell and holler, "The cops are coming. You get the hell out of there." And this guy hollers back, "We are the cops."

Lawyer: (I feel how it must be: I have a gun in my hands. It's loaded. A couple of toughs are beating down my front door. They claim they're the cops. The cops have no business here. I haven't done anything wrong. If I let them in they may rob us and kill us.) What are you saying back to these guys, Danny?

Danny: I say, "You got a warrant?" And the cop says, "You let us in peaceful like and it'll go a lot easier on you."

Lawyer: You must be shaking all over. Probably can't hold the gun steady. You must be thinking, *I never shot a person in my life.*

Danny: Yes.

Lawyer: What happens next?

Danny: I decide to let 'em in. About that time my wife, Judy, comes out of the bedroom. She's been in bed with the flu. She suffers from asthma too. She's coughing and asking me what's going on. She's scared to death when she sees me standing in front of the door with a shotgun and she hollers at me, "Danny, what are you doing?"

Lawyer: You must be thinking, *What else can I do? Maybe they are the cops. But what if they aren't and they try to harm Judy or me, and I have to shoot one of them? Maybe both of them?* You must really be scared.

(The thugs turn out to be cops and show their badges. Then they ask him if they can search his house. He asks why and they say, "For whatever the fuck we're looking for.")

Lawyer: What are you doing now, Danny?

Danny: I'm just standing here not saying anything. I never gave them permission. They just start tearing things apart. I'm horrified. They're pulling out everything in the closets and dumping our clothes all over the floor. They're taking the shoes out of their racks and scattering them wherever they drop. They're pulling out all the pans and dishes, and they break a couple of plates and one cup—my favorite, that my grandfather gave me. They're dumping the cupboards bare and scattering sugar and flour and cereal all over the kitchen. They're emptying the garbage can in the middle of the floor on top of the flour. Judy and I are stunned. We're afraid to say anything for fear we'll be beaten or killed. One of cops, the fat one, already took my shotgun, "for evidence," he says.

Lawyer: Are either of the cops saying anything to you?

Danny: The tall cop says, "You are hiding the meth, you meth head." I'm trying to tell him I don't even know what the stuff is, and they just keep on threatening to wreck our house if I don't tell them where it is.

Lawyer: Danny, what am I seeing when I look at this tall cop?

Danny: He gets up close to me and lights a cigarette and throws the match on the floor. We don't allow smoking in our house. He's hollering in my face.

Lawyer: But what does the cop look like up close, Danny?

Danny: He's got bad teeth in front and he needs a shave.

Lawyer: What else are you observing about this guy?

Danny: I can smell the tobacco on his breath and his mouth is turned down when he talks. Kinda of a high pitched voice like Mike Tyson's. Funny voice for a big man, and when he walks his arms swing around like they're hanging loose at his shoulders.

Lawyer: What is this guy saying now?

Danny: He's saying, "Maybe we should tear up the fucking floor boards. Probably got it hidden down there. You better come clean or we'll tear up this fucking house. Dave, go get the crowbar." Judy is crying and coughing. I say, "Please, officer. I don't do drugs. I'm a Boy Scout leader."

Then the other cop says, "Hey, Dave, this meth head is a fucking Boy Scout leader." They are both laughing and they dump over a chest of drawers to see what's behind it. All of the kids' pictures fall to the floor and the glass in a couple of the frames break.

Lawyer: What happens next?

Danny: The cop named Dave hollers, "Bingo!" He jerks up a plastic bag from one of the drawers with some green leaves in it. He sticks the bag in his pocket, and he snaps the cuffs on me and tells the fat cop to cuff Judy and they haul us off to jail. Judy is still in her nightgown and robe. They let her get her slippers.

(We continue taking Danny's story, *but always in the present tense*. When Danny slips into the past tense we bring him back to the present. We want him to relive the experience, and we want to live it with him.)

Danny: When we get to the jail they dump us into the drunk tank. We aren't drunk. We don't drink. It's cold in there. Judy is sick and coughing and barely able to talk. She lies down on one of the benches. She's shivering and I'm afraid she might die or something. I take off my jacket and lay it over her. She could die in here. Then a jailer comes by and looks in. I'm asking him for a blanket but he says, "We don't give drunks blankets. You sober up in the cold better." I'm trying to tell him we weren't drunk but he says they all say that.

Lawyer: What is it like in there? What do you see and smell? (Nothing creates a more vivid story than the smells and sights and sounds that are encountered.)

Danny: The place stinks.

Lawyer: Of what?

(Danny is looking off into the distance as if he can see and smell and hear it all at this moment.)

Danny: Smells like vomit. And a couple of drunks are throwing up over in the corner making a lot of noise, and a couple are lying on the floor—look dead—and one is screaming like he's seeing horrible sights—screaming and screaming, "They are two-headed dogs and they are coming!" We are both petrified with fear.

I beg the jailer to send someone for my wife's medicine. But he doesn't even answer me. I sit down beside Judy on the bench and put her head on my lap and try to cover her with my upper body as best I can, and I kept checking to see that she's still breathing.

(I see the momentary approach of tears in his eyes that are quickly pushed back. Five days later the cops concluded that the substance was not marijuana and the D.A. dismissed the case, except the assault with a deadly weapons charge, which they agreed to reduce to simple assault if Danny would plead guilty.)

Danny's story was made vivid and memorable because the lawyer put himself into the hide of Danny, tried to feel it as Danny felt it, and encouraged him to relive the experience by having him speak in the present tense. Most stories we hear from lawyers are poorly constructed previews of the story to come, previews that would not compel us to rush to the movie house.

We can tell our story to a fellow worker, or at home we can tell our story to our spouse who will add to it from Judy's standpoint. How is it to be the helpless woman, sick and embarrassed, in a drunk tank? We can tell the story to one of our friends over a cup of coffee, and this time we can become Judy ourselves. As I become Judy and try to understand what she must have experienced I can almost hear her say, "I thought I was going to die, I was so embarrassed being hauled off like that. I've never been in a jail. I've never even been in a police car. It was cold outside and the police car was cold and I was sick. All I could think of was, what will my mom and dad say? What will the neighbors think? What will I tell the boss? Maybe we will both lose our jobs. I was too scared and sick to know what to say or do."

After we tell a woman colleague or friend the story, let's ask her to become Judy before we interview Judy. We will likely garner better insights by this method that will aid us in the interview. Our friend, as Judy, can tell us what it was like to be in jail with a bunch of drunken roughs. We can hear our friend, as Judy, say, "I was afraid I would be gang raped. I was too sick to scream. I thought, my God, what if I get a disease in here? I was having trouble breathing, and some drunk asked me, 'What's wrong with ya, sister?' and I couldn't even answer him."

On the second day Judy was transferred to a woman's holding cell populated with prostitutes and drug addicts. One was banging her head on the concrete wall and screaming. Another woman claimed Judy was a snitch and grabbed her by the hair and dragged her to the floor and kicked her and cursed her. Judy was too sick to resist. When we talk with Judy we will be fully aware of the experiences she no doubt endured. We have become good listeners. If we state facts that are not accurate, she will correct us. But having experienced a sense of Judy beforehand, we will have acquired a knowledge of her experience that will help us with our questions to her, and help her tell her story with more clarity and power.

This is only the beginning of the story for Danny and Judy. We can discover, by becoming Danny and Judy, what it's like to face false charges, the nightmarish prospect of being confined in such an inescapable hell. We will feel what it's like to be dragged into court as a common criminal in those orange pajamas where people gawk at us, probably snickering behind our backs, and where we must look up to see a strange face peering down at us, a bored, unfriendly face on a man in black who is only too ready to pass judgment on us.

We'll discover the anger that wells up, that wants to burst free and strike back. But we're helpless to strike back, helpless to even curse our jailers. Our home—we saw it torn apart, our small castle wrecked. (The guinea pig, while Danny and Judy were in jail, died for lack of food and water.) The whole experience was like a rape.

Already we've seen the jail, its gray, miserable, cold walls of concrete and steel. We've felt the tension of people caged like beasts, and we've known fear and smelled the evil smells of decaying men and lost women. We've heard the screams and the slamming of steel doors and the hateful orders of the jailers. It has been as if we were trapped in the darkest pits of human existence.

We can expand our understanding of the story by asking a friend, "What would you fear most in such a situation?" The friend might say, "I'd be afraid they might dummy up the evidence against me."

Let's tell the story to older people. Ask them, "What would you feel if you were Danny? What would this experience mean to you?" The older person might talk about how the experience would smear a filthy smudge across an otherwise exemplary life and shame him.

Tell the story to children and ask them what would they feel if they were Danny or Judy and what would make them feel the worst. Perhaps the child will cry over the death of the guinea pig.

Tell the story to a tough neighbor and ask, "What would you have done?" He might say he would have shot the cop when he came bursting through the door. Eventually the full spectrum of emotions will come into view. It's not that the story gets longer. It's that it gets more pungent, deeper and more complete than the first view we were given.

The wonder of the method is that rarely will we discover from these diverse sources a fact or feeling that Danny and Judy didn't experience. Like most of us, they are limited in their ability to bring to the surface those myriad fears and feelings that they have difficulty in remembering and expressing. By hearing the responses to this story from so many, we've come closer to experiencing what Danny and Judy went through, the truth of which they will affirm or deny in their final preparation. At last, it is an exercise in exploring the self—in discovering that part of us that seems small, powerless, and frightened, that part that cries for justice. And only when we've discovered it in ourselves will we be ready to tell it in the courtroom when we ask a jury to assess damages for Danny and Judy's false arrest.

The focus group approach. Focus groups have nearly become standard in the last decade—a random gathering of persons in the locale where the trial will be held, people who represent a cross section of the jury one is likely to draw. Professionals who sometimes call themselves "trial consultants" go to some pains to gather several such representative groups to whom both sides of the various issues in the case are presented by the lawyers—usually from the same firm. The deliberations of this "mock jury" are televised for later study, after which the professionals share their insights with the lawyers on how best to present their case. Focus groups are used by the government, by politicians, by ad agencies, indeed, by any who want to know how best to discover the story and thereafter to tell it.

I use focus groups somewhat differently than many. Some see the process as a means to discover the most effective way to deal with a troublesome issue, how to form the lawyer's approach so that he'll have the best chance of winning. Too often it is an intellectual exercise that asks which set of facts and which arguments will best convince these inscrutable rascals we call jurors?

I believe the value of a focus group is to learn how to better tell the story, and the best way to tell the story is always from the inside out. It's hard to tell our story until we know it—that is, until we've *felt it*—heard it with our third ear, seen it with the eyes of our client, until we have been gripped by it in deep places, and have finally lived it. Only then are we ready to tell our story to the focus group—our objective, to learn even more: Have we told the whole story? What part did we omit? Were we blind to areas in the story that others readily saw? Sometimes we're oblivious to the obvious. I have never tried a case to a jury in which, after the case was submitted and decided, a juror didn't tell me something about the case that I overlooked. We all have blind spots in our inner eyes.

Is it necessary to present our case to a focus group? I went for most of my career without knowing much about that tool. Instinctively, I created my own focus group—my wife, family, friends, the cab driver, the local waitress at the coffee shop. The scope of this book does not extend to a detailed discussion of focus groups, but suffice to say we can create our own without the expense of professional services simply by randomly gathering together any group of folks, the friends of the people in our office, or a group we gather from an ad in the paper that might read: "Want to hear an interesting story? We'd like to get your reaction to it. If you have a free day next Thursday, call us. Our phone number." Numerous ways abound to bring people together. The last focus group I did in a death penalty case a few months before this writing cost a total of one hundred dollars for the group's lunch, and from which I gleaned untold riches in new insights.

Telling a summary of the story. Often people will ask what your case is about. Can you answer the question in a short paragraph? If you can't, you haven't discovered the story yet. What, for example, is Danny and Judy's story about?

Perhaps it's a story about rape, since rape occurs when something is taken from us against our will. Here Danny and Judy were first raped when their privacy was taken from them by police who were more like thugs than police officers and who used threats to enter their home. Then they maliciously ripped apart their home and ravaged it looking for illegal drugs. Danny and Judy were thrown into jail with drunks where they were humiliated and frightened, their rights as innocent citizens raped. They were raped because they'd committed no crime and were guilty of no wrong. It's a story about rape by the justice system that, when its rape was exposed, raped Danny and Judy one last time by demanding that they plead guilty (which, fortunately, they refused to do) to a crime they didn't commit.

Discovering the theme. Every case, has a theme—like a title to a song. If we want raises for our school teachers, the theme may be, "Teachers need love too." If we want the boss to give us a raise, the theme may be, "An employee you needed, needs you now." In Danny and Judy's case the theme might be, "The rape of Danny and Judy." As we tell the story the theme will find its way to the surface. When I write a book, the title never comes first. It grows out of the story.

In a recent pipeline explosion case that killed twelve people, all members of the same family, my theme was, "Their profit before people." In a suit against a company that negligently applied metal-working fluids to increase the life of their tools, and caused the permanent injury of its workers, the theme was, "Save the tools, not the workers."

Why do we need a theme for our case? It usually contains the essence of our story—the quintessential statement that continues to emerge from out of the chaos of words, that redirects us to the cause when the arguments lead to other places and fuzz our focus. The theme speaks of the underlying morality of the case—what is right or what is wrong. It is the final argument in a single phrase.

Political candidates shroud themselves with themes and usually smother themselves in the flag. "He's tough on criminals." "The man you can trust." Nearly every advertised product has a theme: "Things go better with Coke," or the Miller slogan, "Less filling, tastes great." Budweiser focuses on our sense of slavery—the working person having toiled all day comes home for his reward—"This Bud's for you." The antiabortionist's theme is "The right to life." Their opposite is, "Woman's choice." Virginia Slims targeted women with a powerful theme: "You've come a long way, baby," her pride represented by a cigarette in her mouth.

The theme is the means by which we focus the justice of our case. Every cause has a theme. "Give me Liberty or Give me Death," was a battle cry of the American Revolution. "Save the Union" was the theme of the Civil War. One of World War II's theme was "Making the World Safe for Democracy."

Perhaps one of the many failures of the Vietnam War was that there was no convincing theme. In short, without a powerful theme we will win no wars, win no cases, sell no products, and advance no causes. A theme becomes the heart of our presentation.

Brainstorming. Clarifying the theme is often the product of brainstorming, a process by which the team sits down in a room without a phone, with lunch served in the room if necessary, and with people uncommitted to anything except the program ahead of them—brainstorming. It's fun because it's creative, and ideas bounce around the room like playing children. I like to assign one person the job of writing on the blackboard or a flip chart in large letters, so we can all see and remember what has been suggested.

The brainstorming team is composed of anyone who is likely to have an original thought. Membership is not directed toward measurable intellect, or impressive degrees. It seeks people with creative minds. I enjoy the fresh minds of the young, the assistants in the office, the lawyers who have had experience in the area but are not drooping from the weariness of the ages. I like women as well as men. Children can offer suggestions that we might otherwise overlook.

The process is without structure. No one is in control. We experience the free association of the members' thoughts, ideas, and emotions as they occur. One person's idea will tickle the creative process of others, and the storm of ideas and images and sayings will grow as the members play off of each other. The most frequently heard phrase is "Yes, *and* . . . ," as an emerging idea is born from one just offered by another. Someone writes the ideas down on a flip chart.

The group, in effect, becomes a single organism, and the individuals composing the group are the cells. Someone familiar with the story, say, Danny and Judy's, will begin. Questions are asked. "How does this story make you feel?"

"I'm pissed off at the police. I had a similar situation three years ago with a client, and the police tried to cover it up."

"Yes, and we should make this sort of conduct public and get it stopped."

"Ask for punitive damages. Big time."

"What about the people of the town worrying about a big verdict increasing their taxes?"

"We have to deal with that in *voir dire*" (jury selection).

"Can punitive damages be given against the city in this case?"

"Better assign that issue to Halley. She can give us an answer."

"This is a civil rights violation and we can go into federal court."

"Maybe. Let's get Halley to look at that too."

"Let's build a model of the holding cell and let the jury go into it. How big is it?"

"Twelve by twenty. Too big to haul into the courtroom; but we can get video shots of the real thing. We can get a court order."

"Yes. And the sounds in there, the drunks hollering and the doors slamming—scare you half to death. We can tape the sounds."

"Maybe we should find out the names of the prisoners who were in there at the time and talk to them."

"And the jail keepers. Subpoena them. Make them talk with depositions."

"We need to look at the police reports. What did those cops report?"

"Yes, and the booking process. We need to show how it feels to be booked, to have mug shots taken of you like you are a common criminal. We need the mug shots to show the jury. Then they fingerprint you and you're afraid to say anything because some cop might attack you."

"It's hard to believe that cops like that have nice families and kids at home and that they go to church on Sunday."

"Yeah, who are these cops? What have they done in the past? Where did they get the idea that there was meth in that house? We've got to take some depositions."

The questions go on and the ideas develop. Several hours can be constructively spent brainstorming the case, and as the case emerges more brainstorming sessions can be held. We will discover the kinds of documents that will be helpful, the investigation that needs completing, and we may even begin to inquire into the law of the case and which lawyer should lead the case. We may consider the court where the case ought to be filed, a choice of the judge, and even how the parties should dress when they go into court—the ideas are as endless and as free as the fertile minds that create them.

Free association brainstorming. Brainstorming can take on yet a different form. Our case may be about a farmer whose crop was insured against hail damage. The insurance company, let us call it the Honest Crop Insurance Company, refused to pay after the hailstorm ruined farmer Smith's crop of oats. The company claimed that the crop had already been destroyed by drought.

Setting the scene. Let's gather up four or five people in a room who know the fundamental facts of the case. First we want to set the scene. We have pictures of the farm and of the oat fields that have been destroyed. The group has seen the pictures. But what do they really show? When these same pictures are shown to the jury they give a one-dimensional view of the place. Isn't there more? If we took the jury to the farm after the hailstorm, say a week later, what would they experience? The picture fails to touch most of what can be experienced at the scene with the five senses. Let's discover what has been left out.

Let's choose a single word that brings us to the case. Let's say, the word *oats*. We might ask the question of the group, "What comes to mind when you hear the word *oats*?"

"I see the field," Joyce, our legal assistant, says.

"What does it *look* like?"

"It's yellow, the oat straw is lying on the ground all bent over. Looks like some giant animal has lain down on it. Oats are supposed to stand up and wave in the breeze."

"Can you walk through it?"

"Yes," Joyce says, already setting the scene in her mind. "But it's like walking on wet, straw-covered ground."

"Take a handful of the oats. How does it *feel* in your hand?"

"The straw is wet and limp and the oat pods are empty. Sort of like holding wet noodles in your hand."

"Is there a *smell* to it?"

"Yes, the smell is musty. The oats have started to rot on the ground. The hail melted and the wet straw and the oats are molding."

"You're standing out there in the field in your shoes. What about them?"

"They're muddy."

"And as you stand there, what do you *hear*?"

"It is very eerie and quiet. Usually you would hear the sound of the farm equipment harvesting the grain. But things are strangely silent."

We may turn to another member of our brainstorming team. We ask Jack, the janitor, what he sees. He sees the distant farm house.

"How far away is it?" we ask.

" 'Bout a quarter mile."

"What does the house look like?"

"It's a tall, two-story, plain-looking house, white siding. Porch."

"Anything on the porch?"

"Yes, a couple of rocking chairs.

"Anyone on the porch or in the chairs?"

"No, but there's an old dog lying next to the rocker."

"Is he friendly?"

"Yes, he's one of those collie dogs. Wags his tail a lot and jumps up on you."

Next we might turn to Cindy, another lawyer in the firm. "What do you see inside the house, Cindy?"

"I see the farmer, Mr. John P. Smith, and his wife, Mary, sitting at the kitchen table."

"What are they doing?"

"They are going through a stack of bills."

"What are they saying to each other?"

"Nothing. They are just looking at the bills and then looking at each other."

"What do you see on their faces?"

"Dismay. Fear. Confusion. Their crop is ruined and they can't make their payments."

We can go on from here introducing the other factors in the case, the worthless insurance policy they paid good money for, the promises that were made to them by the insurance agent before he took their money to pay the premium. How they had saved from their crop the year before to pay the insurance, the money that they would have otherwise used to buy Mary a new set of drapes for the living room, and for John a badly needed repair to the barn roof. We will take the couple through the whole year, the planting of the crop in the spring, the rising hope for a good crop, and their sense of security that if the crop was ruined by hail, they were covered. There was a drought, all right. But the crop was made early in the season. Not as many bushels per acre that they had hoped for, but enough to get by, to pay the bills, and to keep the bankers away from the door. But now this.

Sharing. Each member of the group has had his or her own experience with failure and disappointment, with false promises and fraud. Each has had a set of experiences that, when told, will likely add another facet to the story.

A part of every person is a part of us. And we have experienced a part of every experience of every other person. If we are told of a shipwreck in a hurricane, we have experienced our own near-collision with a truck in a blizzard. The galvanic experiences are the same. We are flooded with adrenaline. We gasp and load our lungs with air against the danger. Our hearts beat faster. Our blood pressure elevates. We sweat.

Hank, the guy who rents the space across the hall and does computer programming, may say, "Yeah, and the fear of the bank coming to take away my equipment, and maybe take away my place, is something I have nightmares about sometimes. I dream about my arguments against them repossessing my house and car, and how I end up even begging, and they don't listen. Just like talking to people without ears."

The stories that each of us have experienced, although with differing details, are the same in their substance. For every story we hear we inhabit part of that story as our own. Each of us has lived a different version of farmer Smith's story in one form or another, and each of us can share our own experience that involves false promises and the injuries that result. By relating personally to farmer Smith's story with our own, we are better able to access the feelings that the Smiths have experienced.

And lest we forget, the jurors, too, as experienced members of the human race, have lived their own stories, which they will vividly relive as they hear the Smith story told by one who, himself, has vividly felt those same feelings. Because the storyteller has, so to speak, been there, he can, with credibility and power, pass on those feelings to the jurors.

But how is all this fantasy relevant to the real facts in the Smith case? When we sit down and begin to talk to farmer Smith we'll find out that he can't tell us very much about what has happened to him. He can't bring it to the forefront of his mind when we ask him simply what happened. He's not good at storytelling. He can't set the scene. About all he can say is that his oats were down from the hailstorm and the insurance company won't pay.

On the other hand, absent our brainstorming session, we ourselves may not know the questions to ask to bring out the facts that will give the story the texture and power that is born of the senses, that will turn the case from a flat, two-dimensional presentation to a vivid, many-dimensional, moving story. Brainstorming has given us a better view of the case than the client can impart to us. It has provided us with a rich source of visuals—all of us think in pictures. We now know the questions to ask farmer Smith, and although his answers may vary slightly from the pictures created by our team, nevertheless, the amended story, as set straight by farmer Smith, will now be manyfold more complete and compelling than the one we would have retrieved from Smith alone.

As the input of our brainstormers escapes spontaneously into the room, we will eventually take on the case of the insurance company as well.

We'll hear things like, "If we pay Smith we'll end up paying a whole county of farmers trying to gouge us. Got to make a stand with Smith. Call in the experts. Get the weather people ready to lay out the facts on the drought. Offer him fifty percent on a confidential settlement. He'll take it. He's in debt up to his ass. Move the case out of the county. Too many farmers and farm businesses there. Get old George Hoffman to defend. He talks farmer talk and jurors will think he's one of 'em. Go out and measure his fields exactly. Dollars to a dime he has overstated his acreage and we can show the jury that he's the one who is guilty of fraud." On and on.

We will discover the feelings of the team members toward the case, both negative and positive, when at the conclusion of our session we hear the feedback of the members in response to a single question: "You have been both the Smiths and the insurance company. How do you feel about this case?" Each member of the team will have varying thoughts about it. Jake the janitor may think the Smiths are asking for too much money, that they are taking advantage of the situation, while Joyce our legal assistant says no, it's the insurance company that's taking advantage of the drought as an excuse for paying nothing. Some may think the case should be settled and others will talk about the possibility of punitive damages to keep insurance companies from doing this sort of thing to other farmers. In the end we have learned what our case is about and in ways know it even better than our client who experienced it.

10. DISCOVERING THE STORY THROUGH PSYCHODRAMA

I F WE CAN SEE ANOTHER person as they see themselves, if we can experience life as they experience it, we can usually tolerate that person as a human being on this earth." So says John Nolte, the eminent psychodramatist. He says our emotional apparatus will vibrate to the emotional apparatus of another in the same way that, if we pluck the G note on a piano, the G note on every other piano in the room will begin to vibrate. He insists that there is no such thing as information, only experiences, feelings, actions, and emotions. And as we have seen, facts are only words, mere symbols for what we have experienced and felt. Emotion bursts up from the *motion*, from the action, whatever it may be. In the end, the process is to go into the self to discover both the self and the other.

So we wish to discover the *whole* truth of, say, a case involving a fifteen-year-old boy charged in juvenile court with the rape of a sixteen-year-old girl. The boy has confessed to the crime, so what more is to be done but to make the best possible deal with the juvenile authorities? But something seems amiss here. Girls are often physically older than boys of the same age, and this girl is a year older still than Buddy, but they are about the same size. They ride home together each day on the school bus and live next door to each other. They're friends. But Nancy has a boyfriend of her own.

Nancy came home one day with a bite mark on her cheek and bruises on her arms. Her parents cornered the girl, who denied that her boyfriend, two years older than she, was responsible. Finally she blamed Buddy. Because of the mother's concern that her daughter might get pregnant, the mother took steps, but by the next day no semen samples were available for the police.

Buddy's parents are in the throes of a divorce. They excel at despising each other, and are vindictive and cruel to the core. In the custody battle between them the mother claims that the father has sexually abused Buddy's twelve-year-old sister. The father denies any such abuse, sexual or otherwise. During the divorce proceedings a court-appointed social worker interviewed Buddy, now living with his father. Buddy admitted the rape of his sister. The mother is insistent that it was her husband who abused the daughter, not her son.

Employing the psychodramatic method to discover the story, we might gather a group in our office, maybe four or five laypersons or lawyers who've agreed to help us.

Choosing the drama. As in the making of a movie, someone will serve as the director and will ask the lawyer responsible for the case what scene, what event or occurrence is important from the lawyer's standpoint to his case. Let's think of it as a screenplay. Where would the movie begin? The scene could begin with Nancy, who is telling her mother of the alleged rape. It could begin with Buddy's mother or father and their vitriolic battle over custody. Let's say the lawyer wants to start with Buddy, because the lawyer believes that Buddy's story has something to do with Buddy's parents capturing the children as the loot of their war. The person appointed director will ask the lawyer who will defend the case to play the part of Buddy as he imagines and understands him. Then the director will ask the lawyer to pick one of the assembled group to play the part of Buddy's mother, who we call an "auxiliary."

We understand that we cannot know whether any part of the play accurately corresponds to all of the facts. What we do know in psychodrama is that our life's experiences and those of our teammates will help us discover the several potential stories that may lead us to a better understanding of the truth. How is it to be a boy of fifteen who is the center of the storm between his parents and who is concurrently being charged as a serial rapist? In the lawyer's several interviews with Buddy, the boy was frightened, confused, and willing to say little more than "I don't know." But perhaps we can begin to understand Buddy a little better if we play through some of the scenes he may have experienced.

Setting the scene. We're told by the lawyer that the first scene he would like to explore will be between Buddy and his mother. It will take place in the kitchen in the mother's small, poorly furnished apartment. In setting the scene, the director asks the lawyer to tell us what he (as Buddy) looks like. He says Buddy is smallish, thin, has white skinny arms, and a head larger than most kids his age, with a mop of wild blond hair on top. He wears thick glasses and his eyes look very large through the lenses. He is wearing a T-shirt with the picture of a current rap singer and he has a small pierced earring in his left ear.

The director asks the lawyer to show us the location of the kitchen table and chairs—maybe using some loose chairs or a small table that are available in the room where the work is proceeding. We will learn the location of the kitchen sink and counter. In response to the director's questions, the lawyer will show us the doorway and describe what is on the wall and on the refrigerator door, so that when he is finished we have a mental picture of this kitchen. Buddy (the lawyer) sits down at the kitchen table across from his mother, one of our auxiliaries.

Reversing roles. Our appointed director now asks the lawyer playing the role of Buddy, "What's going on between you and your mother, Buddy?" Buddy may say, "I don't know." The director immediately asks the lawyer playing the role of Buddy to reverse roles and to now become the mother, so that the lawyer playing Buddy and the auxiliary playing the mother change places at the kitchen table. The lawyer, once playing Buddy, is now playing the mother sitting in the mother's place. The director will ask, "What does the mother say?" The lawyer now playing the mother says, "You know very well, Buddy, that your father is a beast and has done those nasty things with your little sister." Immediately, the director again has the lawyer and auxiliary switch roles and places at the table so that the lawyer is Buddy again and the auxiliary the mother.

"No. Daddy never did that. He never did that. I did that," Buddy says.

"You are just covering for that man, aren't you?" the auxiliary, as mother, accuses. Other members of the team may stand behind the mother and speak as if they were she. For example, one person as an auxiliary to the mother may add (as if she is speaking as the mother), "You know that your father is trying to steal you from me, and I'm not going to let him do it. You better tell the truth, Buddy. And you know the truth is that your father did that to your little sister. Your sister said she told you so." At this point two people are playing the role of mother, as ideas spontaneously come to mind. More team members can come up and, in this way, double for the mother as they may perceive additional input from the mother's point of view.

More than one person can also play the role of Buddy. Another auxiliary may come up and stand behind the lawyer who has been playing Buddy and, as Buddy, provide additional input from Buddy's point of view. "I never did it, and Daddy never did it. Sissy is just trying to get Daddy into trouble. She told me that she wants to stay with you and that she can if she says that Daddy did that to her." As many scenarios as come to the fertile minds of the participants can be played out here, the lawyer reversing roles with the mother as often as may be necessary to insert additional facts that are known only to the lawyer, and the auxiliaries adding to these facts as they may imagine them by doubling behind the mother and Buddy.

Expanding the inquiry. After we have exhausted the possibilities with Buddy and his mother we may want to find out what might have been going on with Buddy and his father. Again, the lawyer may take the role of Buddy and choose one of the auxiliaries to play the role of the father.

"You know I didn't do anything wrong with your sister, Buddy," the auxiliary playing the role of the father might begin.

No answer from Buddy.

"You better tell the cops that you did it, or you know what will happen—they will put me in jail and you will have to go live with your mother."

"I don't want to live with her. I want to live with you, Daddy."

"Then you better tell the cops and anybody that asks you that you did that to your sister."

"I didn't."

"Well, you better tell them anyway, or you know what's going to happen to you."

Maybe this conversation took place or maybe it didn't. All we know is that the possibility exists. For the first time, the lawyer, having played through the role of his child client, Buddy, may begin to appreciate the possible conflicts the child is under, the child's pain, the child's fear. He has a fresher view of what it must be like to experience the feelings of this child that the lawyer never internalized before, because he had been *thinking, not feeling,* his way through the case.

But what about the alleged rape by Buddy of the older girl, Nancy? Something's wrong there—the disparity of age and physical development for one thing. The director may want the same lawyer to play that one out a little more. The director will lead the lawyer through the scene setting in the living room of the girl's house. Her parents are at work. Perhaps the scene will begin with Buddy and Nancy sitting on the couch together.

We remember that the girl claims that Buddy forced her. Yet she was wearing jeans at the time and was older than and as strong as Buddy. We also remember that Buddy has admitted this rape. The director may have the lawyer, in the role of Buddy, now play out the alleged rape scene. The lawyer picks someone to play the role of Nancy.

The lawyer, as Buddy: "You ever do it?"

Nancy, played by a team member: "What?"

"You know."

"Know what?"

She knows. She is coy and she puts a hand on Buddy's leg.

"You want to?"

We remember that Nancy had a boyfriend. The director has the lawyer immediately switch roles and become Nancy—the auxiliary becoming Buddy for the moment. The lawyer, as Nancy, says, "I already got a boyfriend. We do it all the time. I'm not going to do it with a little shrimp like you."

The soliloquy. The discovery process is spontaneous. The soliloquy can be introduced at any point when the director wants to examine the inner working of our protagonist's mind. Perhaps at this point the director can have the lawyer switch back and become Buddy once more, because we want to hear what's going on in Buddy's mind when he's told that he's a little shrimp not fit to play like that with Nancy. The director walks around the room with the lawyer, who now is encouraged to speak as Buddy. As they walk together the director asks the lawyer, as Buddy, to say his thoughts out loud. In his soliloquy we hear Buddy say, "She doesn't think I'm as good as her boyfriend. She's the only friend I have. I'll show her." Or he might be so devastated that he says, "I have to get out of here," and runs home not having touched Nancy. Or he might say, "I want to continue trying to get her to do it with me like they do in the movies." As Buddy speaks his soliloquy aloud, others in the room may walk behind him, adding their own ideas as to what Buddy's thoughts might have been.

Letting the drama set its own course. We, as directors, can go further by setting another scene, the one when the police interrogate Buddy after Nancy's mother makes the rape complaint against the boy. In setting the scene, the lawyer, as Buddy, will show us the interrogation room, the cement walls painted white, the proverbial lights aimed at the accused child, the bars at one end of the room. There is no escape. The lawyer still plays Buddy, and a team member plays the cop.

> **Cop:** Come clean, kid, you better tell me the truth or it can go damn hard on you. You did that girl, Nancy, didn't you?
> **Buddy:** I didn't do nothin' ta her.
> **Cop:** You want to stay on living with your dad, or do you want to go somewhere else? (Intimating that the boy would be taken from his father—maybe sent to his mother. Maybe to some other horrible place.)
> **Buddy:** I want to live with my dad. (He begins to cry.)
> **Cop:** You better come clean, then.
> **Buddy:** (Says nothing.)

Having heard the whole drama, the team members can add further ideas about Buddy and the cop. One team member as an auxiliary playing the cop does just that.

> **Cop:** You want to be a man? Well, Nancy didn't think you were man enough to do this, but I think you were. (The cop puts his hand on the boy's shoulder.) So why don't you just tell me you did it and we can make everything all right again.

Pretending and learning. In many ways we are like children playing "Let's pretend." But we know by having been children, and having observed our own and others', that children often tell us truths we might not otherwise see. When we become as children, and play as children, we empower ourselves to search our deeper selves to discover truths that have otherwise evaded us. We never experience role playing in this psychodramatic method without learning something new.

How does this work? First, the lawyer gets in touch with his own feelings and those of his client. He begins to remember what it's like to be a fifteen-year-old who is confused about who he is and what his role with friends and family should be. He remembers his blooming naiveté. By becoming the client and playing the various other roles, the lawyer achieves insights that he likely wouldn't have understood before. He begins to care for his client, who has become a person to him, not just a name on a kid whose most informative statement is "I don't know."

We will have the team furnish their further insights as we download what we've learned. Maybe the father did abuse the eleven-year-old daughter and the boy is covering for him. But no one on the team now feels certain that Buddy is that evil serial rapist he was once made out to be. Maybe Buddy did sexually molest his little sister. But everyone on the team is pretty sure that he wasn't guilty of raping Nancy. And, what is rape and what is consensual sex between children of this age?

The scope of the cross-examination of Nancy and her mother is now apparent. Nancy may have had a reason to cover for her boyfriend. We need to find out more about the boyfriend and about the problem, if any, between Nancy and her mother concerning that relationship. We can play out that scene if we wish, preparatory for the time when Nancy is on the stand and a thorough cross-examination can be had.

And what about Buddy's twelve-year-old sister? What does she have to say about all of this? She is with her mother. Is it possible that the mother has manipulated the child into accusing her father, and the child, feeling abandoned by the father, is willing to blame him based on some childish idea of justice? At this point in discovering the story, Buddy is as likely innocent of all of the claims made against him as he is guilty. The role-playing has opened up many divergent trails that need exploring before a fifteen-year-old boy is convicted, his confession notwithstanding.

As we remember, all of us have had experiences that in some way relate to those of every other person in the world. Few crimes exist, however evil and depraved, that in some diminished and muted form do not resonate in our reptilian beginnings. By playing out the various roles in Buddy's case, the lawyer understands both his client and his opponent in a way that would have been impossible, but for his playing the parts of the several participants in this family tragedy. The various scenarios may not exist, in fact, but they open up avenues for further investigation and study.

Where once the prosecution had an open-and-shut case against a confessed rapist, the possibility of the boy's innocence will now be investigated. And even if he were guilty of the rape of both his sister and Nancy, we have new insights as to how a child whose fragile psyche has been twisted by the brutal wrenching apart of this family might act out his anger against females over whom he could possibly exercise some domination. No matter how the case is resolved, it will be a different, more complete case than the one we first examined.

For the nonlawyer—using the psychodramatic method to discover the story. The methods we have discussed can be used to discover the story by laypersons in the out-of-court case. Let's take the case of a worker who wants better working conditions at the plant. Suppose four or five of his fellow employees gather at his home one evening. One who has read and understood the methods we've discussed can act as the director. The employee who wants to bring about change can play his own role. Someone else can play the boss. We can already imagine what will be happening.

The first scene could be between the boss and the employee. But a more important scene might be between the boss and his wife. He is telling her how all of this pressure is coming down on him, how he is afraid the unrest at the plant is getting out of control, and how the employees are beginning to gather together and talk about the health problem there. He thinks he ought to find a way to can the employee who seems to be the leader. Someone will play the wife. Someone the boss. There will be auxiliaries' input for both.

We may also play out the scene between the boss and his supervisor. He assures his supervisor that he has things under control. Maybe in the course of the play we will see a better way to argue the case—avenues that had not been apparent before. What will happen when the issue gets up to the CEO? What will the board say? Can we see the CEO trying to explain this to the board? When all of the scenes are set and played out, we will know a lot more about how this issue should be handled and how it can be presented in a way more likely to succeed.

Where does the story begin and end? Whatever the facts of the story, we must have a beginning, a middle, and an end. Where does our story begin?

We'll make that decision after we've discovered the facts. In the case of a business decision, perhaps we start with workers creating the product, or the managers who are in charge of selling it. The story could begin with the product itself. But most likely, the story will begin with the customer. Without the customer, all else becomes irrelevant. In the criminal case in which we are defending Buddy, the story may begin with the war between Buddy's parents for the custody of their children.

Our gathering of people who have aided us in discovering the story will help decide where the story begins and what its components will be. The greatest minds are not the ones that produce those grand, pedantic propositions, the ones with that bulging, sweat-covered, intellectual brawn. The most coveted minds are those that can absorb the fertile ideas of others and put them to work. No single individual can discover every flower in the forest, nor can he fully understand what the law calls "the whole truth."

How is a drama constructed? A rule among moviemakers says that drama is divided into three parts, the setup, the conflict, and the resolution. Putting the rule in its simplest terms, Sam Goldwyn said, "We introduce the hero, we chase him up a tree, and then we get him down again"—the beginning, the middle, and the end—the setup, the conflict, and the resolution.

In Buddy's case, we might see in the setup a smallish, skinny, frightened kid sitting over in the corner cringing as his parents battle. We'll see him on the school bus with his friend, Nancy; we'll see how she's older and toys with Buddy, who is totally infatuated with her. This is the setup. Now Buddy is chased up the tree when he is charged with the rape of Nancy. When the facts come together, perhaps Buddy will shinny down the tree and be saved. The formula is good for nearly every story.

In a trial the jury completes the story. The defendant in a criminal case and the plaintiff in a personal injury suit are presented to the jury. Then they find themselves up the tree when the defendant is charged with a crime or the plaintiff suffers injuries as the result of the negligence of another. The jury renders its verdict, which ends the story happily with an acquittal in the criminal case—or a conviction that converts the story to a tragedy. So, too, in the civil case. The injured plaintiff is awarded adequate damages or is turned away.

I always present my case as a story. The old saw, truth is stranger than fiction, holds here. The story must be truthful or else, as we have seen, the case will surely be lost. The beginning, the setup, as in nearly every movie, introduces us to the hero (our client) in ways that permit us to care about him. Then we experience the difficulty he is in, the conflict, and finally we map out for the jury the resolution, the ending we wish the jurors to adopt.

In our hearts we all love to hear and to tell a good story. Stories, well told, are the engines by which we win.

11. PREPARING THE DECISION MAKERS TO EMBRACE US— THE *VOIR DIRE*

OUR APPROACH TO JURY SELECTION. As we must prepare ourselves to present our case, so, too, we must prepare the jury, the boss, or the board to receive it. I think of it as if I were developing a friendship—perhaps plunging headlong into a love affair.

We can beseech the other, beg, plead, threaten all manner of evil against the other, go on a hunger strike, and threaten to give up chocolate, but unless the person to whom we make our presentation is prepared to receive it, indeed, wants to receive it, we are simply blowing our puny breath into a gale.

Every person has an opinion on everything, from how the government should be run to how long the kids' hair should be. We're experts, even though our expertise may be the product of what mamma told us forty years ago. To our last breath, we're going to go down with those ideas, those faith-based beliefs we've never thought through, that we've always lugged around as part of our psychic baggage. But a person without an opinion on most things is an idiot. Our minds were given in order that we might come to false conclusions on nearly every subject. How dare anyone try to convince us otherwise?

In the trial of a case before a jury, lawyers in the more enlightened jurisdictions are given the right to *voir dire* the jury. In the lazy vernacular of the law, the term *voir dire* has become both verb and noun. Its Anglo-Norman roots simply mean, "to speak the truth." Prospective jurors are placed under oath and questioned, *voir dire*d, as it were, by the lawyers at the beginning of the trial. The professed purpose of the exercise is to determine whether the juror can be fair and impartial. In truth, the lawyers on both sides are looking for jurors who will decide the case for *them.* Both sides weed out those jurors they think will likely be against them, and the resulting twelve are supposedly the least prejudiced and biased that the venire (the panel of prospective jurors) has to offer.

In some jurisdictions (notably the federal courts) judges do all the questioning of the prospective jurors, although these judges know little or nothing about the case and are mostly uninformed concerning the important issues that may effect a fair outcome in the trial. But some of the more enlightened federal judges are now permitting lawyers to *voir dire*, and most state courts allow it. The largest impediment to the exercise of this skill is that too many lawyers simply don't know how to do it. Yet, that problem is not alleviated by letting judges engage in it. I've sometimes observed that if I did a *voir dire* as poorly as the judges I've seen I should be sued for malpractice.

Including, not excluding the jurors. Lawyers hire experts to help them determine which jurors to exclude from the jury. I'm more interested in which jurors *to include.* How does it feel to be questioned, when we know that the questioner, no matter how charming, is intending to expose whatever fact, whatever small secret he can pry from us in order to strike us from the jury? And who wants to be cross-examined? Nothing in this approach invites the prospective juror into the process, and that's where we want him: *with us.* Moreover, since prospective jurors understand the game, they can play it as well—and with a total lack of candidness. Suddenly, the lawyer has unwittingly seated a bunch of jurors who will vote against him at the first opportunity.

I begin with the proposition that everyone has an opinion, but everyone is basically fair. The questioning takes on the flavor of friends talking, accepting the other's opinions and feelings with respect. It is not a manipulation or a strategy. It's simply an attempt to be who we are with each other. I've finished many a *voir dire* examination not wanting to strike a single person from the original jury panel.

The *voir dire* has a profoundly deeper purpose than to exclude those who are immutably biased against us. In subtle ways we want to open up the juror to new ideas, to open him to our position in the trial, and to be open to his.

Cynics of the jury system like to call this brainwashing. That, of course, is not possible. No one can easily remove the stain of long-held opinions or prejudices from another, and it's impossible to do so in the short time that jurors are questioned in the *voir dire*.

Being in the moment. A successful *voir dire* begins with our being *in the moment*. This doesn't mean to fly by the seat of our britches. I'm speaking of being spontaneous. It calls on our ability to listen to the other, to focus on what is happening—the feelings that abound—both ours and theirs. Instead of thinking of the next question we're about to ask, we are lost to the self, to the moment, to the other, to the magic happening around us.

When we stand before a jury for the first time in a case, when we begin our presentation to the boss or the board, we stop and take in the moment. They may be watching us, waiting for our first word, but we're not with them—not now. We're with ourselves. We're tuning in to our feelings: "What am I feeling at this instance?" Likely it's anxiety, a diluted form of fear. I'd rather not be here. This is where the *voir dire* begins—at this moment. With us. With who we are. With what we feel. Then, as if we were speaking confidentially to our best friend as we sit together on a log in a small meadow in the forest, we may begin, "I'm feeling anxious. A little scared. I guess I'd rather not be here."

Already we're spontaneous. We've prepared ourselves to feel, to share, and to follow our feelings like a friendly hound, as we experience our feelings in ourselves and perceive them in the jurors, the committee, the boss. Nothing will turn us aside. No answer we receive will send us into spasms of speechlessness. We invite the truth, that is, whatever the other has to say and whatever we ourselves feel—which is the truth of that moment.

The six simple steps to a successful *voir dire*. An effective *voir dire* has proven to be a difficult, even harrowing undertaking for even the most skillful of trial lawyers. I've distilled my method to six simple steps that anyone, lawyer or layperson, can follow in or out of court. Still, it exacts from the us the highest level of truth and the greatest degree of fidelity. It's an approach that takes courage, because it first begins with an examination of the self concerning *our feelings* on the troublesome issues we face.

Step 1. Identifying the issues we're afraid of. In every presentation some issue lurks that we're afraid of. In the criminal case we may be afraid of race issues, or the way a hard-looking defendant will be seen by the jurors, or the fact that most people believe in the old adage, "Where there's smoke there's fire," meaning that, since the defendant has been charged he must be guilty of something.

In the civil case we may be afraid to ask for a large sum for a dead child, or that jurors see lawsuits as nothing but a shovel by which greedy lawyers scoop up large piles of money at the expense of the hapless taxpayer.

Before the boss or the board. In the same way, before we begin to make our presentation to the boss or the board, let's first discover what we're afraid of. Suppose, for example, we want a raise. We were given one six months ago (not a substantial one—a routine cost-of-living raise). We're *afraid* the boss will resent our request for yet another one. Or maybe we want to change a long-standing company rule that inhibits the free exchange of ideas between the company's employees and its management, and we're afraid we will be seen as troublemakers. (People who seek change for the better are often suspect in the eyes of management.)

The first step toward a successful *voir dire* in or out of the courtroom is to identify the issues we're most afraid of. Let's listen to our bellies where our fear hides out. Let's talk about our fears to our friends. Listen to their reactions against our case or proposal. What prejudices or opinions do these decision makers likely hold going into this case that spell doom for our cause?

Step 2: Experience feeling *the issue in ourselves.* When we identify what we're afraid of we must ask ourselves, why? Isn't it because down there, someplace, our own prejudice is speaking to us? It's the discovery of the issue in ourselves which permits us to understand and deal with that issue in prospective jurors.

Let's suppose that in the trial of a criminal case our client is black. Already we know what the answer will be if we ask the simple question, "Do you hold any prejudice or bias against people of African-American descent?" "Of course not," the juror will quickly reply. We are all politically correct, right down to the white marrow in our bones. We've gotten the answer we expected, and although we may be relieved to hear it, we may put twelve rabid racists on the jury and never know it. So how do we get the juror to tell us the truth, if, indeed, the juror recognizes it himself?

Let me tell you a story: When I was about eight or nine years old, my pal Buddy and I wanted to discover a secret we'd heard about—that there was this mysterious difference between boys and girls. A couple of neighborhood girls, also our age, were with us in Buddy's garage. Would they show us the difference? we asked in our boyish, embarrassed ways. "Are you crazy or something?" was their reply. The fruitless dialogue continued until I got this marvelous idea: "We'll show you ours if you'll show us yours." From that simple proposal new discoveries were made.

From the I'll-show-you-mine-if-you'll-show-me-yours paradigm I illustrate that before you can expect people to reveal their feelings, their biases and prejudices, we must first be willing to reveal our own—openly and honestly. How do we know when a juror is telling the truth? It's when we are telling him the truth. How do we know when a juror is no longer lying to us? It's when we stop lying to him.

Let's continue with the example of racial prejudice: We're *afraid* the juror may be prejudiced. But are *we* prejudiced? Not on your life. But our lack of prejudice is something we've probably taken as a truth without much thought about it. Racial prejudice is a bad thing. We are not bad persons. Therefore, we're not prejudiced—or some such mental process.

Black or white, all of us harbor some racial prejudice, and I distrust those who claim they are Clorox-clean. We're uncomfortable with the differences, and nothing is more obviously different than the color of our skin. We have lived in different cultures, suffered different pain, and adopted a different set of truths on a variety of important human issues. Out of our differences comes a lack of an in-depth knowledge of the other. As white persons, we've never walked in the shoes of a black person, and distrust often arises from a lack of complete understanding. Distrust leads to prejudice, and no matter how we wish it otherwise, we'll likely find ourselves among the masses of good Americans who believe we harbor no prejudice at all, but who actually suffer prejudice at some level.

Hypocrisy runs deep in the culture. It is the principal sin of the pure of heart. It ought not find a comfortable home in us. So, before we begin to question the juror we need to discover and acknowledge, on a *feeling* level, our own prejudice. And it doesn't feel good.

Having discovered what we're *afraid* of, we hone in on how we *feel* about the issue. How does our racial prejudice *feel* to us? Do we own it? How do we *feel* about an employee who demands yet another raise, or argues to change long established company rules? Do we admit that such a person brings up our "enmity in the shadows," shall we call it? When we are aware of such feelings in ourselves we will have a more ready access to the feelings of the decision maker that we did not fully appreciate.

Step 3: Sharing our feeling with the decision maker. We're now ready to begin our *voir dire* to the jury, or our presentation to the committee or the boss, by simply sharing our feelings.

Let us continue with the race issue. We're afraid that because our client is black that he'll not be believed. But what about our own racism? Here's how I might begin such an inquiry:

"Folks, I represent Johnny Jones here. I have to confess something to you. I'm afraid I'm prejudiced against black people." This is a good time for silence, to let this awful truth sink in. Even the prosecutor is likely to remain silent—no time to object, not when opposing counsel is confessing his prejudice.

I continue. "I don't like my prejudice. I don't even know where it came from. It makes me feel ashamed, and I have tried hard to overcome it. Prejudice has a way of creeping back uninvited. I try to be aware of this all the time. But sometimes I'm afraid I might not." I've now had the courage to show the jury mine. It's time for the jurors to show me theirs.

Step 4: Invite the jurors to share their feelings. Still dealing with the racism issue, I look over the panel and ask, "Am I all alone in this?" No one raises a hand. "Am I really the only one who feels this way?" I ask again. I *am* feeling alone, and my feelings are open on my face. Then I see a juror give me a slight nod and a timid raising of her hand. I turn to the juror. "Mrs. Smith," I say with true relief, "I'm so glad there's someone else who's had to deal with this issue. That took a lot of courage on your part. Could you tell me a little bit about how you feel on this subject?"

Mrs. Smith says with refreshing candor, "Well, I suppose that everyone has a little prejudice."

"Thank you Mrs. Smith. Could you tell me something about how you feel toward black people in general?"

"I guess I'm just a little afraid of them, I don't know."

Her answer leads me to ask the next question of the panel: "Do any of the rest of you have any feelings similar to those of Mrs. Smith?"

The ice has been broken. The jurors have discovered that it's all right to be open and candid. And the discussion begins.

We will encounter those who claim they have no prejudice at all. What do we do with them? Although some may, in fact, be prejudice-free, my experience is that, usually, those who claim to be free of prejudice are not in tune with their feelings, or are so intimidated by political correctness that they're afraid to admit the slightest prejudice. They may be people who are patently self-righteous, or they may simply be lying. In the end I want people who can feel, and especially those who are honest enough to "show me theirs." I can trust them, and because I've been open with them they've begun to trust me. We're in this together.

I may ask a juror to tell me how he feels about another juror's response. For example, "Mr. Peabody has just said that he thinks black people are more prone to commit crimes than white people. Do you think that's true?" When the juror says yes, spontaneity will rule. "That scares me," I reply. "Maybe at this moment you see my client, Johnny, as guilty."

Of course, Peabody wants to be seen as fair. "I'll wait until I hear the evidence," he'll say.

But we may ask, "How can we give Johnny a fair trial if we suspect he may be guilty because he's black?" We'll talk about the presumption of innocence, and when it comes time to choose the jurors to sit we'll likely take those who admit some prejudice. The most dangerous people on the face of the earth are those self-righteous prigs who have embraced their prejudices so long that their prejudices have settled comfortably into their souls.

Let's look at several other typical issues we are afraid of in jury trials.

The greedy lawyer: We're always afraid of the appellation that society has placed on trial lawyers—those greedy charlatans who are destroying the system. We will begin by admitting the truth: "Yes, I guess I am one of those greedy lawyers you hear about. It's hard for me to ask you for money for a dead child. Hurts me. But (looking up at the judge) his honor will tell you that money is the only justice I can ask for. No one goes to jail here. We don't put Kiddie-Corp (the maker of a dangerous toy) in jail for its negligence. There's no other justice available but money. I wish it were otherwise. But I want all the justice I can rightly get for Baby Jane. I am greedy. How do you feel about that, Mr. Mayweather?" And an honest dialogue begins after we have identified the issue we're afraid of (step 1, above), felt it in ourselves (step 2), shared our feelings about it with the jurors (step 3), and invited them to share their feeling with us (step 4).

The juror may say that ten million dollars seems like a lot of money. We agree. It is a lot. The dialogue continues. We might emphasize our distaste for substituting money for a little child, and we might ask, "How would you suggest we replace Baby Jane in this system that only permits us to do so with money?"

"It hurts Baby Jane's parents to ask for money. But money is the only justice the law will give them. Would you be willing to consider what amount might reasonably stand for justice here?"

We might continue with questions that further point up the problem: "Should her parents just forget this?"

"Should they go home without asking for justice?"

"If Kiddie-Corp put out a dangerous toy, should they go scot-free?"

A juror may ask how I came to ten million dollars. My honest answer will be, "I don't know. There is no measurement given to us by the law. We can only use our best judgment, our most considered, thoughtful decision as to how much money rightfully represents the value of Baby Jane's life. I may not have asked for enough. You're free to decide on a greater sum if you wish."

Another juror may say, "I don't think the parents should get rich because of her death." If that question isn't asked, it is one we are afraid of and that we will bring up ourselves (step 1). We might say: "I am repulsed by the idea that parents can become rich over the death of a child. Seems wrong to me. Seems even barbaric" (steps 2 and 3). We ask if anyone else on the jury has a feeling about this (step 4). Others may express a like concern.

Perhaps we will say, "I think if you ask any parent, they would not trade a little finger on their child for a million dollars, much less ten of them for ten million dollars. Little Jane's parents feel the same. We are made rich with our children—the most precious of all riches. That this most precious of all wealth has been taken from Baby Jane's parents requires us to try somehow to bring justice. Money is all there is. Just money." And an open, free discussion continues. We follow it wherever it goes relying, in the moment, on our spontaneity.

The jurors' distrust for lawyers. I might say to the jurors, "I hear a lot of lawyer jokes these days. Any of you know one?" (If so, let the juror tell it to us.) "I have to tell you that these jokes hurt me. It's true I asked for it, but the jokes say that people hate or distrust lawyers. And I can understand why that is. I have met lawyers I distrust.

"But when we talk of the distrust of lawyers across the board, does that include Mr. Ketchum (the prosecutor or the defense attorney in the civil case)? I am not going to ask you to trust me. I think we have to earn our trust, just like anyone else. After all, there are some very honest used-car salespersons, too, aren't there?" A little laughter.

"Because I am a lawyer I become one of those men who people dump into the bucket with all the other lawyers in the world. To get out of that slop pail we have to earn our way out. But let me say something I would like you to think about: Without me, Shirley White (my client) will have to face this judge and this jury alone with no one to speak for her. Without me she will have to cross-examine the experts who have been hired against her, and she has no training to do so. And without me you will have to take their paid expert's word for what they say, because there will be no one to show you the whole truth.

"Without me there will be no one to stop Mr. Ketchum from dumping improper evidence into the case and there will be no one to argue the law on her behalf to his honor. And without me she will have to argue her case by herself against the likes of Mr. Ketchum, who is a powerful lawyer with power people behind him. So, Mr. Black (a juror), is it all right with you if Shirley has chosen me to fight for her rights?"

The client looks guilty: Suppose our client has the unfortunate look of one who's guilty. We're afraid he will be prejudged as we prejudged him (step 1 and 2). We will say the truth: "I have to admit that when I first met Jimmy in jail I thought, 'Oh, no, not another guilty one! I have to represent *him*? Anybody can tell just by looking at him that he's guilty.' I said as much to Jimmy" (step 3). "He said, 'Well, Mr. Spence, you don't look so innocent yourself.'" (Maybe a little deserved laughter.)

"I'm wondering if you'd all take a good look at Jimmy and tell me what you think. Mr. Hayworth (a juror), so you think you can tell whether a person is guilty or innocent by looking at him?" (step 4). Our discussion continues. Other jurors may argue you can't tell guilt or innocence by a person's looks.

Sometimes the innocent-looking person turns out to be guilty, and along the way we will come to the conclusion that we have to decide the case on the evidence, not on the looks of the accused.

Big verdicts mean insurance rates go up. Some courts won't permit this issue to be aired to the jury. Yet the insurance industry has launched a national crusade against trial attorneys and their alleged big-money verdicts in which the insurance industry threatens every American with unaffordable insurance. How do we begin any civil case for an injured person on an even playing field? Assuming a fair and intelligent judge will let us talk about this, let's start by simply telling the truth.

Following the steps I have outlined above, we might begin by saying, "When it comes time for me to pay the insurance on my car I wonder if I can afford it. I've heard all about big verdicts causing insurance rates to soar, and that also bothers me, because I'm going to ask for a lot of money in this case. What do you think about that, Miss Haberstab?"

Perhaps she says, "I think that big verdicts and you trial lawyers are the ruination of the country."

"I can certainly understand how you might feel that way." Then I might ask, "Does anyone here question whether big verdicts have anything to do with rising insurance rates?"

Blank looks from the jurors.

"Have any of you heard that the big losses insurance companies experience may actually come from the bad investments they've made in the stock market, and they want to blame someone other than themselves?"

Maybe a nod from Mr. Black.

Following up with the juror. "Suppose, Mr. Black, I knocked on your door just before this case took up and asked if I could come into your living room and discuss the amount of money I'd like to get in this case for the injuries done to my client. Wouldn't you turn me in to the judge and call the sheriff for jury tampering?"

He agrees.

"Do you think that insurance companies come into your living room though their TV programs and newspaper ads in the hopes of affecting the outcome of cases and increasing their profits?"

He says that might be so.

"My client's never been to your living room to talk to you about it, has he?" Again the discussion can continue and the final question may be, "How many of you would agree that we're not here to protect insurance companies and their profit? We are not here to protect ourselves. We're here to provide justice for the parties in this case." Then we might add: "And how many of you believe that in the scheme of things a verdict here for $10 million would actually increase your car insurance one penny?" (I can hear the screaming objection of the insurance defense attorney all the way out here.)

Step 5. Accept (and honor) the gifts the jury gives us. Remember, whatever answer the juror gives is a *gift* to us. It took courage for the juror to open up and tell us the truth about how he or she feels. The juror trusted us enough to tell us. We must honor that. And we need to thank him as we would any who have bestowed a gift on us.

Once I asked a jury panel if anyone knew or heard anything about me that, in polite company, they might not wish to say? One juror raised his hand: "Yeah, Mr. Spence, my dad says you represented him once and sold him down the river."

I was shocked to speechlessness for a moment. But my response had to be real. I said, "Well, Mr. Brown, I asked for your answer and I got it, and I thank you for being honest with me. But I have to tell you how embarrassed that makes me feel to have someone say that in front of all of these people."

His reply was immediate: "Oh, don't let it bother ya, Mr. Spence. He says stuff like that about everybody."

When the hurtful answer smacks us in the face other jurors will help us. We may turn to them and ask, "Do you agree with Mr. Bellows?" (who's just said that if the defendant confessed, he's probably guilty). Some juror will rescue us by saying, "He may have been coerced." How much better to face the problem openly—the gift—than to avoid the issue, leaving the jurors free to crucify us in the jury room when we'll be helpless to deal with it at all.

Step 6. Continue sharing our feelings and invite the jury to share theirs. As we've already seen, the exchange between the lawyer and the jurors becomes an open discussion that includes not only the lawyer talking to the jury, but the jurors talking with each other, so that how the jurors feel about the issues can be revealed to both sides and to the jurors themselves.

The irascible judge. Yes, but what about those cranky kings up there on the bench? They are cranky for various reasons. Some feel underpaid, that all they have is power and they're going to use it. Some feel bored. Some are old insurance company attorneys or former prosecutors and can never be free of their experience and training, never get into the hide of an injured person or understand that those accused of crimes are entitled to a fair trial.

Some judges are put off by lawyers who won't tell the truth or those who are incompetent or who don't fully represent their clients. Some will be poised like a hungry leopard ready to spring on an innocent chicken when they get the slightest inkling that there is "that touchy-feely stuff" going on in their courtrooms. Judges like this believe the law is something mechanical or scientific, that certain formulas must apply to justice—a concept they've never understood in the first place, since, as we have seen, justice is a feeling and these judges are afraid of their own feelings. Therefore they do not want anyone else to feel.

When we encounter this kind of judge we can do nothing but press on as best we can. To retreat is defeat. Judges who, at the objections of our opponents, interrupt our *voir dire,* sustain objections to our questions, and generally raise havoc with our attempts to deal with the issues are, all the while, being observed by the jurors. Jurors want to know what's being hidden behind the objectives. They want to be fair. They often want to hear what we have to say. They may not feel kindly toward a judge and an opponent who attacks obviously fair, honest questions.

We must be ourselves, even to the point that our confusion, our fear, or intimidation becomes apparent. My experience is that if we are honest and straight, jurors will take care of us. At the bench or in chambers I have asked judges who limit *voir dire* or who are impatient with the process, what if the tables were turned? What if, say, the judge's daughter were being tried for shoplifting? Surely he wouldn't want his daughter placed into the hands of twelve strangers, persons he wasn't permitted to know even superficially, who might be prejudiced against her but who would blandly assure the court that they could be fair.

On the other hand, some judges will be amazed at this open process that can reveal prejudices to the enlightenment of both sides of the case. Some will be appreciative of the learning experience the jury is going through. Some will be relieved to see an attorney up there telling the truth and soliciting the truth from the jurors. The six steps to a successful *voir dire* I have outlined above offer the best opportunity for litigants to obtain jurors who are candid and fair to everyone. What I call the magic mirror has been at work: We're in touch with our feelings and our prejudices and we've been honest with the jurors. Their honesty has been reflected back. We've been open with them, and their openness has been reflected back. It's that simple.

For the lay person—how to *voir dire* the boss or board members. So we want a promotion? Slipping into the hide of the boss—becoming the boss for a moment—we begin by realizing this is a touchy issue. It's about money. Standing in as the boss, we know that this employee must be handled in just the right way. If we flat turn him down it can cause resentment. He's a valuable employee and he may seek another job. As the boss, we know that a negative attitude on our part will cause the man to feel unappreciated. He's worked hard. We have to be fair. Yet our own job is at issue. We have to hold down expenses and we may be looking for a promotion ourselves, earned as a result of our good and efficient management.

How does it feel to become the boss? There's a tension there. But the mirror, as usual, is at work, because as an employee we feel the tension too. At this point we've (1) identified the issue we're *afraid of*—that the boss will not only turn us down but he'll resent our asking for a promotion, or that our position in the company will be weakened or perhaps our job eliminated altogether. We've (2) experienced the issue in ourselves when we reversed roles and became the boss. How do we (3) share this experience with the boss?

Our approach might be as follows: "Mr. Harmon, I'd like to talk to you about a promotion. I notice that Jim Jeffries has gone up the ladder and his position is open. When I thought about asking for the job it made me pretty uneasy. I've been afraid you might rightly resent my talking to you about this. You have a lot on your mind. On the other hand, I know you are a fair man and I wanted you to know I'm interested in advancing in this company." We look at the boss and give him a minute to gather this all in.

Harmon may be as straight with us as we've been with him. "Actually, what you want is more money, isn't that right, Dick? You want a raise."

"That's right, Mr. Harmon, but I'm willing to take on more responsibility and do you an outstanding job. I know we need to keep expenses in line and, more than that, I want to support you in your management here." We may wait now and let him say something. The power of the pause.

He will likely say, "What you say is true, Dick." And no matter what the boss adds, positive or negative, we'll see it as a gift. He's beginning to talk to us. We'll listen. His candid response to our own openness gives us the opportunity to deal with the issues we must confront.

Suppose he finally says, "Well, Dick, if we give you the new job, how much of a raise are you looking for?"

The truth is we want as much as we can get. And to get a fair raise we know we'll have to ask for more than we'll get, even if we deserve every penny we ask for. Maybe we'll say, "It makes me uncomfortable to talk about money. I deserve the raise. I need it. My family needs it. I have a boy just entering college. But on the other hand I know we have to stay locked into the budget. I'm looking for twenty thousand."

The boss has been prepared for our presentation. He knows we are sensitive to his position, that we feel in conflict, and we've been honest with him. And we've judged him as a fair man—the kind of man his response must demonstrate. We've laid it all out in the open. We've shown him ours. Now it's time for him to show us his.

We will never argue with any point Harmon makes. We take any negative as a gift, understanding it from his point of view. If I were speaking to a juror and asking for a multimillion-dollar verdict, I might say, "I know what I'm asking for seems too much—even outrageous. But it's my duty to prove to you that we're entitled to that amount. Will you give me a fair chance to do that?" The answer is almost always yes. So, with the boss: "I know, Mr. Harmon, that what I'm asking for seems unreasonable. But will you give me a few minutes to show you why I'm entitled to it?"

We will talk to the board members in much the same way that we *voir dire* the jury. We identify the issue we're concerned about, the issue or issues that will most likely stand in our way of success. Again, we experience that issue in ourselves as if we were a member of the board. Then we share our feelings as a board member with the board. When we understand the decision makers, when we can feel what they must be feeling, it closes the gap between us and helps us connect. It leaves us feeling as if this board is ours, this boss is ours. Such is the environment of winning.

How we've won through the *voir dire*. We've learned that to win we must persuade the decision maker to be open to our case. But before we can be heard with ears that accept rather than reject, we must reverse roles with the decision maker. Once there we can test our own feelings as we, ourselves, take on their role and spontaneously, in the moment, share those feelings with them.

We see the *power persons* not as adversaries, not as those we are attempting to exclude, not as rascals who are hiding some insidious truth from us, not as the enemy, not as persons to be manipulated, not as persons to be brainwashed, not as persons whom we must fear, but persons we respect and whose opinions are gifts to us. Then, at last, we will have created a relationship with the decision makers that opens them to us. Therein lies the power of the *voir dire,* in the courtroom, the boardroom, and everywhere else.

12. TELLING OUR STORY—THE OPENING STATEMENT

THE APPROACH—THE CRITICAL CHALLENGE. If we walk into a car lot and before we've taken two steps from our car door we're met by a waiting salesperson whose approach is akin to the hungry piranha, we know exactly how we do not wish to approach this jury, this board, this boss. We have something to sell, all right, because every successful presentation grows out of the skill of selling, but it isn't a used car. It's justice, it's the right thing. The war—and it still is a war—is with the other side that wants to sell its cause, its ideas, which are, as we see it, unjust and wrong.

Let's suppose that we have a prospect, a juror, a customer, a board member who, somehow, has maintained a blank mind, one without overriding prejudices. How would we approach that person to make the sale? In the simple paradigm of the salesman, we would tell the prospect what a fine product we represent, why it is better than all the other products on the market, and why the customer will be happy if he buys our product. This said, the salesman will present the product itself—the proof—with a demonstration. In the same way in a jury trial, after the *voir dire,* the next step will be the opening statement that sets out our case, that is intended to demonstrate that the case we are about to show the jury will fulfill the jurors' expectation of justice.

But there is competition—always another side, another viewpoint. Our competitors say they have a different but better product. Both sides will attempt to show that the claims of their competitors are overstated, or not complete, or defective in some way, or that although the competitor may have a good product, it is not as sterling as our own. If we are proposing a change in an administrative process, our competitor may be stodgy precedent, the eternal retort, "This is the way we've always done it." The competitor may be the silent fear of the decision maker to take the risk of change. The competitor may be money, the reluctance of business to spend it, even for the safety of its workers or the health of its customers. Evidence will be presented. But the time arrives when the sale must be made or lost. This is the final pitch—the final argument, we call it in the courtroom. Considering these typical elements in any sale, be it of a product, an idea, or justice, which of these all-important steps is the most critical?

I say it is the opening statement. If we have no product to sell in the first place, obviously no sale can be made. If we have nothing to offer we should stay home and paint the backyard fence. If the decision maker has no reason to embrace what we want to sell, nothing will happen except a wasteful expenditure of our time and theirs. But once the idea is implanted that what we are selling is worthwhile, the customer (let us always include the juror as customer) will be automatically moved to the next step, which is our proof that what we have said is true. We say we have this new, wonderful product? "Prove it to me," they will say, either aloud or to themselves. We have this concept of what is profoundly just—show me the facts that support it, the jurors say.

I have often said that if I am given the opportunity to engage in an effective *voir dire,* that is, if I can open up the jurors to the issues in my case and create a trusting relationship with them, and if thereafter I can make an effective opening statement, the case is mostly won. First impressions of a case are hard to overcome. If our opening story is sound and honest and reveals the injustice for which we seek retribution, the picture it creates in the minds of the decision maker will be hard to erase. Indeed, research reveals that something like eighty-five percent of jurors make up their minds in the case by the end of the opening statement.

The danger of deceit, the power of honesty. But for the salesman who wants us to believe that his product is the best, it is imperative that he has told us the full truth about it. If it does not meet our expectation as he set it in our minds during the opening pitch, the sale will surely be doomed. Trust is the foundation of every sale. Once betrayed all will be lost.

I am talking about credibility again. It is the most important word in this book. *Credibility*. At last, credibility is all the lawyer or the salesman or any of us has to sell. Without credibility we become isolated from the human community. Consider two lovers who have vowed their love for each other. One fully believed the declaration while the other was less than sincere. When the cheat is later exposed, the deceived will come down on him (or her) with a horrible vengeance born of hurt. Nothing is more painful and more detested than the cheating heart. So too in the courtroom, the boardroom, or any other room: When we've gained the trust of the customer, the juror, yes, our partner in love or business, and thereafter betray that trust, no matter how we try, the stain of deceit can never be fully bleached.

The opening statement must always be a true statement. If we make an opening statement and the jury accepts us, and the jurors decide that this is the person we want to follow through this forest called a trial, and then along the trail the jurors find out that we have been untrustworthy, the case will be lost at that moment.

I've seen it many times in the courtroom—the overly ambitious opening statement, the assurance of counsel that his proof will establish a certain truth. We often endure wall-to-wall ballyhoo, the lawyer hoping that somehow the jury will go on to believe him, despite the fact that in his opening statement he misled the jury. But the lawyer's case will be lost when the first credible witness takes the stand and contradicts him. In the courtroom the contest is often simply over the credibility of the lawyers. Has either lawyer lied to us or misled us? Who has been fully open and candid with us? I am careful to the extreme not to say anything in my opening that I cannot prove. I have my opponent's opening taken by the court reporter and I refer to it repeatedly during the rest of the trial, reminding the witnesses (sometimes obliquely) what my opponent said in his opening when I know the witness will take issue with it.

If there is a set of facts that is hurtful or embarrassing to my case I hasten to present it in my opening. I want the jury to know the facts against me. I want to expose what lurks beneath in order that the jurors will trust what lies on top. I never want the underside of my case revealed by my opponent. When that happens the jury's trust vanishes like dew on a hot griddle.

From the standpoint of a sale, nothing is more trust building than a sales-man who will tell us about the weaknesses of his product. The other day I was considering the purchase of a new car. I ended up buying one that cost less money and in which the salesman's commission would be less, simply because he was honest enough to tell me that the more expensive car I was about to buy would give me repair problems—parts were slow to come from the for-eign manufacturer. His honesty in putting my interests ahead of his own cre-ated a credibility that will serve him well in the future with both my business and the business of my family and friends. So it is in the courtroom and every-where else.

What about facts that are in dispute? Let's tell the jury that the facts are in dispute. Let's tell them our position and our opponent's and then explain why our position is better. What if there are hurtful facts that cannot be explained away? Let's tell them that. There may be regrets that need be expressed, apologies made and shared with the jurors. But the overriding justice of the case still rests with our side.

I remember the case of an oil field worker who was killed as a result of a negligently installed blow-out preventer at the well head. The pressure of the well erupted and blew the man into parts. His wife sued the company that in-stalled the preventer for the loss of her husband, his financial support, her loss of his "care, comfort, and society," as the law refers to the relationship of spouses. But the facts were that they'd been separated at the time of his death and he was not providing support. I told the jury the truth. "You need to know those facts in order to make a just decision in this case. But one cannot make amends in a marriage with a husband blown into bloody bits. Reconcil-iation? Did they ever try? No. But when the drilling company killed Jim Smith with their negligence it stole from both Jim and his wife, Ann, the *chance* to make a go of it. They had the right to sew up the wounds of their marriage. The drilling company had no right to deprive Ann of that right. It was a right that did not belong to the company. And Jim Smith had a legal obligation to support her. You cannot enforce legal obligations against a dead man with no estate."

Later in the final argument I was able to make my case. "But there was a letter, one small note she had written that after his death was found in his bill-fold, smudged and worn. It was her handwritten note with those few simple words, 'I need so terribly to love you.' We struggle in our relationships. Romance is just that—romance. It exists mostly in the thin, swift mist of our memories and dissolves into the sweat of reality. But we reach out for love. We are proud, and we don't know how to ask for it. We are afraid, and we don't know how to trust. But it is our right, it is a part of the human condition to seek love and often forgiveness, to forget our pain and to go on—to make our lives. The drilling company deprived a man of his life and a woman of the right to fly back to strong arms that were aching to embrace her."

The jury found for the widow, and justly so. The award for her was diminished but not denied. The case seemed important to me because all of us thrashing about in this hostile, dangerous world are so poorly equipped to deal with the painful challenges of relationships.

That a negligent drilling company should be able to take advantage of our inborn disability seemed to me to be wrong. The jury agreed. The result would have been otherwise, had I attempted to fiddle with the facts, to deny them, or to present them in any way other than as they were.

Telling the story. Already, as in previous chapters, we have discovered our story and set the theme. Now we will tell this story in the opening statement. I like to think of the story in its simplest form. As children we heard the stories begin, "*Once upon a time* there was a little girl with beautiful golden hair whose name was Goldilocks. She went for a walk in the forest and before long she came to a house. She decided to see who lived there and knocked on the door. When no one answered, she walked in."

In all stories, in every novel we've read and every movie we've seen, the story begins by creating the characters and setting the scene. In every case there are principal characters—our client, his family—and the bad guys, the greedy, negligent corporation on the other side. Good stories have heroes and villains. Indeed, our lives are lived so that from time to time we, too, occupy the role of either hero or villain, depending upon who is telling our story.

In the case of Jim and Ann Smith, the story began with a young couple who had fallen in love, that kind of ecstatic love that leaves us giddy-headed and fluttering in the heart. We learned who Jim was, the strong, tough, physical kind who could never back down, because to survive as a boy without a father, and one of five poor kids born in a tough part of Chicago, he had to be strong to survive. He knew no other way. But if we were able to take out his heart and examine it under a magical microscope that could reveal the capacity of a heart to love, we would find that his heart was soft and spongy, that it could soak up huge quantities of love, and that he was vulnerable there, which made it all the more necessary for him to protect it with his hard outer armor. We would go on to describe how he was honest and hardworking and protective, and how he struggled to better himself by labor and loyalty to the company he worked for.

We previously discovered the story of Jim Smith by having acted out his role as a man at work, one who played hard, as well as who fell hard, like a stricken soldier, when he met this wife-to-be, Ann. By the time we get to court we know his viewpoints, understand his weaknesses, and know where his "tenders" lie. We have consulted with Ann in the workup of the opening. She has played both her role and his in our office where we have unraveled the story of their love and their trouble through the methods described in the chapters on discovering the story. By the time we walk into the courtroom we have become both Jim and Ann Smith. We have also become the foreman of the drilling company who was trying to make a three-thirty flight to Vegas on the day he was installing the blow-out preventer. We have taken on the role of the president and owner of the drilling company, who is now faced with liability for the death of Jim Smith, and who is both angry at the suit and afraid.

After we have set the beginning scene in our opening statement—the first meeting of Jim and Ann—we will go on to the other chapters in this book called the life of Jim and Ann Smith, the other scenes, the time of their marriage, the thrill of their honeymoon and their first years together. We will see the scenes where they had problems and how they dealt with them—not always appropriately. Finally there will come a time when we tell the jury, flatly, about how they separated.

Often we use the first person in telling the story. A certain power rises up out of a first-person narrative that cannot be duplicated in third-person storytelling. And it is easy to move in and out of the first person. It can happen like this:

"That day they were having breakfast. Jim was feeling hung over. They had a quarrel the night before and he'd stormed out of the house and escaped to the bar where he'd taken on a load. Yet he was up the next morning having his breakfast and headed out for work." Suddenly we can launch into the first person. "If Jim were here we would hear him say: 'I didn't know what to say to her. I felt bad. My head was pounding and my stomach was hollerin'. Then she said, "I suppose you think we can go on like this." I didn't know what to say. I knew we couldn't. But what was I supposed to do? Get down on my hands and knees and beg, or what? Then she said, "Well, aren't you going to talk to me?" and I still didn't know what to say. I didn't say anything. She said, "I don't think I want to live with a man who won't talk to me." I got up and walked out, and I burned about it all day. Hurt me, what she said. And that night when I came home I still didn't know what to say. She just stared at me with her hands on her hips, and so I packed up my stuff and moved out. We never got back together.' "

Although we obviously can't offer proof of all this soliloquy, and we may hear objections, nevertheless what is said is a fair inference from the evidence that will be presented, because Ann can testify, and, through our lips in our opening statement she can tell it in the first person as well.

We can move into the first person in our opening statement simply by saying: "My name is Ann Smith." She might go on to say, we speaking for her, "I loved that man. He was so tough and so tender, and I shouldn't have spoken to him as I did. Yeah, we had a fight and he went out and got drunk. I knew him. When he got up the next morning to go to work he was feeling bad. You could tell it. His eyes were blurry and he looked pale and he was messing with his eggs and not eating. He wouldn't speak to me. He was that way when he was off base. I mean, he should have stayed home and we should have worked it out. But he didn't know how and I didn't either. Although he was sorry, he never knew how to say it. So I tried to pick things up and I said, 'I suppose you think we can go on like this?' And he didn't answer. When he didn't know what to say he usually said nothing. Then I pushed it. I said, 'Well, aren't you going to talk to me?' and he just looked down in his plate like he was embarrassed and kept stirring his eggs. Not only had we had this fight, but after that he went to the bar and got drunk. So I pushed it further. I said, 'I don't think I want to live with a man who won't talk to me.' I shouldn't have said that. It hurt him, I know, and then he got up and walked out, and that was the last I ever saw of him alive. We never got back together. And it broke my heart, because I didn't know how to say I was sorry any better than he. Then I wrote him that letter that said that I loved him. And then they killed him."

It's immediately apparent that the first person is more effective in showing what was going on between this couple than if the lawyer had said something like, "Well, the next morning Jim and Ann didn't talk about what happened the night before. Jim walked out and he never came back."

Again, I insist lawyers must become good storytellers. We should tell stories to our kids every night, and to our wives and friends when we have a chance. If we ask anyone, "Would you like to hear a story?" the answer is almost always yes. We crave good stories—even bad ones—because our genes crave stories. Usually the good storyteller can tell the story better than the witness can on the stand, which is not to say that we are not telling the truth.

Most often I tell the story in exquisite detail, such as my first-person narrative of the Smiths. When Ann takes the stand, despite our preparation of her, she will be nervous. She will undoubtedly hear objections by the opposing counsel and the rulings of the court, and her story will be disrupted and fragmented, and after that twisted and torn when she undergoes cross-examination, all of which argues for the presentation of a thorough and detailed opening statement to support the story she will attempt to give on the witness stand—but only if we can present our story in an interesting, yes, a compelling way. Nothing deadens the bones more than listening to a long, mumbled, boring tale.

Our fear of objections, our intimidation by judges. Lawyers have an indigenous fear of objections like birds fear snakes. *Objections will be hurled* at this kind of storytelling. But I argue, and I hope I am heard again: If we risk nothing, we gain nothing. Objections do not hurt us. I have never seen an objection kill anyone. I have never seen a judge's ruling delivered in a shrieking "sustained" do anything more than pierce the eardrums. Judges often holler because they feel so powerless. Judges may snarl like junkyard dogs because they are tied to the bench and cannot physically thrash the lawyer who is boring them to death. Judges may be nasty because they suffer a congenital temperament defect. Judges may be bullies because as little boys their fathers shamed them and called them sissies. Whatever the cause, the foul, nasty, intemperate, uncivilized judge is how he is because of *his* defects, not ours. We must remember that.

And why are we afraid of objections? The judge is like some bullying father against whom we have no power. We quake inside when the berating begins.

And we're afraid of looking bad in front of the jury. The browbeating judge can humiliate us. But if we do not react to him things usually will change in the courtroom.

"Your Honor, I object to Mr. Spence's theatrics." He is referring to my telling the story in the first person.

"Yes, Mr. Spence," the judge bellows. "You know better than that!" The clear implication is that I have now crossed a well-known line and trespassed into some forbidden place—that a damnable foul has been committed.

A smile for his honor. Not a smirk. A kindly smile, and in a quiet voice, "I didn't know until you told me. Thank you, Your Honor." But within minutes we will be back in the first person again.

The judge interrupts: "What did I tell you, Mr. Spence?"

"Yes, Your Honor?"

"You are doing that again."

"What is that, Your Honor?"

"You know what you are doing."

"Yes, of course, Your Honor, I am telling the jury what our evidence will be from the standpoint of the principal witness in our case."

"Well, tell it then."

"Thank you, sir." And in a few minutes we again launch into the first person, which is not improper in the slightest. The impropriety is being foisted on us by the judge. But a polite, gentle, smiling response is so disarming. It is difficult for a judge to be too violent with a peaceful person in front of him. If we show no anger in return, none, the way is often easily cleared. In fact, a little good humor, nothing smart, will often work wonders. The lawyer who fights with the court is going to lose in this power struggle. Nothing is more intimidating to a judge than a lawyer who contests the judge's power, and the judge will come down with all of his power to keep it.

The *fear* (loss of power), the *pain* (the pain of fear), and the *anger* (anger that replaces pain), a progression that is so prevalent in all of us, is also at work in judges. We do not wish to frighten our judge, nor put him in pain, nor call forth his anger in response to his pain.

Of course, some judges are not so easily frightened, and therefore are not likely to be so easily converted into tyrants. I have seen many a good judge simply overrule the objections of the opponent, which leaves him caught in a malignant paradox. By not objecting, our opponent permits us to tell our story in the most effective way. By objecting, he may well incur an unfavorable ruling by the court, which only adds power to the story we're telling.

When the opposing lawyer has joined in the melee against us and piles on with more objections, the resulting match-up—the opposing lawyer and the judge against us—does not display a fair fight. Imagine the referee during a boxing match smacking one of the fighters in the back of the head when the fighter is fully engaged with the other combatant. Jurors possess a critical, instinctive awareness when a fight is not fair, and will readily react against what appears to be a judge-opponent conspiracy.

Moreover, jurors have an insatiable desire to hear a well-told story. So, probably, does the judge. The story will get out. And when all fails, nothing has failed. The judge has shown himself to be unreasonable. He has not laid us bare. He has run naked before the jury, showing what no one wanted to see—his most ugly parts. We should not be afraid of objections. Our overriding fear should be that we are not doing our job as fully and fearlessly as we should.

As we know, the opening statement has for its avowed purpose outlining what our proof will be—to inform the jury what our case is about, to create a road map, as many lawyers like to say, so that as the evidence is submitted, as the witnesses take the stand, the jury can understand where each piece of evidence fits. I know no rule of law that says the opening statement must be brief, although it should fairly state what the intended proof will be. In one of my cases my opening took five hours. If the story is complicated, there is no better place to explain it and to make it understandable than in the opening statement. We have to understand that when judges want us to be brief, their demand is more for the benefit of their calendars and the comfort of their beleaguered rear ends than for justice, because justice cannot be rendered to either side if the jury does not have an in-depth understanding of the facts of the case. When a judge limits an opening statement he is saying that his time is more valuable than justice.

On the other hand, a shorter opening is sometimes more effective, depending on the facts and issues that require understanding. Imaging, my wife, tells me that I am at my best when I'm forced to make a shorter opening. There is a power in the short, but well-conceived opening. Remember Lincoln's Gettysburg Address took less than two minutes and became immortal, while the words of those who spoke from the same podium for hours were soon forgotten. When a long, detailed opening is given, the risk is that we'll make representations that we'll fail to prove during the trial, so that during final argument our opponent will take our overstatements and shove them up into dark and painful places. Still, in balance, I favor the longer, detailed story. The jury is still relatively fresh. They are eager to hear our side of the case, and we must remember that the opening is our first opportunity to establish the justice of our case in the minds of the jury. It is the most important single address we will make in the case.

The opening in the criminal case. How well I remember the advice we used to glean from the old heads as we struggled to find some way to win a criminal case. The state was so powerful. The rights of the accused seemed substantially nonexistent. The prevailing wisdom then was that the defense should reserve its opening until after the state rested its case—the theory being that, since the defendant didn't know what the evidence against him would be and how it would play out to the jury, the defense should wait until the state's case was in, analyze it, and then prepare a response that would fit the situation.

This approach, like so many strategies that trial lawyers hold dear to their breasts and smother with the reverence (and ignorance) of habit, is almost always wrong, and for several powerful reasons.

There may be other strategic reasons why the opening should be made at the outset in the criminal case, but here are five very good ones:

Reason 1. Sending the wrong messages to the jury. The judge now turns to the defense lawyer after the state has completed its powerful opening that has left the jury gasping at the heinous crime our client has been accused of.

"You may make your opening statement, Mr. Spence," the judge says to us.

We rise, the heat of the prosecution's vile story still steaming in the courtroom, the jury stealing hateful glances at our client with a loathing that only the executioner's needle can cure. The prosecutor has told us how the hapless victim, Too Big Smith, was stabbed forty-three times, his throat cut, and his heart punctured three times, not to mention that he was stabbed in the right eye and that his left ear was cut off and shoved into his dying lips. We now rise up with all our towering magnificence and mumble, "The defense reserves its opening statement."

What message have we conveyed to the jury? (And, of course, everything we do or say is a message to the jury.) First, the message is that we have no ready, honest answer to the charges, to the whole truckload of horrors the state has just dumped on the jury. Second, the message is that we are games-men. We are going to play a sort of waiting game that keeps the jury in the dark as to what our defense will be. This is not the way supposedly trustworthy lawyers gain the trust of the jury.

Reason 2. Leaving the jury with a one-sided story. But the worst of it is that as the state lays out its case, witness by witness, exhibit by exhibit, the jury has no theory of the defense by which to test the evidence as it comes in.

A simple example: The state's star witness says, "I saw Billy Ray (our client) about eleven-thirty that evening (the night of the murder) and he left the bar just ahead of me." The state is establishing the fact that Billy Ray was up and about and near the vicinity of the killing on the night in question. The circumstantial evidence is piling in. But our defense is that Billy Ray got in his car and drove home that night. His family will vouch for the fact that he arrived home a few minutes later and remained home the rest of the night. And his employer at the garage will say he came to work as usual the next morning.

We can already see the error of a reserved opening statement. If the jury had heard us say that Billy went home that evening and that his family would be here to testify to that fact, along with his employer who would say he was at work the next morning, the jury would be alerted to the possibility that the state is mistaken in its accusations. On cross-examination of the state's witnesses, our questions and the answers might sound like this:

Q: After you saw Billy Ray leave the bar, did you follow him?
A: No.
Q: When you came out of the bar to go home, did you see him on the street?
A: No.
Q: So you don't know where he went?
A: No.
Q: You say you saw Billy Ray follow Too Big out of the bar that night?
A: Yes.
Q: You don't know that Billy Ray was following Too Big, isn't that true?
A: Well, he was following him all right.
Q: By that you mean that Too Big went out of the bar and that Billy Ray left the bar at about the same time—behind Too Big.

A: Yes.

Q: And you left the bar behind Billy Ray yourself.

A: Yes.

Q: Were you following either of them?

A: No.

Q: And no one is accusing you of murdering anyone, simply because you came out the bar door behind both Billy Ray and Too Big, isn't that true?

If we have reserved our opening, our cross-examination is essentially without roots. The problem the defense attorney faces in the criminal case is that every innocent fact will usually be attributed some sinister meaning by the prosecution. The murder took place in the alley behind the bar. That Billy Ray was at the bar establishes his opportunity to commit the murder (along with scores of others who were also there). That Billy Ray had an argument with Too Big is further evidence of motive (but Too Big argued with others and was a known troublemaker and bully). It was well known that Billy Ray often carried a knife, but no knife was ever found, which suggested that he threw the knife away (whereas he may not have taken a knife that evening). Besides, it was a short-bladed knife, while the coroner's report showed that the puncture wounds were five inches long. These facts will come out during the cross-examination of the state's witnesses, but they will have little meaning unless the defense made a complete opening following the prosecution's story of horrors that introduced the jury to these facts.

Reason 3. The jury's early decision making. Still, a better reason exists for the defense to make its opening immediately following the state's. We've already seen that jurors often make up their minds after having heard the opening statements. If we make none, the jurors have the state's case in mind and only their case. Their minds are pretty well set in concrete at the moment we say, "The defense reserves its opening." In fact, in the minds of the jurors, the burden of proof has shifted from the state to the defense. Believing the state's case, and despite the judge's instructions to the contrary, it now becomes the burden of the defense to dislodge the inculpatory facts from the minds of the jurors—to provide reasonable doubt, rather than enjoying the protection of the constitution that requires the state to prove its case beyond a reasonable doubt. Not only that, the judge himself needs to know where we are going in our defense, so that his rulings can be fairly made from a complete under-standing of the issues in the case.

Reason 4. Relinquishing control of our case to the state. I have never wanted to put the state in control of my case. For us to attempt to create a defense that fits the state's case is to abdicate control of our case to the prosecutor. How much better to lay out the defense in exquisite detail, which will then require the state not only to present its case, but to attack our defense all along the way. We are in control. Reasonable doubt arises out of the courtroom clashes, out of strident arguments fairly made. Reasonable doubt is the product of cracking open the door of truth so that the jurors can peer in and see enough to wonder what they might see if the door were flung wide open? It's the state's duty to slam the door. When the state fails, when the door is still ajar, the pros-ecutors must pack up their boxes of evidence, shut their briefcases, and plod on back to construct other cases, we must hope, against guilty defendants.

Reason 5. The silent defendant. But something even more fundamental to the defense in a criminal prosecution is the defendant himself. I most often de-cline to put my client on the stand. Whether to have his client testify is a deci-sion every criminal defense lawyer must make in every case. Lawyers usually put their clients on the stand because of two compelling motivations. First, the client himself wants to take the stand and protest his innocence. For an inno-cent man, nothing flogs at the soul more than to sit silently by while the prose-cution impales him with lying witnesses, witnesses who tell only half truths, with cops who have forgotten the facts that would acquit him, with prosecutors who point their long, accusatory fingers at him and claim they have brought be-fore the court the most heinous monster in the history of the human race.

But the jury, too, wants to hear from the accused. If a person is innocent, doesn't he protest? Doesn't he want to tell his story? Every seated juror knows if he or she were in the shoes of the defendant, and if innocent, it would take a bulldozer to shove him off the witness stand. And when the defendant fails to take the stand, the obvious conclusion is that he must be guilty.

But those who make such judgments have never been an accused in a crim-inal case, where their lives or their freedom are at stake. Although the accused argues to take the stand—and it's ultimately his decision—things grow grim when he gets up there and the prosecutor begins his long, laborious, detailed, well-prepared cross-examination that will frighten the accused, then make him angry, or sometimes leave him with a loss of memory and good sense. By the end of the cross he'll be shown as one who can't keep his story straight, who is evasive, and who gets hostile too easily, thus confirming the prosecution's argument that Billy Ray lost his temper and murdered Too Big Jones. When a skillfully prepared cross-examination is complete the prosecutor will often leave the most innocent appearing to be guilty—a murderer, a thief, a two-bit fraud, and a dastardly liar, which, in the hierarchy of all crime, and to many jurors, is the worst crime of all, since we have been taught that only the guilty lie.

The truth is that we can tell Billy Ray's story better than he. Our lives are not at stake. We haven't sat in a smelly concrete box suffering a year of nightmares about this moment when we must win on the stand or perish. We've not facing a prosecutor with greater communicative skills than our own. As lawyers, our business is to tell true, compelling stories. And the story we tell will likely not be severely interrupted in the opening whereas in his cross-examination the prosecutor will chop up Billy Ray's story like chicken liver. As skilled storytellers we have prepared the accused's story, remembering that every story has a beginning, a middle, the climax, and the end. We will be able to tell that story to the jury and support it with evidence during the trial, and put it all together again in the final argument much more effectively than Billy Ray will ever be able to do under fire.

Of course there are cases in which the accused must take the stand. Indeed, the prosecutor will often attempt to inject evidence into the case that only the accused himself can rebut, which always puts the defendant in a dilemma: The defendant must either take the stand and suffer, perhaps fatally, at the hands of the prosecutor; or we must attempt to rebut the evidence, and often can't, because no witness except the defendant may be available to do so. For example, the prosecutor persuades the judge to permit evidence that Billy Ray was engaged in some sort of barroom scuffle in the past in order to show our client's propensity toward violence. No one except Billy can explain that he was defending himself against the onslaught of another drunken bully. If he fails to take the stand to rebut this evidence, the jury's conclusion may be that Billy Ray is a violent thug who hangs out with churlish mobs in slummy saloons, waiting for the chance to do physical damage to any available human being. If he does take the stand to explain the situation, he of course submits himself to a full range of cross-examination by the prosecutor covering his entire life—from his first unfortunate breath in this world to the very moment he is found sitting there on the stand.

Telling a story you do not intend to prove. I remember a murder case in which I told the jury about my client, who'd been in the Royal Canadian Air Force during World War II, flying Spitfires out of Britain. I told the jury he was an ace, flying those flimsy fighter planes into the jaws of the enemy, and he was among those who stood receiving honors from Churchill when the British prime minister made his famous speech, "Never in the field of human conflict was so much owed by so many to so few." I created the scene for the jury based on my client's statement to me. I needed to put this good-looking man on the stand to testify to these facts, because what he'd been charged with was a dicey case to defend.

Let me tell you the story: My client, who had been working out of town, drove back unannounced one night and parked his car some distance from his residence where he and his girlfriend had been cohabiting. He went into the house and sat in the living room with his loaded pistol awaiting the return of his girlfriend and her newest lover—a bull rider of some local fame. After a night of conviviality the two of them staggered in. As they entered my client suddenly turned on the light, pistol in hand, but somehow the two men got into a wrestling match from which the bull rider emerged shot through the heart. In my opening statement I had explained all of these facts to the jury, including the heroic history of the defendant as an ace fighter pilot.

Then serendipitously, and before I called my first defense witness, I found out that the prosecutor had a witness from the Canadian Air Force department of records who would testify that during the entire war my client had never left Canada, where he had only been engaged as an aircraft mechanic. When the state rested its case, I hurriedly rested as well. I of course did not call my client to take the stand, since I had discovered that his testimony concerning his life in the Royal Canadian Air Force would have been false. And I rested my case without putting a single witness on the stand. Of course, since I called no witnesses there was no testimony for the state to rebut, and the state's star witness from Canada's department of records sat mutely in the courtroom and returned home having never testified.

Had I known that my client's statement was false—the one I passed on to the jury—I would have been guilty of a serious breach of ethics. Before the trial I had my client examined by a psychiatrist, who also had questioned him carefully on this subject and who came to the conclusion that his entire story was true.

In those days in the still-wild West, there was this somewhat quaint but prevailing notion that any man who would dare trespass into another man's house and partake of his woman shouldn't complain if he finds himself dead in the morning. The jury acquitted.

This story, however instructive, not only illustrates the additional risks we face when we put a client on the stand, it admonishes us that if we intend to do so, we have an ethical duty to tell the truth in the opening statement to the best of our ability.

Preparing the jury for a defendant who fails to take the stand. I have never seen a jury that doesn't expect to see the defendant take the stand to defend himself. His taking the stand is something the jurors look forward to—the climax, as it were, in the trial. We have been trained as voyeurs. If it were otherwise, the television and movie industries would be out of business and the sports stadiums would be vacant. Jurors anticipate with a sort of voyeuristic glee the moment the poor wretch, the defendant, takes the stand to try to save his neck.

After all, we as jurors are supposed to be able to tell who is lying and who is not. That notion is at the heart of this business called the jury system. We will hone in on every question the accused must answer. We will watch his every move, how he grips the arms of the witness chair, how he blinks at a hard question, how he hesitates—thinking of new lies—before he answers. Does he get angry when he is cornered? Aha! You *see*? He *is* lying! He has his arms tightly folded across his chest and his ankles are crossed and he is all hunched up and red-faced—the body language, you know. We have always wanted to see what a murderer looked like. Look at his eyes. Are they cold and calculating? How would you like to meet that devil in an alley someplace? I'll bet he could stab you in the belly and never blink an eye, just wipe the dripping blood from his knife, put it back in his pocket, and go whistling on down the street. And if we the jury are deprived of the right to make our judgments of the accused as he wrestles for his life on the stand we will be sorely disappointed.

In the opening I will tell the jury that there's a reason why the defendant is not required to take the stand. It's his constitutional right—our founders understanding that we can never prove our innocence. We can only give the prosecutor the opportunity to prove an innocent man guilty. I might say, "You expect Billy Ray to take the stand and tell you what happened that night. You want to know. Yet if he takes the stand you'll wonder if he isn't just lying to save his hide. On the other hand, if Billy Ray does not take the stand and testify, you'll wonder why an innocent man didn't want to tell his story—any innocent man would. So you can see, either way we go we're in trouble. I cannot tell you at this moment what our decision will be. If Billy Ray does not testify here, the court will instruct you that you are not to consider his failure to testify as evidence of his guilt. That is as much protection as we can get as we face this dilemma."

For the nonlawyer—the opening in the boardroom, the council room, the boss's office. We have already learned that the opening is the most important of the several important elements in presenting our case. First impressions stick like a catsup stain on a white shirt. The first pitch—the salesman's story of his car, the art dealer's story behind the painting he wants to sell—is the first and best chance the seller has to close the sale. I wager that few would be as enthralled by Van Gogh's wild, childlike attacks of the brush on canvass without also knowing something of his struggle as a person. Every good salesman has a story about his product.

The opening tells the decision maker what to watch for, what the issue is. It tells the story before proof is offered—such as testimonials, the actual calling of colleagues who will make brief statements (also in story form), and the handing over of written documents, brochures, and the like.

Before the school board, say, the opening is not laid out in the abstract, about how we do not have enough qualified teachers to fulfill our obligations to our children because of teachers' paltry pay. Instead, our story begins with a real person, a woman who has devoted her life to teaching.

Standing before the board, we may begin our presentation in the first person. "I want to tell you the story of Molly Carpenter. I am fifty-eight years old and have spent thirty years teaching the fourth grade at Hot Springs Grade School. I love my job. My children beam when I walk into the classroom. You can see it in their eyes, a sort of love that children have for those who care about them. My class has had the highest evaluations of any fourth grade in the city since I have taught there. My kids have gone on to become doctors and engineers and lawyers. Dr. Mary Littlefield, the famous neurologist, was my student. So was William Sloan, who has been a key scientist in our space program. You all know Robert Hardesty, the lawyer, who is well known for his fight against the pollution of our streams and rivers. Each of these former students will tell you that Molly Carpenter introduced them to themselves. She taught them that they were special, as each of us is different and perfect, and she encouraged each of them to follow their passion.

Now the presenter, as Molly Carpenter, says, "I have had to leave my beloved work. I just cannot make ends meet. I couldn't pay my electric bill, and the power company was threatening to turn off my power. I had to take a job as a waitress in the Broadway Café, where I make more on tips in a day—by nearly twice—than my teaching salary provided. It breaks my heart that I had to leave my children behind. But I have my own family to feed. We have lost over two hundred highly qualified teachers this year because we are not paying them a living wage. The damage to our children is nearly incalculable. We will show you how our classrooms are so crowded that children can do little more than occupy their space and hope to survive the day."

Nowadays even journalists avoid the old, mechanistic approach of reporting, and often begin their articles by telling the story through the life of a living person. Abstractions do not best inform us, move us to action, or cause change or reform. We care little about an epidemic of SARS, with an equally abstract name, Severe Acute Respiratory Syndrome, the dangerous new respiratory disease caused by a heretofore unknown virus, until, of course, we see some person who is suffering from it—say, a child. A little girl name Jenny Ann Wilson, age five, is at Disneyland with her parents. She has been coughing a little, and has not wanted to go on any of the rides. Her parents begin to worry when the little girl becomes confused as to where she is. Her eyes are becoming glassy and she seems feverish.

Her father, Paul Wilson, decides to take her back to the hotel. He says, "I called for a doctor who finally came to the hotel room. By this time Jenny Ann has a fever of 105, and she is coughing so hard I think her lungs are going to come out, and you could see her chest heaving like she was dying from lack of air. The doctor came and we took Jenny Ann to the hospital." The story can go on with all of the visuals of the doctors trying to save Jenny with every known treatment and device known to medicine. If we read the whole, frightful specter of the child's fight against SARS and the helplessness of the medical community against it, the disease becomes alive and meaningful to us, where before it was little more than a vague acronym.

The cold, hard, lifeless stone of abstractions. Remember, we think in pictures—not abstractions. We have empty ears for abstractions. Professors spout abstractions like an eternal fountain, and even they have no ears for other people's abstractions. Why do we take notes? Because of the professor's affliction—his inability to speak other than in the tongue of abstractions. His inability to tell us a story requires us to remember words instead of word pictures.

Concerning such simple things as gravity, we can proclaim in our deepest authoritative voice, "That, as a consequence of a certain force that has been the source of argument among scientists for centuries, a force between objects that pulls them toward one another, a universal force that affects the largest and smallest objects and all forms of matter and energy, and as a consequence of which the victim descended to the surface of the earth . . ." or we can simply say he was gazing up at the stars, tripped over an empty whiskey bottle, and fell on his keester. Both describe the forces of gravity. The first is an abstraction, the second a word picture.

When we face a problem, when we worry, we do not think of it in abstract words. I worry about my wife Imaging when she goes out on the highway to drive—not that she isn't a skilled and careful driver, but because there are more people killed on highways than on battlefields. In my mind I see myself waving good-bye to her and then, hours later I hear in my mind's ear the telephone ringing. I pick up the telephone and it's somebody saying, "Your wife has been in an accident, and she didn't make it." In just a fleeting part of a second I experience horrible, flashing scenes of the mortuary. I am picking out the casket and then I'm trying to figure out what I'm going to do with the rest of my life without her. These scenes come and go so fast we cannot recognize them as scenes. But our thoughts, all of them, are in pictures.

Invariably, in court, I have experts on the stand who talk in abstractions. Experts are comfortable in the cloistered halls of their intellects, which provides them a wide and easy illusiveness. To such an expert, my standard response is, "Whoa, wait a minute. Give me an example," which is to say, tell me a story. I cannot follow language adorned with abstractions—no one can, unless those stone-cold words somehow bring up a picture.

Preparing the opening. I begin preparing the opening statement for the trial (along with the closing, which we shall see is a different creature) at the very outset. How do I prepare the opening? I type it word for word into my computer. Am I going to read it? No. Will I memorize it? No. Again, what I'm doing is loading up another computer—the mind. If that old, dry sponge of the mind hasn't been wetted with our creative juices, our word pictures, the powerful action verbs, then there's nothing much that can come out. If we're going to be spontaneous, as I say we must, we cannot find spontaneity floating around in a dry sponge. But if we have soaked the computer brain with creative preparation, our opening will come flooding out whenever we squeeze the sponge. People sometimes ask, "How can you be so spontaneous about this and that?" It's because I have over fifty years of the stuff I am talking about soaked up in there, together with the fully developed story of the case I'm presenting.

We harbor bits and pieces of trivia in the mind that if extracted and piled up would look like a mammoth junk pile. The contents of the mind aren't classified, nor are they indexed. To make what we know available for immediate use, we have to fill the computer of the mind with our current story so that it is on top of the pile. We have to provide it with an index, an outline, and a form that will become readily available when we stand to deliver. If we know the story inside and out, if we've written and rewritten it, outlined it, and, with heroic tenacity, outlined it again, magically we will become spontaneous. We do not deliver a memorized statement. We do not read from notes. We simply have a loaded mind computer with a narrative that includes an outline, a beginning, a middle, and an end, and—trusting the wonders of the mind to now tell the story in an exciting and compelling way—we will give a winning opening statement. As a side effect of our untiring preparation, we will have shed a good deal of our fear and replaced it with an eagerness to tell our story.

As soon as I take a case I begin to correlate the opening statement with the witnesses that I will be calling to support it. As the witnesses' anticipated testimony expands, or as new facts are discovered, I go back and work some more on the opening statement. By the time I walk into the courtroom to deliver my opening, I know the story so fully I could deliver it in my sleep. In fact, I have.

Winning in the courtroom is not so much a reflection of the genius of the lawyer but of that lawyer's preparation. Among the comments I have heard about my work in the courtroom, the one I most value is, "I have never seen him come into the courtroom unprepared."

No story is truly banal. We may have tried a dozen of those all-too-frequent soft-tissue injury cases that arise from a whiplash caused by the common rear-ender. But each case involves different persons with different histories, medical and otherwise, who have reacted in quite different ways to the low-speed, rear-end impact. If the story is trite and worn out it is because we are dull and insensitive to the nuances that surround each individual case.

If we think of the stories we have heard or told around the campfire they will provide us an excellent example of the form and texture of our opening statements, those stories we should tell in the courtroom, the showroom, the boardroom, and every other room where we want to win our case.

13. TELLING OUR STORY THROUGH WITNESSES—DIRECT EXAMINATION

I
N OUR OPENING STATEMENT WE have told our story. The complete story. Now we're here to prove it. But remember, the key to direct examination, as in every element of the trial, is we. It begins with us. Everything, everywhere, begins with us. We are it. If we haven't discovered our story and its theme we can't lead a successful direct examination. If we physically haven't been to the scene we can't do a direct examination. If we can't live for the moment inside our client's hide, we can't do a successful direct examination. If we haven't spent the necessary time preparing our direct examination will be of little value. And most assuredly, if we can't tell the story effectively, our direct examination will be more confusing than enlightening.

The direct examination is also storytelling—telling the story through the lips of the witness. Our job is to help the witness tell the part of the story the witness knows.

Preparing, not coaching, the witness. Let's first disabuse ourselves of a myth designed to sully this whole business of the preparation of direct examination. The preparation of a witness to testify is not the ignominious, illegal, immoral act often referred to as "woodshedding" the witness, or coaching him, as is often the attack by our opponent if he has nothing better to say on cross-examination. As we shall see in the chapter on cross-examination, this attack on the witness is virulent and, unless the witness is prepared, it can do him and our case great damage.

It is something approaching malpractice for a lawyer to fail to prepare his witness to take the stand. For the lay witness, his first experience on the witness stand can be daunting. The witness has likely never before tried to tell a story in a place as unfriendly as a courtroom. Slip inside the witness's shoes for a moment. You are called to the witness stand. You look around you. The place looks more like the chapel in a funeral home than a place in which to tell your story, and you begin to feel like you may be mistaken for the body. The judge is not your friendly undertaker. He is not there to comfort. He is there to fulfill his own agenda, whatever it may be.

The judge, in black, looks down on you with an appalling dark countenance. Across from you sit the opposing counsel, crouched like tigers about to spring on you, the helpless prey caught in a dead-end crevice. Your own lawyer looks pale and nervous and begins asking you questions you had not anticipated, questions you have to think about. Sometimes he doesn't even look at you when he asks them, his eyes glued to his notes like a choirboy. One thing is certain: Your lawyer isn't listening to what you're saying because he can't listen to you and read his notes at the same time. "For God's sake," you say, "I wish somebody had prepared me for this nightmare, and if not me, that someone had at least prepared my lawyer."

Tutelage is divine. Coaching, on the other hand, occurs when the lawyer tells the witness *what* to say, despite what the truth may be. Such a lawyer should have his license lifted and be prosecuted for a conspiracy to commit perjury. A witness who would tell a lie that was foisted on his lips by the lawyer should face the same music.

Preparing the witness to testify is something quite different. We first want to discover the story from him. We've seen in a previous chapter how that can be assisted through psychodrama. But another review of the process may be instructive. Let's suppose our case is one in which our client Derrick Smith has been wrongfully assaulted and beaten by two police officers. The suit is for damages against the city for the officers' brutality. Our witness, a passerby, is going to testify about what she saw.

Let's take on the role of the examining lawyer, remembering that in direct examination, as distinguished from cross-examination, the star of the drama is not the lawyer but the witness. Let's first have the witness take us to the scene. Shirley, we'll call her.

"Where does this incident take place, Shirley?"

"It's an apartment complex on Bath Street."

"As you face the building from the street, tell us what this apartment house looks like?"

"It's a brick building with three stories—one front door. The bricks are smudged with a lot of smoke and grime. There's graffiti under one window. Some of the windows on the third floor have no curtains over them, and some have cardboard to cover where panes of glass have been broken out."

If the witness can't produce this kind of detail, then we have to go with the witness to the scene and point out all of the details of the surroundings that we will want her to testify to in the trial. We could use a photograph. But a detailed picture from the lips of the witness provides us with the assurance that the witness has been there and that the witness is observant. Moreover, having her describe the scene in detail is a way for the witness to become comfortable with this peculiar way we are required to communicate with people in the courtroom.

We'll continue setting the scene. "How do you get to the front door of the apartment house?"

"A concrete sidewalk leads to the front door through a gate."

"As you look at the gate, what do you see?" Note, we are not asking the witness to tell us from her memory what she saw. She is there, now.

"It's broken and hanging on one hinge."

"What's it made of?"

"Sort of iron work. You know, with those scrolley designs in it."

"Open the gate for us."

"It's already open and hanging on that one hinge."

"What do you see beyond the gate?"

"The front yard. Small, about this big." She motions to the size of the fifteen-by-twenty-foot room we are in.

"What do you see in the yard?"

"I see a poorly tended lawn, mostly brown."

"Is there a smell about the place?'

"I suppose."

"What do you smell?"

"Oh, I guess it's a stale, heavy odor that comes from the street, the cars whipping by—it's hot and muggy smelling. I think there is a taint of garbage there as well."

"As you approach the scene, what do you hear in the background?"

"The droning of traffic, the gunning of car engines. The hollering of people across the street."

Perhaps there will be objections to this kind of detail. The court and counsel may not be used to a thorough scene-setting that takes into account all of the senses. But we already see that this brand of scene-setting not only creates credibility for the witness and helps her become adjusted to the courtroom, it also does a good deal more than a photograph could do, which is merely a two-dimensional image that cannot recreate sound, smell, and feel. I am not suggesting we not use a photograph, but that our scene-setting go beyond it.

"What time is it now?"

"It's two in the afternoon."

"What month and day of the year?'

"July twenty-eighth. It's hot."

"How do you know?"

"Because I can feel the heat."

"Are you sweating?"

"Yes.

"Exactly where are you in this scene?"

"I'm walking along the sidewalk of the street. I am at the intersection of that sidewalk and the smaller concrete walk that leads to the gate and to the apartment."

"Perhaps you can get up now and stand where you were standing." The witness can get up from her chair and choose a spot as the place where she was standing.

"Where are you going at this moment?"

"To the store to get some groceries for dinner."

"What's going on at this moment?"

"I see this African-American man trying to get into the door of the apartment house."

"How far away from you is the door to the apartment house?"

"About twenty feet."

"Show us where the door is." She walks about twenty feet to a place she designates as the front door.

"Let's put a chair here to designate the apartment door." These simple visual aids help make the scene real.

"Describe this man."

"He's thin, about thirty I'd say, about five-feet-eight. He has balding hair."

"What is he wearing?"

"He's in a pair of floppy brown pants, a pair of worn, white tennis shoes, and a white T-shirt."

We are about to ask our witness what she is seeing (not what she saw). Keeping this in the present tense allows us to bring the jury into the action.

"Where's the man you've described?"

"He's at the door of the apartment house. The man is trapped at the door. He's trying to unlock it and one officer is running around the apartment house from one direction and the other from the other direction."

We ask the witness to take the position of the African-American man as she saw him. She walks over to the place designated as the apartment door and lies down on the floor where she remains during the following questions.

"What happens *now*?"

"A couple of police officers are holding him down and beating him with night sticks."

"Do you recognize any of the officers today in this courtroom as the ones you are now seeing at this scene?"

She looks up from the floor. "Yes." She points to the two officers who sit at counsel table with their lawyers, their ferocity hidden behind glumness and scowls.

"Do you recognize Officer Bates?"

"Yes."

"And Officer Harlow?"

"Yes. They're the ones beating on this man."

"Do you recognize the man who is being beaten?"

"Yes. He's at your table."

"How do you recognize him?"

"Like you recognize anyone. He is himself. I would recognize him anywhere." Our witness is still on the floor.

"What is happening to you?" The "you" then serves to convert the witness into our client, Derrick Smith.

"I am being hit over the head and across my body by Officer Bates."

"What are you doing?"

"I am yelling, 'Don't hit me! Don't hit me. Please don't hit me again.' And I am crying and screaming."

"What is office Harlow doing now?"

"He is hitting me as well."

"What are you doing?"

"I am putting my hands over my head like this. Then when they hit my body, I try to protect my body."

I ask Shirley the witness to get up, and I hand her a ruler. "Assume this is the night sticks of the officers, show us what Officer Bates is doing to Derrick Smith who is still lying there on the ground."

"He is striking Mr. Smith with his nightstick like this." She beats at the place where she previously lay.

"And will you show us what Officer Harlow is doing now."

"He is striking Mr. Smith like this." Also beating the imaginary man on the ground.

By this process the witness has taken the roles of four people in this drama, the client, Derrick Smith, the two officers, and herself. She is testifying to what she saw, but it is testimony that is *put into action*. Had she testified in the usual manner of an eyewitness, she would have simply told what she saw—"I saw the officers beating on Mr. Smith and he was yelling for them to stop." But putting the scene into action creates a more vivid, accurate picture. In truth, we are not coaching the witness, she is educating us.

And remember two simple things about the direct examination: Again, the star is the witness, not the lawyer. And secondly, the lawyer *directs* the jury to the star with open-ended questions, the who, what, where, why, when questions, the how questions. The lawyer does not lead unless he must—in response to a blank face from the witness, or because the witness is straying, or when emphasis is called for. The leading question is always there to save us.

Facing potential objections. Of course, I'm interested in the objections that are made to this kind of testimony and the lawyers' fear of their embarrassment at the hands of an oppressive judge. But in the courtroom there are forces at work that inhibit objections. First, the court isn't likely to interpose an adverse ruling without an objection from our opposing counsel. Our opposition may or may not object. Often he will be taken into the story and see no valid opposition to it, except that it is something new. He may be curious. More to the point, he may be concerned that his objection to this interesting form of giving testimony—words in action—may cause an adverse reaction by the jurors, who want to see what is going to happen and will resent his interrupting it.

We hear objections like, "This is not testimony, this is acting." The response is that we are interested in the truth. Words with action provide us with a much more vivid view of the facts than mere words alone. Often witnesses are not especially articulate. They have to choose the correct words to tell what happened, and many are not good at this, especially under the unrelenting pressure of the courtroom. When we see the action along with the words, the picture becomes more clear.

The objection may be that the action of the witness cannot be recorded by the court reporter. But a better picture of what happened, brought to reality by action, ought not be victimized by the limitations of courtroom technology. If there is an honest concern that the action of the witness can't be accurately reported for the appellate court, then the trial court can order that the testimony of the witness be recorded on video, which the appellate court can review and which is much easier and informative for them than reading the dry, impoverished transcript that is void of most of the truth. The printed word in the transcript does not reveal voice intonations, nor the emphasis on words that can change the entire meaning of those words, nor the facial expressions and body language of the witnesses. The experts tell me that less than twenty-five percent of meaning is conveyed by the spoken word itself. A much smaller percentage is conveyed by the cold word on the page. And the attorney can always make the standard report to the record, "Let the record show that the witness is . . . [whatever the witness is doing]."

Back to our courtroom drama: "Perhaps, Shirley, you can retake the position where you are watching this scene take place." She walks back to the place on the sidewalk where she witnessed this assault. "Could you tell us what you are thinking now as you watch this?" This question probes into a richer source of truth. Her thoughts will show us a deeper understanding of the facts. Her interpretation of what she sees is not only relevant but tells us what is otherwise unknowable.

"I am thinking, what is going on here? This is horrible. They are killing this man. He is surely going to be murdered in front of my eyes. I have never seen a murder before. I had better run and get out of here. Maybe they will kill me."

"Do you say anything to the officers?"

"No."

"So, what do you think you should do?"

"The first thing I think is, I had better call the police. Then I realize that they *are* the police."

"What do you do next?"

"Suddenly, I don't know why, but I run over to them and grab that Officer Bates's arm and holler at him, 'You are killing that man.'"

"Show us."

She goes to the place in the room where the officers are beating Derrick and shows us how she grabbed the arm of the officer. At this point this drama can be acted out with others taking the role of the police officers and our client. And even in the courtroom the witness can be asked to use, say, one of our attorneys at the table to stand in for Derrick and the bailiff to stand in for the officer to show us what happened.

"How are you feeling as you grab the arm of Officer Bates?"

"I'm scared. I'm afraid he might hurt me."

"What happens next?"

"He throws me aside with just one big swing of his arm, like this. [Showing us.] He knocks me away about five feet."

"And what, if anything, is he saying?"

"He says, 'Get the fuck out of here, bitch.'"

"What is he doing now?"

"He is beating at Derrick again."

"And what are you doing?"

"I grab his arm again."

"Show us. And what is Officer Bates doing now?"

"He gets up from where he is beating on Derrick and he pushes me up against the wall and he's saying, 'I'm going to arrest you for interfering with the official duties of an officer.' "

"What are you thinking now?"

"I am thinking, 'What am I going to tell my mother if he puts me in jail?' He is holding me up against the wall of the apartment house and he is putting handcuffs on me. He says, 'What's your name, bitch?' and I tell him, 'Shirley MacCall,' and he says, 'Where do you live?' I say, '324 West Park.' And he says, 'Okay bitch, how old are you?' I say, 'Seventeen.' And then he takes off the cuffs from me and says, 'Get the hell home to your mother.' "

"What is going on with Derrick?"

"They have quit beating him. He is lying on the concrete walk uncon- scious, face down."

"How do you know he is unconscious?"

"Because he isn't moving. He is bleeding from the nose and mouth."

"What are the officers doing?"

"Officer Harlow is calling an ambulance on his walkie-talkie radio."

"What are you doing now?"

"I'm running home."

When Shirley appears in court as our witness she will have had the oppor- tunity to reexplore in depth what happened at the scene. She will go into court nervous, but ready. She knows what her testimony will be, the story that she will be telling. Her testimony will be elevated a notch above what we might ordinarily hear in court—a witness groping for words to express some- thing that took place in the past, a scene that is rendered in the usual abstract, sometimes-fuzzy language that leaves the jurors to create their own mental picture that will not accurately portray the events.

For years I have suffered and struggled with direct examination. I repeat- edly, habitually, found it necessary to lead the witness who, under the heat of the courtroom, suddenly couldn't tell what he knew. But I found that the use of the psychodramatic technique opens the doors to discovery. The witness of- ten doesn't know all that he knows until he plays through the scene. We learn it along with the witness. We are not coaching the witness. Once more, the witness is teaching us.

Being upfront with the jurors about our preparation. What happens to our case if, after having prepared our witness to testify in the manner just illustrated, opposing counsel asks on cross-examination the following, and in the following manner.

"So, Miss MacCall, have you met with Mr. Spence and gone over your testimony?"

"Yes." Some of the less sophisticated jurors are now aghast. Mr. Spence, the supposedly upright and ethical lawyer, has been coaching his witness.

"And when did you meet with him?"

"Last week. In his office."

"Who was there?"

"Mr. Spence and his son Kent."

"And did you put on this dog and pony show there for them?"

The questioning goes on in this manner, creating an unnecessarily mortified witness. (The Latin root of the word is *mortis*—death.)

We easily could have avoided this disaster. At the very beginning of Shirley's testimony our questioning would go this way.

"Shirley [some courts object to calling a witness by his or her given name, in which case it is Ms. MacCall], have you and my staff met before you took the stand today?"

"Yes. We met at your office a week ago."

"What did we do there?"

"You asked me to show you what happened. And what I saw."

"Did you show me?"

"Yes."

"How did you do that?"

"I showed you where this happened, and I showed you and told you what the people there did and said."

"So, did this help prepare you for your testimony today?"

"Yes."

"And I can say, Shirley, that you helped me understand it as well." An objectionable but harmless comment that puts the preparation into correct perspective.

The client as witness. I have already discussed the inherent danger of calling the client as a witness in the criminal case. But in the civil case the issues are different. If we don't call the client, which we must, the defense surely will. In the civil case, the client is an imperative part of our case—he is what the case is about. We are not, as in the criminal case, defending. In the civil case we are the prosecution. We are going forward with the evidence. We are *It*. The burden is on us. Our client is the victim, the injured, and we want justice—all the justice we can pack into the verdict. The client's story is at the heart of our case. The client *is* our case. Often I hear lawyers talking about their search for experts and for witnesses who will buttress their case. I think of the wise doctor who understands that his patient knows more about his patient's condition than the doctor, that the first source of information about the patient's case is the patient. And so it is with our client.

When I hear lawyers seeking answers in their cases I ask them, "Why don't you just go talk to your client? Your client is the expert in his case. He has lived it every day and dreamed of it every night. He has explored untold dead end alleys. He knows the forest out there. He may be confused. He may not know the law. He may be clouded with a haunting anxiety about it. He may be harried by outside forces, but he knows his case better than anyone in the world."

Too often lawyers see their clients as those bothersome, whining pests who are always demanding and always unreasonable. They may be all of the above, but they know their case the best. They are the wellspring from which all knowledge originates. They are not just somebody who happened to stumble through our office door and signed a fee agreement, and who now is constantly bothering us about why the case is moving so slowly.

If we are to do a direct examination, and do it right, we ought to go sit with the client at his house. That's where he spends his life. Let's look at his bedroom, his bookshelf—even inside his refrigerator. Let's see what he does with his painful days and lonely, misery-filled nights. If we represent a quadriplegic we ought to spend the night. Bring a sleeping bag. See the family. See their caring, their struggle, and how his damnable injury has imprisoned them—and see their heroic cheerfulness and love as well. We should watch our client struggle into bed at night and out again in the morning. See how they insert the various tubes into his body. See how helplessness is really defined. He cannot lift a spoon to his mouth. He cannot move his bowels without assistance. His state of being demeans every essential quality of human existence. His lust for life is buried beneath pain and misery and degradation. If we want to know what his case is about, we should live with him for at least one day and one night, especially considering the fact that he will live with it until the grace of God intervenes. If we want to know what it is like to be a quadriplegic, let us become one with our client. If we do, we will not only learn what it's like, our lives will be changed by it. We will go into the courtroom having visited the heartland of our case, the dark, haunting, lonely interior where our client lives and will live the rest of his life.

To prepare for this witness we must to go to the accident scene. If we know little about the scene, how can we begin to understand the story? So the accident took place at an unguarded railroad crossing? What do we see there? The long, steel curve of the tracks and a train barreling down on the unguarded crossing. What about the high weeds the railroad let grow up at the crossing? Let's wait until a train roars by. Can we hear it? The frightening, descending sound. What are the smells in the air? Can we smell the diesel from the engines? If we have not been there we cannot accurately bring the scene into the courtroom.

I am amazed at how often counsel have never been to the place of the accident. I am appalled at how many lawyers go to court and have never sat in the automobile that crashed. We lawyers are bookish by training, and many think we can learn all we need to know about the case by reading the reports of the experts and glancing at the photographs.

The idea of helping our client on with his prosthesis, or slogging through the mud where the car rolled over, the very notion of getting hands or feet dirty, or the lungs filled with the reality of the scene, is often abhorrent to those who see themselves as the ladies and gentlemen of the bar. And when the verdict comes in against them these same ladies and gentlemen sit in their plushy offices and appeal their lost cases to other ladies and gentlemen who occupy soft-seated thrones on the courts of appeals.

I recall as a young lawyer representing a woman who lost her daughter in an accident caused by a defectively manufactured automobile. Her daughter was the hub of her life. The mother was devastated by her daughter's death and bore a deep hunger for justice. But when she got on the stand and we began to discuss what it meant to her to have lost her daughter she seemed cold and distant. The jury returned a verdict for her, but it was ten percent of what the verdict should have been. I talked to one of the jurors after the case, who told me that the manufacturer was negligent and that the company ought to pay, but the mother seemed not to care much about her daughter. She seemed so mechanistic, so matter-of-fact about it. Not a tear, not even an approaching tear, not a quaver in her voice. My client had been so afraid of showing emotion, so fearful of being herself, that she froze into emotional ice.

We must spend time with the client, emphasizing that they have our total permission, and the court's and jury's as well, to be who they are. I am not talking about maudlin sentimentality. I am talking about being real. Real persons have feelings. Real persons cry. Real persons even show anger when it is appropriate. Real persons can smile though their tears. It is all right, indeed, it is imperative, that we be who we are in or out of court.

Preparing the witness for cross-examination. The prospect of our opponent's cross-examination can be frightening. Nothing protects the witness against fear and anger better than preparation.

The witness who takes the stand becomes the target. In many ways his function is that of the soldier on the front line. If the opponent can kill him it brings the war that much closer to an end. We are still barbarians who use words instead of swords. The courtroom becomes an arena of human struggle. But, if we understand the nature of the trial, we can prepare ourselves and our witness to survive and prevail.

Here is something we might say to Shirley, or even to a seasoned expert— perhaps especially to one of them.

"You are going to testify. As you know, our opponent will likely try to attack your testimony in some way." (Before we are finished with our preparation we'll have subjected our witness to our own cross-examination.) Continuing, we might say, "When we are attacked, it naturally makes us afraid. When we're afraid, we sometimes get hostile. We want to hit back. We strike back. We fight. It's only natural to be angry.

"If Attorney Jones can make you angry he will have won. Remember the three Cs of a good witness: It's for you to remain *courteous, calm,* and *considerate.* The more hostile he gets, the more anger you see from him, the more you know you are winning, and the more courteous, calm, and considerate you become. Anger in the courtroom is the blood of the battle. I want it to be theirs, not ours."

Then I might add: "Now, let's talk about the reality of a trial. Although a trial has monumental consequences, I have never lost a witness. Nobody ever really dies on the witness stand. If it were otherwise, they would have to kill

me first. In the end, there is nothing for us to be afraid of and therefore no reason to react to our fear. The only thing we really have to be afraid of is ourselves, and as long as we remember the three Cs and never let the truth be
tainted, we're going to win."

I tell the client it is proper to say, "I don't know," if the client doesn't
know. I say, "Don't guess and don't add anything that is unnecessary to give a
full and honest answer. If you make a mistake, simply say you made a mistake.
The truth is always the safe port, even when it hurts. Don't be afraid of the
cross-examination. I will be there to protect you against any improper questions. And one thing for sure. Be absolutely as fair and friendly to the cross-
examiner as you are to me. Remember the three Cs."

To ignore that last bit of advice is a form of courtroom suicide. I give it a
name: the "my team" syndrome, which is to say that if you are on my team I
will be kind, generous, and courteous—always courteous. But if you are not,
I'll turn into a raging scold and I'll fight you on every word—about everything
and anything. I do not want my client or any of my witnesses to be stricken
with the "my team" syndrome.

We readily see how it works: We are coasting along with our direct examination, telling our story, and making our points. It all looks so just, so reasonable. Smiles and sweetness and all manner of brotherly love prevail between
our witness and us. Then, up jumps the other side's lawyer to cross-examine,
and in response to his first question everything changes. I acknowledge that
it's hard to be well mannered and courteous with opposing counsel shaking
his long, bony finger in our faces. One tends to get snappy. Indeed, too often
our witness's face tightens, his voice lowers about two octaves, and he turns as
sour as old socks. If he were a dog his hair would be standing straight on end.
He is ready to fight. He is all but baring his teeth—and I have seen witnesses
bare them. Horrid sight—watching our dear, avuncular witness transformed
into an attack dog before our eyes. Our witness meets the cross-examiner's
first question with an answer tainted by poorly concealed loathing, and he
quibbles over every word. The war may be lost right there.

If our witness had been able to treat the cross-examiner in the same tone
and with the same openness and grace as he treated us when we were asking
the questions, the tide would have immediately turned. The cross-examiner
would likely get testy himself, frustrated that he could not shake this witness's

cool nor pierce his sober honesty. The harder the examiner tries with this kind of witness, the worse trouble he gets into, leaving the jury to believe he is the inquisitor on a witch hunt.

The need for the preparation of our client and all of our other witnesses is only too clear. The last words I say to my witness before I call my witness to the stand are, "When Mr. Jones gets up to cross-examine you, pretend that he is your friend, someone you can trust, a nice man who has to be gently straightened out on a few things. View him as one who is somewhat disadvantaged because he doesn't know the truth of this case. I do not mean that you should patronize him. No. I mean that you should treat him kindly—as you would treat me if I made an error concerning your case." Often this provides the witness and ourselves with a vision of the cross-examiner that can guide the tone of our witness's answers to the cross-examiner.

The critical interplay. We are watching the typical direct examination in the courtroom. Our witness is sitting on the stand clutching the arms of the witness chair. His knuckles are white. Then he crosses his arms as if to protect himself from the spears the attorney is about to throw at him. The lawyer asks his first question:

"State your name." (Is that friendly?)

"John Peacock."

The lawyer is looking at his notes as he asks the next question. "Where do you live?"

"Twenty-six Broadway." The lawyer is still looking at his notes, groping for the next question he has written out, notes to which he is welded like the second head of a Siamese twin.

"So, on the night in question, where were you?"

"I was over in Jersey visiting my sister."

"So, what did you see at your sister's place on the night in question?"

The questioning goes on, the lawyer bound to his notes and never listening to what the witness is saying, because he cannot listen and read his notes at the same time.

The critical interplay between the witness and the lawyer has been destroyed by the lawyer. He is not interested in the witness, so why should the jury be? He isn't listening to the witness, so why should the jury? Nothing is happening between them. From the witness's standpoint, the witness feels as if he has been abandoned by the lawyer—dumped up there on a hard, unfriendly chair and then interrogated as if he were dead meat and the lawyer a blind butcher.

A critical interplay exists between all of the parties in the courtroom. We want the jury invested in this—especially the jury. So the questioning may go like this:

"And so, Mr. Peacock, tell the ladies and gentlemen of the jury what is happening now?" We are looking directly at the witness as we ask the question, and we will gesture from the witness to the jury so that the witness now turns to the jurors to answer. Question after question is prefaced with, "Tell the folks on the jury . . ." this or that. We should also bring in the judge when it's appropriate. "Explain to his honor . . ." whatever the issue is. I have even brought in opposing counsel by saying, "Tell Mr. Jones seated over there what you're actually seeing." Such a question is designed to refute something the opposing counsel has said, for example, in his opening statement. The goal is to bring all of the parties to the party. Leave no one out. And remember, if you leave a juror out, he will likely leave you out.

Listen to what the witness has to say! We ask, "What was really said?" I see lawyers who let the witness lead them into deep, unfocused forests from which there is sometimes no return. We listen with a focused ear, so that if the witness strays like an exploring puppy we can bring him back. And we listen to hear what the witness may be saying beyond or behind his words. When we listen and both the lawyer and the witness are in the moment, a connection occurs that can touch the sublime.

Formatting the drama—whom do we call first? In a civil case I often hurl myself directly into the battle. I, the plaintiff, carry the burden of proof. What better tactic than to launch a frontal attack. But the attack must be gracious and fair. It must not be bellicose and belligerent, because the moment we bully, the tide has already turned against us.

The jury has just heard our opening statement and the defendant's in response. Who is right and who is wrong? The jury is waiting to see. If we call the opposing party as our first witness with a well-conceived cross-examination we may make magnificent leaps forward. Often the opposing attorney has not taken the time to prepare his witness. Often the witness is shocked and takes the stand soaked in anxiety.

I want the order of witnesses to tell the story in a logical and persuasive way. Just as we cannot tell the whole story in one sentence, so, too, the story of our case cannot be told with one witness. Our story has already been told to the jury in the opening. The order of our witnesses should complement that.

In a civil case, the story usually begins with a happy, healthy person who one day is met with the negligence of the defendant and is injured or killed. The dramatic format of most movies is instructive. We observe how the director wants us to care about the protagonist before the horrible events descend upon our hero. If we do not care about him, no matter what happens to him the movie will be a flop. Heroes have a role. Their role is to be admired, even loved. Villains have a role. Theirs is to be rejected, even hated. Most drama is couched in this simple formula. If we do not care about the hero or do not wish all manner of evil to befall the villain, we have no drama and, in court, we have no case.

Considering this, the director in the movie shows the hero coming home to his little house, giving his adoring wife a kiss, and tussling with his children before he tucks them lovingly into bed. The director smears the hero with his super-good-guy brush. We see him as the kind of person we might want to be ourselves. We may see him struggle against unreasonable odds, see him rejected or scorned for his heroic stand. We want him to win. The dramatic conflict is always between the hero with whom we identify and the forces of evil he must overcome. In the movie we become the hero. We experience his fear. His fear becomes ours. And the drama moves step by step, just as it does in the courtroom, witness by witness—until the climax is achieved.

We like movies with a happy ending. In the civil case our plaintiff has been injured, perhaps killed. The injuries the plaintiff suffers are severe and shocking. In the criminal case our innocent client has been charged with some horrible misdeed and faces prison or execution. But the movie director has the power to cause the story to end happily, so that the audience walks out of the theater feeling good, fulfilled, and inspired. Our story in the courtroom can end happily as well. In the civil case the jury can return justice in an award of dollars that will compensate the plaintiff for his injuries or the loss of a loved one. In the criminal case, the happy ending can be the jury's delivering freedom to the accused. But none of this can occur without our having first made our client the hero.

We remember the old saw, "Heroes are made, not born." We make our hero at the outset. We have told his story to the jury in the opening, where he is portrayed as someone we, as his attorneys, care about; because we care about him our caring is transferred to the jurors. Now, as we call the witnesses, we hear live people describing our client as an attractive person. If he suffers from certain warts of life we present them. He, as we, is not perfect, but we understand him and we want him to win. So, the order of our witnesses and the telling of their stories is usually scripted for us.

In the civil damage case where the plaintiff has been horribly injured we might begin by calling a friend or a member of the plaintiff's family to explain to the jury who this man was. We will show him as a happy, caring father, a man devoted to his family, and a hard worker. Perhaps we will call his former boss or a fellow worker. Perhaps we will call a child to simply testify about how Daddy was before he was hurt and what they did together. (We may have to recall the child later on to testify about how all of this has changed, how Daddy is no longer able to go fishing, to go to the ballpark, to teach him how to pitch or swim.)

After we have created our hero we will then take him to the scene of the event that injures him. Maybe we will call his wife to the stand to tell how she said good-bye to him in the morning and how they were to each other as he left, not knowing what fate lay ahead. (Again, as with the child, we may have to recall the wife at a later time.) There will be witnesses to testify as to what happened in this tragedy. We will re-create the negligent acts of the defendant, the scene, the horror, the injuries, the pain, all of the facts surrounding this preventable accident.

We will likely put our client and the damage experts on the stand at the end. We will not overdisplay our client's injuries because, as humans, we have the ability to become callused to the pain of others in order to save ourselves a mirrored pain. We display the stump of our client who has lost his leg in the accident, or we witness the horrible disability of a brain injury, or the utter helplessness of quadriplegia. But to flout these horrors to the jury leaves them feeling that their emotions are being manipulated, and a backlash can occur. People do not want to be used. We love heroes who, although horribly and unjustly injured, smile through their tears. We want to come to the aid of those who bravely face their unjust fate. We, as jurors, want to exercise a power over fate and deliver justice. And, in the end, the lawyer, not the client, will demand retribution.

For the lay person: direct examination and its application out of court. As we have already seen, calling witnesses to support our story is not a function limited to the courtroom. In a sales meeting where we want to know what is going on in the field, we call a salesman to tell us. If there are defects in the plant processes, management wants to know them firsthand and calls a worker. In a city council meeting where the issue is a zoning change, the proponent, a citizen, may ask a neighbor to stand and speak on the need for the change. Before the hospital board, a patient whose diagnosis was missed may appear when called by the staff to illustrate the need for newer equipment. The use of testimony in out-of-court proceedings is a powerful way of presenting the case.

We have already discovered the story. We have told our story as our opening statement. Now we call the witnesses to support the story, remembering that the principles, the ideas, and the techniques we've discussed concerning the presentation of our witnesses in court for their direct examination, apply in most part in parallel to out-of-court cases as well.

14. EXPOSING THE HIDDEN TRUTH— CROSS-EXAMINATION

ROSS-EXAMINATION IS THE ONE best pry to disgorge the whole truth. We see old TV shows of the great cross-examinations by Perry Mason that end with the witness jumping up from the stand and screaming, "Yes, I did it! I did it!" and television's scintillating modern equivalents that are entertaining but unreal. Both the bar and the public see cross-examination as the ennobling accomplishment of the great trial lawyer. Whole libraries have been written about it. A deep hunger persists in the breast of every young lawyer to become the great cross-examiner and thereby the great trial lawyer.

The witness's words are murky and misleading, not quite a complete lie, but plunked into the courtroom like a rotten fish, the underside of which must be exposed. Along comes the great cross-examiner. No truth shall escape him. No furtive fact shall remain uncovered. But in an entire career I have yet to experience a Perry Mason moment—the witness on the stand disintegrating into a blubbering confession—which does not comment as much on my failures as a cross-examiner as it exposes one of the myths of cross-examination.

Indeed, cross-examination is the instrument by which the truth often can be gleaned. The lack of its use in telling the whole story is evident, as public opinion convicts nearly every accused person based on the bare, unchallenged allegations of the prosecution, which are consistently laid out in the media in their most venal forms. Before the trial (except in the preliminary hearing, which is usually perfunctory), the defense rarely has the opportunity to cross-examine the alleged witnesses who will supposedly support the prosecutor's press releases. By the time of trial, most of the jurors have been so long exposed to the prosecution's case that they've become surrogate prosecutors themselves, hungrily awaiting the moment they can hang the guilty devil. Cross-examination is the one, best remaining weapon that has not yet been wholly purged from the jury trial.

Cross-examination outside the courtroom. The principles of cross-examination that I propose for the trial lawyer are applicable to many situations outside the courtroom, and the nonlawyer should absorb these sections with an open mind. Although we often cannot perform a cross-examination outside the courtroom setting, nevertheless as we approach hostile persons we can learn much from the art of cross-examination.

The myth of the ethereal art—cross-examination. In the furtherance of their status, the so-called experts usually imply that cross-examination is a nearly unattainable art that only the chosen few can master, an art that can rarely be accomplished by mere human beings, unless, of course, we take their courses and spend a great deal of time (and money) in reading their books and listening to their tapes. Absent the guidance of the experts, we are told that a skillful cross-examination is something that the ordinary lawyer cannot do, ample proof of which is abundantly provided in nearly every trial we might witness.

Rarely do I see a lawyer who knows how to cross-examine, although most have engaged in that supposed art from the moment they were haplessly excreted from their law schools, utterly ignorant of its basic, simple principles. The reason lawyers rarely learn how is because they've been told they can't. But I'm about to reveal a well-kept secret: *Anyone can be taught how to successfully cross-examine in about five minutes.*

What is cross-examination? *Cross-examination is simply storytelling in yet another form*. Cross-examination is the method by which we tell our story to the jury through the adverse witness and, in the process, test the validity of the witness's story against our own. The proper, standard cross-examination questions contain two parts: first a statement that forwards our story through that witness; for example—"No one, to your knowledge,

Officer Jones, has been able to connect that gun to Mr. McIntosh, . . ." followed by the second part of every question, "isn't that true?" Note again: the question itself is simply, "Isn't that true?" The statement either is or is not true.

Basic cross-examination is nothing more than a true-or-false test administered to the witness, in the course of which our story, as it concerns that witness, is told, question by question, to the witness. It makes little difference whether the witness answers yes or no. Question by question, our story is being told. It's for the jury to determine whether the witness is telling the truth when he denies the statements contained in our questions. If we took each statement out of our cross-examination and joined them, we would have presented our story for that witness.

So, if cross-examination is simply a method by which we tell our story and thereafter test it against the witnesses, must we not first have a story to tell? Every day I see lawyers march up to the podium ready to perform the noble art by challenging every word the poor witness has uttered, and, with an unrequited lust for drama, the lawyer attacks the witness with some marvelous irrelevancy like, "So, you say, Mr. Applebee, that he was wearing a blue tie when we all know he was wearing a red tie?" But the part of our story that needs to be told though this witness, or the story we believe this witness should tell instead of the one he's dumped on the jury, has been forgotten, or worse, was never considered by the cross-examiner in the first place.

Discovering the story we wish to tell through the witness. For many, one of the most difficult tasks of preparing for a successful cross is simply discovering the story we want to tell through the cross-examination. Yet it can be the easiest of all. For example, the witness, a deputy sheriff we shall call Brown, tells the jury that the defendant, Jimmy McIntosh, a sixteen-year-old, confessed the murder to him, and offers a document that purports to be Jimmy's signed confession. The deputy claims that he read Jimmy his rights before the confession was given and the document signed.

Jimmy is not able to tell us much. He has a severe learning disability. We learn from his mother that he has not been to school since the second grade. He cannot read or write. He has stayed at home with this mother because he cannot fend for himself, and on the night in question was on the way to the grocery store to buy a loaf of bread and some beans and some other grocery items. The list his mother gave him was in his pocket when he was arrested.

The shooting, the killing of an officer, took place in front of a bar near the grocery store. We learn from Jimmy that as soon as the cops saw him they asked him to come to them. Jimmy could hardly be described as eloquently articulate. "I was scared, an' I run. I never shot nobody. I don't have no gun. They told me ta sign an' I could go home, else I was gonna go to the gas chamber." That's all we could get from a boy impoverished of the ordinary intelligence we take for granted.

We learn from his mother that Jimmy has lived at home with thirteen other siblings, most of whom have been in trouble with the law from time to time, and that the family is known to the cops as "That McIntosh Mob," a family that, to the local police, represents trouble from the parents down to the youngest child. They are seen as vermin that should be eradicated for the safety and well-being of the community. Jimmy's mother tells us that a deputy sheriff told her once that "We (the cops) need to get rid of the McIntoshes like we need to get rid of rats."

The basic cross-examination. Once we've discovered the story that we want to tell through this witness, Deputy Brown, we can simply state it, sentence by sentence, with the question attached, "Isn't that true?" The cross-examination will now sound something like this:

"Deputy Brown, you know of the McIntosh family from past experience, isn't that true?"

"Yes. I know the family."

"You know that Jimmy McIntosh has thirteen brothers and sisters?"

"Something like that."

"And often you in the sheriff's office refer to this family as 'That McIntosh Mob,' isn't that true?"

"I've heard that said." (He is being generous.)

"You have heard some of the sheriff's officers make a joke that the McIntosh family should be made smaller as soon as possible, isn't that also true?"

"No, I've never heard that."

"You've heard officers in the department say that the McIntosh family is a source of continuous trouble with the law?"

"I know there's been trouble with them."

"You've heard your fellow officers say that the family gets bigger faster than you can put them in the penitentiary, isn't that true?"

Objected to as hearsay and irrelevant. Sustained by the judge.

"The attitude of the department is that the McIntosh family are vermin who should be eliminated from the community, one by one, at the first opportunity, isn't that true?"

Objected to on the grounds that there is no foundation for this statement. Sustained.

"Even you have said, 'If there is a McIntosh on the street there is trouble on the street'?" (The "Isn't that true" part of the question is implied.)

"I have never said that." (Do we care if he doesn't admit it?)

"You know that Jimmy has not been to school since he was in the second grade?"

"That's what I've heard in this case."

"And you know that he has a severe learning disability?"

"I don't know that personally."

"You know he cannot read or write, isn't that true?"

"So I am told."

"But he can write his name?"

"Yes."

"You also know that he stays close to home with his mother, isn't that true?"

"I don't know about that. I don't know where he stays."

"You have had this beat for how many years?"

"Four years."

"You have never arrested this boy for anything before, isn't that true?"

"Yes."

"You have never even seen him on the street before this incident, isn't that also true?"

"I don't know. I may have seen him."

"And you discovered from your investigation that Jimmy only goes out when his mother sends him out for something, isn't that true?"

"How would I know that?" (We don't answer questions.)

"On the day in question you know that when he was arrested he had a list for the grocery store that his mother had given him, that's true, isn't it?"

"Yes. He had a list."

"That list is Defense Exhibit A?"

"Yes." (Exhibit A is shown to the officer and offered and received into evidence and shown to the jury.)

"Now officer, the scene of this shooting was about three doors down from Milly's Market?"

"Yes. Three or four."

"In front of a bar known as Peep's Bar."

"Yes."

"No one that you know ever saw Jimmy in the bar or in front of it, isn't that true?"

"I don't know." (He's not answering the question and we're not fighting with him about it. We know where we want to go.)

"When you arrived at the scene of the shooting you saw Jimmy standing there, isn't that true?"

"Yes, Officer Jones and I saw him and I asked him to come to me and he turned around and ran."

"And you chased him?"

"Yes we did."

"When you caught him he was terrified, isn't that true?"

"I wouldn't say."

"You caught him and threw him up against the wall and said to him, 'All right, kid, you shot that cop. Where's the gun?'"

"Something like that."

"He had no gun?"

"No. But then he probably tossed it while we were chasing him. We chased him a couple of blocks and he was in and out of alleys along the way."

"You searched for the gun, didn't you?"

"Yes."

"And you found none, isn't that true."

"Yes."

"No witness saw this supposed shooting by this boy, isn't that true?"

"We didn't find any."

"So you took him in and began to question him?"

It's our turn to question the cops who questioned the childlike boy. We will proceed in open court with a judge watching to make sure the questioning is fair—hardly the decency provided this disadvantaged child. This point can be brought out nicely like this:

"I am going to continue to question you, Deputy Brown, but my questions are being asked in the presence of his honor and your lawyers to make sure that my questions are fair. Did you even call in Jimmy's mother before you began to question him?"

"No."

"Was she even aware that you were questioning him?"

"I don't know."

"My questioning of you is being recorded by the court reporter. Did you make any effort to record your questioning of Jimmy?"

"No. He just blurted it out."

"You are surrounded by lawyers over there who are here to protect your rights, and there is Judge Lewis up there to make sure that the questions I ask are proper. Did you attempt in any way to provide this sort of protection for Jimmy before you began your questioning?"

"Hardly."

"You told Jimmy that he could go to the gas chamber if he didn't tell you what you wanted to know, isn't that true?"

"No, we never said any such thing."

"And if Jimmy says you did, you would still deny it?"

The defense objects and the objection is sustained.

"And you told Jimmy that if he didn't sign the paper you put in front of him that he could never go home again to be with his mother, isn't that true?"

"No, that is not true." (We and the jury know he wouldn't admit it, even though he knows it is true.)

"The boy can't read, that's true, isn't it?"

"I don't know."

"Did you read the confession to him?"

"No."

"Did he read it?"

"He had a chance to read it. I suppose he read it."

"You never made any attempt to determine if the boy would read or not?"

"He signed it."

"You told him that if he signed it he could go home to his mother, isn't that true?"

"No, it is not true."

"And if he signed it you wouldn't put him in the gas chamber, that's true, too, isn't it?"

We have told our story a sentence at a time, adding only the words, "Isn't that true?" It makes little difference what the witness answers, as long as our story is honest and based on the facts as we know them in the case, or on facts that can reasonably be deduced from the evidence already before the court. It is for the jury to determine which story is true: the story Deputy Brown gave on direct examination, or the alternative story that the cross-examiner presents and tests against the witness's story. As we see, the cross-examination has become a vehicle by which we tell our story through the opposing witnesses that have been presented against us.

Two major types of cross-examination. Although there are other variations of cross-examination techniques, we should be concerned here with two major techniques that serve two distinct purposes.

The controlled cross. This method is intended to keep the witness under a tight rein, to require the witness to answer the cross-examiner's questions, one question at a time, concerning one fact and one fact alone, so that the witness is led down the path to the conclusion the cross-examiner wishes to achieve.

Let us suppose a case in which two officers, Smith and Jones, enter a house on a call from a wife whose husband is threatening to kill her. The husband ends up dead. We believe that one of the officers, Officer Smith, overreacted and shot the unarmed husband and then placed what is known in law enforcement as a "throwaway gun" under the deceased where he fell. The suit is by the widow against the city and the police for damages resulting from the wrongful death of her husband.

Absent a careful, controlled examination, the bottom line of Smith's testimony might sound like this: "We went to the house where we got this call. The wife said the husband was threatening to kill her and was drunk. We went into the house and the husband came out of the bedroom. He had a gun, and Smith shot him in self-defense."

In a controlled cross each question is tightly framed concerning one fact and requiring a yes or no answer to that one fact. Here we may be referring to some of the facts contained in the police incident report.

"Officer Jones, you were at 35 Park Place on June 23, 2003, isn't that true?"

"Yes."

"About twelve midnight?"

"Yes."

"You and Officer Henry Smith had been called there, isn't that true?"

"Yes."

"You entered the house, isn't that true?"

"Yes."

"When you entered the house, Officer Smith was in front of you?"

"Yes."

"And as he entered you heard some shots?"

"Yes."

"You entered through the front room?"

"Yes."

"When you entered the front room you saw the deceased?"

"Yes."

"He was lying on the floor?"

"Yes."

"He was facedown?"

"Yes."

"He was bleeding?"

"Yes."

"He appeared dead?"

"Yes."

"You were, of course, somewhat excited?"

"Yes."

"It's true you didn't examine the deceased at the moment you entered the house?"

"Yes."

"Officer Smith told you to check the kitchen?"

"Yes."

"To see if anyone else was in the house?"

"Yes."

"And Officer Smith said he was going to check the bedroom?"

"Yes."

"You became satisfied that no one was in the kitchen?"

"Yes."

"You then returned to the living room where the deceased lay?"

"Yes."

"Officer Smith was out of your sight while you were in the kitchen?"

"Yes."

"When you came back from the kitchen you looked at the deceased?"

"Yes."

"You discovered the gun at that time, as shown in Exhibit 23?" (This is a photograph showing the gun mostly hidden under the deceased body on the right side where he presumably fell.)

"No. I saw the gun there when I came through the front door."

We can't prove anything more with the cross of this witness concerning our contention that the officers shot the unarmed man and placed the throw-away gun as shown in the photograph. We can now only suggest our theory of the case by adding a couple more questions:

"You know that Officer Smith carried an extra pistol with him, isn't that true?"

"No, I didn't know that."

"You've heard him say so, haven't you?"

"No." Other witnesses have already made reference to Smith's bragging about carrying a throwaway gun—"just in case some bastard who needs to get shot gets shot," as he daintily put it.

Here the controlled cross prevents the witness from running all over the place with his answers. Every question has been carefully constructed to allow only a yes or a no answer, and even as to the last two questions in which his answers are no, the jury considers whether he is covering for Smith and that his answers, truthfully, should have been yes.

The compassionate cross. But there's another way to cross Jones that is more likely to lead to the truth and that will better serve our case. In this cross we'll tell our story about what happened through the leading question, without attempting to argue with the witness and without being much concerned about

177

his answers. The officers are partners. They have been sued along with the city. Their jobs are on the line. If there was a throwaway gun placed under the deceased to cover themselves neither of them will ever admit it, oath or no oath, and the best cross-examination ever conceived will never get the witness to bow his head and whisper with all due contrition, "Yes, he put that gun under the guy."

Our client, the widow, wanted protection. She did not want to become a widow. She was entitled to police protection from a drunken spouse. She was not entitled to a dead husband with a throwaway gun stuck under him. The widow knows for certain that her husband had no gun. He despised firearms and was a gun-control advocate.

As we have seen, the legitimate purpose of cross-examination is to test one's bona fide theory of the case against the testimony given by the witness. The story of the witness and that of the cross-examiner will be laid against each other. Which story do we believe? The witness has told his story on direct examination. He is implacable, even hostile to the idea that the gun was planted. His story is pat. He has been well prepared. His story matches the police incident report. There's little to grab hold of, and, *if we can do nothing more than offer up questions that permit the witness to retell his story, we shouldn't cross-examine at all.* We see it all the time—lawyers, not knowing what to ask or how to open a small tear in the cloth of the witness's story, get up and re-ask the same questions, or argue with the witness about the facts on which he can't be shaken—which only reemphasizes the witness's story and convinces the jury that what may only be a well-prepared fabrication is, instead, true.

Our strategy will be to cross-examine the witness with what I call the "compassionate cross," simply a cross-examination that takes into account that this witness is a decent, ordinary human being facing a moral dilemma. We want to understand him and, before the cross is ended, to speak for him in ways that he cannot speak for himself. The key is to understand what this police officer faces, and to present him to the jury as a man facing a dilemma from which he cannot extricate himself.

Discovering the facts for the compassionate cross. Without the aid of a professional psychodramatist we can simply imagine ourselves as Officer Jones. We ask ourselves, what is it like to be this cop who has seen an unarmed man shot to death, who has been called to the scene of a domestic dispute to keep the peace and who, instead, has become a witness to a homicide? What emotional misery must the witness suffer, realizing that they, the officers, have not only failed in their mission, but have killed a man who did not deserve to die. After months of sober contemplation awaiting the case to come to trial, after the nights of nightmares about the trial and the worry about his job, his reputation, perhaps even his freedom, can we really blame him for the stand he takes, even though his testimony may be a lie?

The officers did not intend that anyone be killed. And these officers were buddies. They have backed each other up in many a dicey situation and relied on each other's loyalty. But this situation in the courtroom is the most dangerous of all of their encounters—one in which they have no control over the consequences—and they have no choice but to stick to their fabrication. No one can prove it false. No one was there except them and, of course, the widow. Sure, she is going to say her husband was unarmed, and a bunch of their friends will probably come to court and claim that the dead man hated firearms and never had any, and sure, the gun was not registered to the deceased and the cops can't otherwise tie the gun to him; but, after all, the widow is the one trying to get a lot of money for her husband's death and she's calling on her friends to stick it to the police and the city.

We have become the witness. If we play the part of Jones and, later, Smith, we can readily understand the dilemma Jones faces. We can get to the story easily by discussing the case over coffee with a trusted friend, say, Rob. Our conversation might go like this: "Rob, if I were Jones I would probably think, 'I have to stick with Smith on this thing, but I sure hate it that we have to falsify a report. If they ever find out I'll be one done-for sonofabitch.' "

"Yeah," Rob says, "but you gotta stick with your partner. And there's that kind of unwritten code among the police about the ends justifying the means—that sometimes you face a dilemma—you hate to lie, but lying is best in this case."

"Yeah," we say, "and if you can't rely on your partner to back you up no matter what, well it would be too dangerous out there." Then we might ask Rob, "Just before trial, what do you think Smith and Jones said to each other?"

"Well," Rob might offer, "Smith says, 'Jonesy, we gotta stick together on this. Here's what I'm gonna say happened.' And then they go over their stories." Out of these several scenes we'll discover much of the truth of the story that would otherwise remain unfocused and unrecognized in the recesses of a mind wallowing in the mass of distractions and details that can drown us in every case.

But we might do a psychodrama—say, one recreating the scene itself. A professional psychodramatist would be most helpful in leading this drama, but someone familiar with the psychodramatic process that we've visited here can fill that role. We'll become the psychodramatist for the purpose of this demonstration. We'll have the lawyer who will do the cross of Officer Jones play the part of Jones, and from time to time the role of Smith as well, so that the lawyer can get some sense of who these men are and what they're facing. We'll have someone stand in for Smith as we need his input.

Now as the director of this drama we'll have Jones (the lawyer who will be doing the cross in court) do a soliloquy. We say to Jones, "You've just been at a scene where a man has been shot by your partner. What are you thinking?"

Jones says, "I'm thinking, my God, the poor sonofabitch is dead. I can see the hole through his chest and the blood is rushing out. He's not breathing. Our asses are in a jam for sure. I'm scared."

"What are you seeing and hearing?"

"The wife is screaming, 'You killed him, you killed him.' [We know this from what the wife has told us.] She's beating on Smith. He's still got his gun in his hand. Smith tells me to take her out in the kitchen and see if anyone else is there while he checks out the bedroom. I tell the wife to stay in the kitchen. When I come back I see the gun sticking out from under the guy."

"Do you have a conversation with Smith?"

"Yes."

"Let's hear that conversation."

Jones (our lawyer) and Smith (someone playing his part) face each other. "Jesus, Smitty! What the hell?" Jones says.

Smith says, "I thought the sonofabitch had a gun."

Now we ask the lawyer playing Jones to reverse roles with the person who has been playing Smith, so that our lawyer is now playing Smith and the other person is playing Jones. They also physically switch places with each other. We ask Smith, "What are you thinking, Officer Smith?"

180

"I'm thinking, I fucked up. I thought the bastard had a gun. I been shot at before [a fact from Smith's earlier deposition] and I'm not going to get shot at again. I'm thinking, I gotta get this thing fixed up or my ass is grass."

We ask the players to switch roles and places again, our lawyer once more playing Jones.

Jones says, "You stuck that gun under him, didn't you, Smitty?"

They switch roles and places again. Smith says, "Yeah, I had to. You gotta back me up on this, Jonesy."

Again and again we have them switch roles and places—our lawyer playing both Smith and Jones, a procedure that will aid him in better understanding the case.

We ask the lawyer in the role of Jones, "What are you thinking?"

"I'm thinking 'I gotta back Smitty up, false report or not. If he goes down, I probably go down with him. And besides, he's my partner. Man's gotta do what a man's gotta do.' "

We've discovered the cross-examination we can make. We have the ethical duty as cross-examiners not to ask questions that suggest an answer we know to be untrue. But we have the right to ask bona fide questions, the answers to which can be fairly inferred from the facts. We are approaching this cross as if we're still rummaging around in the hide of Jones. The approach will not be confronting. It will not be ugly or hostile. It will not be accusatory. It will be one couched in understanding, and it will be one that tells the jury our interpretation of the facts so that the jury can make a fair decision as to which story is the truth.

How the compassionate cross-examination might sound: "Officer Jones, this must have been a very unhappy experience for you."

"Yes, sir."

"You certainly are not a man who goes around shooting unarmed citizens."

"Right."

"And the death of Mr. Hansen must have saddened you a good deal?"

"It did."

"You are a long-standing member of this police force, a man with a good record?"

"Yes."

"And you didn't pull the trigger on Mr. Hansen in this case."

"No I didn't."

"Your partner Officer Smith did."

"Yes."

"And he has been your partner for several years?"

"Yes."

"I suppose you have been in some tough spots together?"

"Couple of times, yes."

"And you care about Officer Smith? He's not only your partner, he's your friend?"

"Yes."

"You are a loyal friend?"

"Yes."

"You wouldn't betray a friend, would you?"

"No sir."

"And that is part of the unwritten code of the police—to back up your partner when he's in trouble, isn't that true?"

"Well, yes." (He can deny it if he wants, but the jury and everyone else knows about this unwritten code.)

"Officers face dangerous situations frequently, even situations where their lives are at risk?"

"Yes, we do."

"One of the dangers is to come into a strange place facing a stranger who may or may not be in his right mind and who may or may not be armed. That's true, isn't it?"

"Yes."

"And officers are trained not to panic, to be cool and careful and observant in those dangerous situations, isn't that true?"

"Yes."

"But I suppose that officers are like other human beings. Despite their training, they can panic and make mistakes?"

"I suppose so."

"Officer Smith came into the Hansen home ahead of you—he was the first in?"

"Yes."

"He had his gun drawn, of course."

"Yes he did."

"And so did you?"

"Yes."

"You thought it might be a dangerous situation?"

"Yes. The caller said her husband was going to kill her."

"So the adrenaline was up a little, so to speak?"

"If you want to put it that way."

"Well, at least, it must have been a situation that caused you to be quite alert, let us say." (The phrase "It must have been" is one that tells the witness we are trying to understand the situation he found himself in.)

"Yes."

"And you have been trained to be prepared to defend yourself in face of an armed subject?"

"Yes."

"So when you heard your partner fire his gun, you must have been shocked and surprised?"

"Well, yes. I heard him holler, 'Come out of there,' and then I heard the shot."

"You didn't see Mr. Hansen when he came out of the bedroom?"

"No."

"You of course didn't see him when he was shot?"

"No."

"But later on you say you saw a gun under Mr. Hansen?"

"Yes, I did."

"You must have been in a very tough situation, Officer Jones. I mean, if Officer Smith placed the gun under Mr. Hansen, what would you tell the jury?"

Opposing counsel objects on the grounds that the question assumes a fact that is not in evidence. The judge sustains the objection.

"You know, of course, that if Officer Smith shot Mr. Hansen, who was unarmed, that would cause both of you considerable problems."

"Well, maybe."

"Have you ever talked with Officer Smith about a throwaway gun?"

"No."

"You have heard him talk about throwaway guns before, isn't that true?"

(Based on the testimony of two other witnesses who heard such talk from Jones before.)

"No, I haven't."

"And you knew, did you not, that he carried a throwaway gun?"

"No."

"Would you tell the jury what a throwaway gun is?"

"It's a gun that cannot be traced to the officer who tosses the gun down on a subject who has been accidentally shot by the officer."

"And the idea is for the officer to make it look like the shooting was in self-defense, isn't that true?"

"Yes."

"You of course didn't search Officer Smith for a throwaway gun before you entered the Hansen residence?"

"Of course not."

"You knew that Officer Smith had been shot at once before."

"Yes. He told me about it."

"To be shot at is a very frightening experience, isn't it?"

"Yes it is."

"Have you ever been shot at?"

"No."

"And if the subject has a gun out you'd better shoot first and ask questions later?"

"Could be."

"You have told us that you are a loyal friend to Officer Smith."

"Yes."

"If he made a mistake and shot Mr. Hansen, you would never be heard to say that he planted a throwaway gun on Mr. Hansen, isn't that true?"

The opposing counsel objects. The court sustains the objection.

"Officers have to stick by each other?"

"If it is honest, yes."

"A situation like this must be very hard for you. Would you turn Officer Smith in if he made a mistake, shot Mr. Hansen, and then planted a gun on the dead man?"

"Yes, I would." (Does the jury believe this?)

"You had a talk with Officer Smith before you took the stand?"

"Yes."

"When did this talk take place?"

"Last week."

"Where?"

"Jason's Steak House."

"He buy you dinner?"

"Well, yes. It was his turn."

"So at that time he, of course, told you what he was going to say?"

"No."

"You never talked about his testimony or yours?"

"No." (Does the jury believe this?)

"It would be important to you that his testimony and yours matched?"

"I never thought about it."

"You want everything to come out all right for Officer Smith and the city in this case, isn't that true?"

"Of course."

"You would feel badly if the jury decided that Officer Smith planted that gun on Mr. Hansen, isn't that true?"

"I don't think it would be right."

"After all, he's your friend and your partner."

"Yes."

"And you would do what is necessary to help him in this jam?"

"Not if it requires me to lie under oath."

"If you were going to lie under oath about it, you certainly wouldn't tell us, would you?"

Objection by opposing counsel as argumentative. Sustained by the court.

"You heard Mrs. Hansen screaming that her husband never had a gun—that you, the officers, put it there, isn't that true?"

"She was hollering about something."

"You took her to the kitchen right after the shooting?"

"Yes."

"It was when you came back from the kitchen with Mrs. Hansen that you first saw the gun under Mr. Hansen?"

"Well, no, I saw it when I first came through the door."

"You are not able to tell us exactly what Officer Smith did while you were in the kitchen, isn't that true?"

"Yes."

"And you never saw Mr. Hansen until after the shot was fired by Officer Jones, isn't that true?"

"Yes."

"So you can't tell us from what you saw with your own eyes whether Officer Jones put that gun under the victim or not, isn't that true?"

"I know he didn't."

"You or Officer Smith, or anyone in the department, have not been able to connect that gun to Mr. Hansen, isn't that true?"

"Yes."

"Throwaway guns are guns that cannot be connected to anyone, isn't that true?"

"Presumably."

"That is the kind of gun that officers sometimes use in this kind of case?"

"Not to my knowledge."

"Thank you, Officer. I know you're on a spot here. I'm sorry we had to call you."

No one could force Officer Jones to admit anything about the throwaway gun that was likely planted on Mr. Hansen. Nor can any cross-examiner, no matter how brilliant, how hostile, how facile and quick, make any witness say what the witness is unwilling to say—even if it is the truth—cross-examinations by Perry Mason notwithstanding. The witness has his own agenda—in this case, Jones's loyalty to his partner and his desire to remain in good favor with the rest of his fellow officers and the department. That agenda outweighs the officer's concern about telling a lie under oath.

The need to lie outweighs the truth in many circumstances that we encounter daily in our lives—from the little white ones to, occasionally, the powerful lie that can change our lives. Juries know this. That is why we have juries—to test the story of the witness and his demeanor against the jurors' own everyday experience in life.

We know, for example, that a parent will lie to save the life of a child, a spouse will lie to protect a marriage, a president will lie to save his legacy. And where money, or freedom, or deeply held principles are at stake, even the most upright witness may lie, since that which he protects with his lie—freedom, marriage, money, a sacred principle—may be more important to the witness than remaining true to his oath to tell "the truth, the whole truth and nothing but the truth, so help me God." Only the deluded or naïve believe that somehow the taking of an oath prevents witnesses, even honest witnesses, from lying where they must.

Even in our case above, where Smith likely planted a gun, what would we think of Officer Jones if he said, "Yeah, I knew Smitty carried a throwaway gun. He's carried it since the day that guy shot at him. He is touchy, that Smitty. I saw that the man was unarmed. I saw that Smitty made a terrible mistake. He was panicked. And he had me take the wife out in the kitchen so he could plant the gun under him. Yeah, we talked about it, and we agreed to keep our stories straight." In certain respects, it might be argued that Jones was more honorable by having lied—by remaining loyal to his partner and to the department—rather than turning his back on his partner and throwing him to the dogs because he took an oath and had to tell the truth. But the cross-examination displays the moral dilemma that Officer Jones faced, and leaves the jury to understand his dilemma and to come to a conclusion as to what the facts likely were in the case. And the facts that have been developed from the several methods above are all properly inferable from the known facts of the case.

The loquacious witness and the misguided judge. Every day we come face-to-face with those effusive witnesses in the courtroom who simply find it beyond their ability, no matter how they try, to answer a simple yes-or-no question with a yes or no. There is something in the human composition that abhors giving a yes or no answer. Often, to a simple yes-or-no question, the witness volleys forth with great globs of verbiage, and when we object the judge, sleepy-eyed, intones in fossilized words of his own, "The witness may explain."

Explain what? This is cross-examination! I frequently hear such a response from the court as if it were part of the sacred judicial liturgy—"The witness may explain." When this happens it's time for a bench conference, or, if one is not allowed, it's time for a recess—somehow we must talk to this judge. Our statement to his honor might be as follows:

"Your Honor, I have asked a simple yes-or-no question. What I have stated to the witness is either right or it is wrong. His answer is either 'yes, that is true,' or 'no, that is not true.' Counsel asked his questions of this witness and, during direct examination, the witness was permitted to explain his answers in detail. He'll have that opportunity again on redirect examination. If he is permitted to explain his answers still again during my cross, it becomes clear that it would be malpractice for me to give the witness the opportunity to tell his story three times without a fair cross-examination ever being allowed. I have not asked a single question that needs explaining. And if I have, the proper venue for such explanation will be the redirect after I have finished my cross-examination."

The judge will likely say he is the judge and for me to continue in my examination or sit down as I chose. But the judge is now alerted to my theory of cross-examination, which is correct, and his rulings in the future will perhaps be somewhat more sympathetic to the true function of cross-examination, which is, once more, to test the story of our case against the testimony the witness has given.

What do we do when the judge lets the witness ramble? We have already been to the bench and we've made our objection in the record. But the judge continues to let the witness ramble on and on in a manic state of verbal ecstasy. I have often used the nursery rhyme of Jack and Jill to illustrate how this word-laden witness can be dealt with. The cross-examination sounds like this:

"Jack and Jill went up the hill, isn't that true?" (Note again: The statement is "Jack and Jill went up the hill." The question is, "Isn't that true?")

The witness does not answer yes or no. He answers with a storm of blather: blah, blah, blah, blah.

When the witness has finished we politely say, "I'm sorry, I must not have asked my question so that it can be understood. Let me ask it again, "Jack and Jill went up the hill, isn't that true?"

Again the witness answers with his endless chatter. We listen patiently.

Now we might turn to the reporter and ask the reporter to read our last question to the witness. The reporter obliges, turns back pages and pages until he finally gets to our question and we hear him flatly intone the words, " 'Jack and Jill went up the hill, isn't that true?' "

"Could you answer that question, please, Mr. Witness?" we implore.

Again the witness answers with more interminable prattle.

Finally, one might walk to the blackboard or a flip chart and write, "Jack and Jill went up the hill, isn't that true?" and, having written the words on the board, we might ask the witness to read the words aloud with us, "Jack and Jill went up the hill, isn't that true?"

To which he again gives us the abysmal, never ending blah-blahs.

By this time it is amply clear that the witness does not intend to answer the question. We have been polite. We will go to the next question with this comment:

"Perhaps you would be willing to answer this question, sir: 'Jack and Jill went to fetch a pail of water.'" Again we get the same endless drivel. This kind of questioning with this kind of witness is wearing on everyone within earshot. But we are not to blame, as the jury can readily see. The witness simply will not answer a fair question.

I recall a case against a large corporation in which I was cross-examining the CEO of the corporation. He refused to answer any of my questions, always inserting at length his own endless colloquy. When the judge called a recess I went out into the hall to walk around a little. There I met the witness. "Well, Spence," he said, as he puffed on his cigarette, "I never answered one of your damned questions."

"Right," I said. "You sure didn't."

Back in the courtroom this process went on for nine days. Each recess it was the same, the CEO boasting that he had still not answered a single question for me, and I admitting that he had not. When the jury returned a multimillion-dollar verdict against his corporation he couldn't understand why. He hadn't answered a damn question, not one. How could the jury do that to his company?

The angry cross. It is rarely productive for a lawyer to attack the witness with an angry cross-examination. Unless the witness is truly a miserable monster, I'm not interested in trying to convert the witness into one, nor to show up the witness as some species of idiot, because in the process the magic mirror always works. Too often I will also be revealed as a cruel ruffian, and in the process of trying to display somebody as an idiot, I will be seen as one.

We have a case, yes. We think the other side is wrong, fraudulent, criminal, rotten, scheming, an amalgam of every known evil attributed to the human species. We feel anger. We do not wish to treat the enemy with kindness. We want to destroy him, to expose his filthy underside, and we attack him with all avidity. The witness smiles—the bigot, the beast, the brute! The witness lies in a quiet voice—the sire of all scoundrels! But the jury does not share our feelings, not yet. The jurors have agreed to be impartial. They take pride in the fact that they are trying to avoid prejudice. They're attempting to be open to both sides, to hear the evidence fairly and to come to a just decision. Our harshness, our vitriolic, noisy attack of a witness who appears to be telling the truth, who seems to be decent enough, will surely turn the jurors against us in the same way that we are repelled by anyone who attacks the innocent, whose bullying and whose bellicosity is uninvited. Simply said once more, we do not like angry people.

I have often told the following story, and I tell it here because I know of none that better illustrates this point. When I was a younger lawyer I was trying a case for a man named Bill Mattilanin, who had worked as a hand on a drilling rig. You can imagine the derrick of the rig that he worked under. It was new and shiny and painted up a pretty yellow, and at its top were those cables and spindles. One of them gave way and fell on Bill's head. From that moment on he never knew who he was or where he was. The company men who designed the machine took the stand to cover their negligent design. We know what they look like—those expensive silk suits, the black silk stockings, and shoes with those little do-dads that flap when they walk. Their faces are pasty and flabby, and when they walk, their cheeks jiggle. There are these little blood vessels on their cheeks that look like miniature red rivers. I call them martini rivers. And these company men are so pure, so antiseptic, that as they walk past you, you get a whiff of something like Lysol.

They took the stand and I wanted to kill them. So I began to kill them with my angry cross-examination. I killed them and killed them and cut them and sliced at them. I chopped them into little pieces like a chef dicing the stuff that goes into the salad. Then I threw the pieces on the floor and I stomped on them. I felt like I had won. How could I not win, having so thoroughly destroyed these witnesses?

After my day's work in court I would go to the hotel with my partner, Bob Rose, and I'd say, "I sure fixed him," the company's witness I had just finished butchering. And Bob with his sad eyes would say, "You sure did, Gerry. You really fixed him good." But something was lacking in his enthusiasm. Still, I knew I had destroyed the witness. Company witness after company witness. At the conclusion of the case the jury was out about fifteen minutes and returned a verdict against our client, Bill. How could they do that to this innocent man? How could they do that to me, this lawyer who had slaughtered my opponent's witnesses?

As I was leaving the courtroom one of the women on the jury came up to me. She had tears in her eyes. She looked up at me and she said, "Mr. Spence, why did you make us hate you so?"

I see Bill Mattilanin lying on a grate someplace to keep warm. If he's alive, which I doubt, he lived without justice, without care, with no one to love him, and no one to show him how to get to the dinner table or to bed or to tell him who he was. He lived that way because I did not know what was going on in the courtroom. I was too taken up with my own anger, when the jury had yet to discover the good reasons for my being angry. I tell this story over and over again in memory of and respect for Bill.

Revisiting the issue of anger: When we begin to cross-examine a witness we despise, who we want to show up as a fraud or a fake, we must remember that the jury doesn't know him. The jury isn't angry at him. At this point the jury can only get angry at us. To be sure, there's a proper time in the courtroom for anger. There's a proper time in the courtroom for every human emotion. But each emotion must be appropriate for the dynamic in the courtroom—where is the jury with their emotions? I am not suggesting that we cook up false emotions. Our feelings must be real. On the other hand, we can't explode in the middle of a trial, shaking our finger at opposing counsel, crying, "You filthy representative of those damnable insurance companies. You are lying and you know you are lying," all of which may well be true, but an appropriate time for such an outburst is not at hand.

I have discussed previously that anger is a valuable emotion, one I embrace, one that reflects my caring. I would not be without my anger. Properly contained, it drives me toward a just decision for my client. I feel it. I'm glad for it. It is precious and belongs to me. However, rarely will I give the gift of my anger to an adversary.

Again, if I were to lay all of the emotional weapons out on the tabletop, like displaying the tools in my toolbox, and given a choice of but one, I would choose love. Love is the most powerful emotion in or out of the courtroom, and the next most powerful is Love's cousin, Understanding.

Not until we have been able to prove, one patient question at a time, that the witness is who we know him to be—this devil all done up in angel's dress—do we dare attack. Only when it is clear, very clear that the witness deserves to be confronted with anger do we dare angrily attack. And even then, a strong but fair confrontation is the most effective; although, as we have seen, if the jury wants the witness disemboweled it is our duty to do so, quickly, efficiently, and gracefully. We must remember that the decisions of the jurors, like our own, will be coming from the gut. A drama is in process. There are still the good guys and the bad. Rarely will jurors find for the bad guy—the person the jurors do not like—even though the cold hard words in the record may support his equally cold legal position.

What is the whole truth and nothing but the truth? Every witness is sworn to tell the whole truth and nothing but the truth. But few do. If they did there would be no cause for cross-examination. But the human mind does not grasp whole truths. It grasps only those truths that serve it.

When we have a difference with another we often see him as testy, inconsiderate, arrogant, mean-spirited, or simply just a damn jerk. But that, of course, is not the whole truth. We will have forgotten that we may have disappointed him, showed our disrespect for him, or whatever we did without evil intent, which brought on his unpleasant conduct. I sometimes talk about this phenomenon with a witness on cross. The examination of the expert might sound like this:

"Most science has many facets, many considerations that are not all bundled up into a single answer, isn't that true?"

"I suppose so."

"For example, in this case, we are concerned about what caused Baby Jane's injuries that were first detected at the time of her birth."

"Yes."

"You have given us your theory of what happened. And our doctors have given theirs."

"Yes."

"The whole truth is that, although a doctor may be mistaken in his final opinion, all of the opinions given here were based on some facets of truth, yours and theirs, isn't that true?"

"Perhaps."

"In your opinion, no one is lying here."

"That's true."

"These opinions that we have heard are all based on some fact in the case."

"I suppose so, only partially, in my opinion."

"So you believe that our witnesses have not told the whole truth. Just part of it?"

"I would say they were misguided in their conclusions."

"Which brings me to my question, Doctor. Dr. Cutter, you took an oath here to tell the truth, the whole truth, and nothing but the truth. What does that mean to you?"

"Just that."

"Does that mean that you can leave out those facts that don't support your opinion?"

"Of course not. I took into account all of the pertinent facts in this case."

"Yes, and who determined for you what facts were pertinent and what were not?"

"I did."

"Would you permit any other authorities on this subject to tell you what facts were pertinent?"

"If I thought they were authorities?"

"You leave room for the possibility that there are other authorities in this field that might disagree with you?"

"None that I would respect."

"Are you acquainted with [here we refer to a well-known authority in this field, who is deemed the father of whatever the field is]?"

"No, I am not acquainted with him."

"Before you gave your opinion, did you search the authoritative literature to determine if any authority on this subject agreed with you?"

"No I didn't."

"So, do you claim to be the only person in the world upon whom we may rely?"

(Probably an objection.)

"Surely, Doctor, you wanted to be up-to-date on this matter."

"I am up-to-date."

"When was the last time you searched the authorities on this subject?"

"I don't remember."

"Would it have been in the last month?"

"I don't remember."

"Well, could it have been in the last year?"

(Maybe another objection. We don't care. The point of our argument is developing.)

"Could you possibly share with us the name of a single authority in the world who agrees with your opinion in this case?"

(He may or he may not remember one. If he does, then:)

"What book or periodical did you read this in?"

(He won't remember.)

"Do you happen to have the article or book in your office?"

"I don't know."

"Would it be possible for you to bring it to court in the morning?"

(He'll probably make an excuse.)

"Do you leave room for the possibility that Dr. [whoever the authority is that he has named] disagrees with you on any part of your opinion?"

"Possibly."

"What part would that be?"

(He doesn't know.)

"But when you read this article or book, whenever you read it, you must have noted that he had taken positions somewhat different than yours that you express here."

"I don't remember."

"Did you forget to tell the jury about that?"

(Whatever his answer, it doesn't matter.)

"So, did you comply with your oath, Doctor, to tell the truth, the *whole* truth, and nothing but the truth?"

"Yes I did."

"The whole truth includes the parts of Dr. [whoever]'s article that you can't seem to remember, isn't that true?"

And this cross-examination can go on following this basic line until it is exhausted. Continuing, one might ask:

"Do you think there is another authority in the world, other than yourself, who has opined on this subject?"

"Yes, of course."

"Who would that be?"

(He names someone.)

"Did you talk to Dr. [whoever he named] about this case?"

"No."

"Did you try to confirm your opinion with any other expert in this field?"

"No. I didn't need to."

"You think patients should usually get a second opinion when they are facing serious medical decisions?"

"Not necessarily." (The jury knows better.)

"So you didn't think a second opinion was necessary in Baby Jane's case?"

"No."

"You didn't even bother to read the current literature to see if your opinion was supported by any other medical expert, isn't that true?"

"Yes."

"Thank you, Doctor. No further questions."

The wisdom of juries. Our species' most prominent characteristic is our peculiar kind of intelligence. Since we all have it to one degree or another, and since members of our own species are our greatest threat, we must have a means by which to judge others who may do us harm by deceit or device. We have that ability. As we have seen, we are given the psychic tentacles to test the sounds, the expressions, the out-of-order sort of hints, the intonations, the expressions, the body language—all of the ingredients that help us conclude whether the witness is genuine, indeed, the good guy or the bad. Some call these feelers "intuition." We all have them with varying degrees of sensitivity. When they become too active we say the person is paranoid. When they are underdeveloped we say he is naïve. The biological advantage they provide, like the speed of the antelope or the shell of the turtle, is to aid the individual to survive. We are one of the few species on the face of the earth who must protect itself first against our own members.

195

I have said that jurors rarely find for the bad guy, even though the cold legal record may support his case. Nor can an apparent sweetheart, a lovely, smiley nice guy win if, in the end, he is not real. Twelve people on the jury with an average age of forty years have the combined wisdom and experience of a sage who has lived a life of nearly five hundred years. Taking the jurors as a whole body, and a unanimous verdict as the law most often requires, we can appreciate the good judgment of our founders in requiring jurors to determine the facts—the truth. No judge alive, even the best of them, has such wisdom, and those who claim otherwise provide us only with a wealth of pretension. Judges are merely members of the species—persons in whom we have vested great power. But I warn against confusing such power with wisdom. We have longed for their infallibility and, at last, have mostly been rewarded with our disappointment.

Discovering what is going on—with us. I have previously noted that when we are engaged in a courtroom battle it is difficult for us to accurately understand what's going on. When I find myself in a vigorous cross-examination, I want to know: Am I being too harsh with the witness? Am I making my points or am I coming off as angry and argumentative? Am I believable? What is going on?

I first try to be aware of what is taking place in the inner sanctum—with me. I need to be aware of my own feelings, including my anger. But just as much, I need to know what is happening to the jury and the judge—those who do not know what I know about the witness I am cross-examining. The same question keeps coming back as I wrestle with the witness: What is going on? Is my cross-examination winning the battle but losing the war? I ask my associates, my wife, my secretary, and other trusted persons who will tell me the truth. I pass them a small slip of paper that says *What's going on?* and I wait until I have an opportunity to speak to them at a recess or on a quick break to find out the answer. The feedback from those observing on the sidelines is usually better than my own—like the trainer who watches his fighter in the ring, who, between rounds, tells his fighter how he's doing and what he must do in the next round.

Impeaching the witness. Impeaching a witness is different, of course, than impeaching, say, the president of the United States. The latter is a trial of the accused. The impeachment of a witness, in short, describes the process in

196

cross-examination in which the witness is discredited. It's an attack on the credibility or integrity of the witness. Since it is an attack, it needs to be done with care and as kindly and matter-of-factly as possible, without sarcasm, anger, hatred, or the bad-tempered aloofness of the strutting cross-examiner we see in the movies, and, sadly, sometimes in court. Impeachment is available in a variety of situations that permit the cross-examiner to displace the halo with which our opponent has surrounded the head of his witness.

The expert. Let's say, in a medical malpractice case in which the insurance company's expert doctor is on the stand, the questions in our cross-examination may cover the following appropriate impeachment issues:

—the witness's interest in the outcome of the case.

—that the witness is a paid witness in the control of the opposing side.

—that the witness may not be fully acquainted with the medical history.

—that he has no interest or responsibility in the patient's treatment.

—that his "independent medical examination" is not independent at all.

—that he is an expert in testifying, rather than an expert in treating the patient.

We have asked our questions in a patient, courteous way, which by the very tone of our questions underlines the fact that we are not attempting to embarrass the witness, but simply trying to get to the truth. And all of the questions we ask are honest questions that the jury should consider in evaluating the witness's testimony.

"Dr. Mercy [the opposing expert], you, of course, get paid for your work here?"

"Yes."

"We all get paid, hopefully."

"Yes."

"Your fee here for testifying is one thousand dollars an hour, as you told us in your deposition?"

"Yes."

"You couldn't charge that much unless your testimony was worth it to the defendant, Dr. Payne, isn't that true?"

Objection from the defense and sustained as argumentative.

"But we all have to make a living, and this is, in part, how you make yours, isn't that true?"

"In part."

"I see by your deposition that you spend a good deal of your time in court—that is, over half of your gross income is derived from examining injured people on behalf of lawyers who hire you for that purpose?"

"Something like that, I suppose."

"Do you like to testify?"

"Not especially."

"But you choose to do these examinations and to testify?"

"I see it as my duty."

"You have the right to turn this work down, don't you?"

"Yes, and sometimes I do."

"Of course. If you can't find something to say on behalf of the people who hire you, you wouldn't take the case, isn't that true?"

"Yes."

"You don't, however, hold yourself out to be the last word on the medical questions in this case or any other case, isn't that also true?"

He doesn't answer.

"You know that other doctors and experts can have opposing opinions, quite opposite from yours, and that they may be right?"

"I don't think so in this case."

"Your opinion is based on your honest belief, and I suppose that you make room for the possibility that Dr. Primely, who has testified for us, has an honest, contrary belief?"

"I suppose so, but I believe he is wrong."

"So, what we have here are experts who believe opposite from each other, each holding an honest opinion."

He nods.

"We lawyers are the same. Mr. Pinchum, for the defense, and I don't agree on this case at all. That is sort of the way you doctors are too?"

"If you see it that way."

"So you make room for the possibility that experts can hold honest opinions that are opposite from each other?"

"Yes."

"Yes. And so, in fact, you have an interest in the outcome of this case, isn't that true?"

"No, I don't believe so."

"You will receive no more compensation above your one thousand dollars an hour for your testimony here if you win, that's true, isn't it?"

"Yes."

"So, even if your side wins the case, your fee will remain the same?"

"Yes."

"This is also true if your side loses the case. Your fee remains the same?"

"Yes."

"But we know that if the jury finds against your side and refuses to follow your opinion and follows instead the opinion of our doctor, Dr. Primely, that you may not be hired again, or at least as frequently as you have been in the past?"

"I think that is an unfair question."

"I don't mean to ask unfair questions. But being fair, we know that the people who hire you are not likely to hire a doctor with a losing record in court, isn't that true?"

"I have no idea."

"Let's talk about another issue: If you wake up in the morning after testifying here and discover that you are wrong, what would you do?"

"I would tell you so."

"May we count on that?"

"Yes."

"And if we don't see you in the courtroom tomorrow or the next day, we can assume that your opinion is as we have heard it?"

"Yes."

"Instead of thinking about this case overnight, won't you be preparing to testify in the next case?"

No answer.

"And your fee is the same in every case—a thousand dollars an hour?"

"Yes."

"Win or lose?"

"Yes."

"I want to take you back to the time when you decided to go to medical school. Can you remember that far back?"

"I suppose so. Yes."

"Why did you decide to go to medical school?" (This is an open-ended question that is safe to ask. He will never be heard to say, "I went to medical school to make a lot of money.")

"I decided to go to medical school because I was interested in medicine."

"Of course. Your idea wasn't to go to medical school so you could get out and make a lot of money testifying, isn't that true?"

"Yes. I didn't know much about the real world then."

"You were somewhat idealistic, I suppose?"

"Yes. I suppose."

"You wanted to heal, to help the injured and the sick?"

He nods.

"You did not specialize or try to become an expert in testifying *against* the injured and the sick, isn't that true?"

"I took no courses in forensics."

"You intended to be a regular practitioner like our Dr. Primely—someone who has patients of his own, who tries to help them and make them better or well, isn't that true?"

"Yes."

"It must be somewhat discouraging to you that you spend so much time writing reports and testifying in the courtroom, rather than treating patients."

"I don't know. I try to do my work."

"You have three children, I see by your deposition?"

"Yes."

"Your oldest daughter is in college?"

"Yes."

"We all know it costs a lot to put our kids through college these days."

"Yes it does."

When opposing counsel objects I promise the judge to tie it in with the next question. But the court sustains the objection. I ask the follow-up question because it seems relevant as an impeaching question.

"Does the fact that you are facing additional personal costs in your family with kids going to college lead you to choose testifying for money, rather than treat patients for money?"

Objected to and the judge sustains the objection.

"To put it another way, if you didn't need the money, would you choose to spend your time testifying instead of treating patients?"

Objected to and sustained.

"But hour by hour you can't make as much treating patients as you can testifying, that's true too?"

"I don't know about that. Never thought of it."

"Well, you have only so many hours in a day, Doctor, and you and you alone decide how you will invest them, that's true too, isn't it?"

"I suppose. I also have a regular practice."

"Yes. Now Doctor, when you leave this courtroom, your responsibility and Dr. Primely's will be somewhat different, isn't that true?"

"I suppose so."

"Would you tell the jury how your respective responsibilities as to our client, Henry Hurt, will differ after you both leave the courtroom?" (Another open-ended question that we would rather see the witness struggle with.)

"Well, I don't know."

"Will you have any responsibility for the future care of Henry Hurt after you leave here?"

"No."

"You never had any to begin with, that's true, isn't it?"

"Yes."

"But after this case is over Dr. Primely will have the well-being of Henry as his responsibility for some time to come?"

"I suppose."

"So, in effect, all you do is make an examination that took, I believe you said about twenty minutes, testify as to what you saw, and collect your fee—that's fair, isn't it?"

"You can put it any way you want."

"I see by your report here that you call your report, Exhibit 22, an 'Independent Medical Examination'?"

"Yes."

"Why do you call it an *independent* examination?" (Let him struggle with this one. And note that all the time we are speaking to him in a kindly voice.)

"Well, that is what we call these reports."

"But his honor, here, Judge Bloom, didn't order this, did he?"

"No."

"He had nothing to do in choosing you?"

"No."

"You were chosen by the defense, here, by the lawyer, Mr. Pinchum, isn't that true?"

"Yes."

"And neither the judge, nor the State of Wyoming is going to pay your fee?"

"No."

"It will be paid by those who hired you, right?"

"Yes."

"You were chosen, hired, and will be paid by the other side in this case, that's all true, isn't it?"

"Yes."

"And we didn't choose you?"

"No."

"Nor did we even agree that you could examine Henry, or report on him, or testify against him."

"Yes."

"So your report isn't an independent medical examination at all. It's an examination on behalf of the defense in this case, that's true, too, isn't it?"

"As you want to put it."

"Doctor, we have mentioned your daughter in passing. And we have talked at length about your qualifications. If your daughter had the same injuries as Henry has suffered in this case, would you choose a person with your qualifications and experience in treating such injuries over those of Dr. Primely?"

"I can't answer that. It is too hypothetical."

"Well, your expertise is in testifying, not treating this injury, isn't that true?"

"I hope I have expertise in the medical field in which I testify."

"Yes, of course. [No sarcasm in my comment.] Now, being utterly fair with the jury, who do you think has a better understanding of the facts in this case, a doctor who has treated the patient day after day, month after month, or one who has just seen the patient for twenty minutes and has read the record of his care and treatment?"

We don't care how he answers this question. The jury will know that the treating doctor has the best insight into the patient.

A word to the wise in cross-examining experts. We may learn a great deal about the expert's field by simply reading the medical textbooks on the subject. I have often said that the lawyer can know as much or more as the experts about the limited field in which they testify if the lawyer will take the time to read. The learned treatises and medical texts are easy to find in any medical library (our own doctor probably has them), and when we come into court to testify we can be as informed as the expert. I often encounter the expert who has not kept himself completely current in his field. The scientific fields are moving targets.

Cross-examining the expert from *learned treatises,* as the law permits, can be effective. But it is also dangerous. Most well-schooled experts will refuse to admit that a given text is a learned treatise. They will call the book an opinion or one written by an author who is not generally accepted as an authority in the field. Still, the law permits one to cross-examine the expert from a learned treatise, and the opportunity to do so should not be overlooked, especially in depositions where we can discover in advance what the witness is going to say concerning opposing opinions from the texts. A lawyer who comes into court without knowing the full extent of the science surrounding his case is a well-coiffed charlatan.

There is no wealth greater than the wealth of mind filled to brimming with the facts and science of one's case. But I see the expert as a caged lion. We can get in that cage and wrestle with him if we want. But he will devour us. We can argue all day and deep into the night, and despite our superior current academic knowledge he will win the argument, because the argument seems to be, as it is, an argument between a lawyer and a scientific expert. The jury has to decide who is to be believed—the lawyer who is an expert in the law, or the witness who is an expert in his science. The winner is preordained. We argue and it sounds like argument. We protest and holler and it sounds like that—and the winner, still, is the expert. There is a built-in futility in demeaning the knowledge of the expert by attempting to show our own superior freshly acquired knowledge.

I believe we should get involved in scientific arguments only when we have the clear, undisputed advantage: Has the expert given contrary testimony at some previous time? Has he written papers that are contrary to his present position? Has his mentor or one of his professors contradicted his testimony in prior works? Has a world authority made a clear statement to the contrary? We can attack him when he or other undisputed authorities have taken a different position than he now espouses. Under these circumstances we are not arguing as the expert. We are arguing, though. I say, keep out of the lion's cage. We can prod the lion with our sticks from outside the cage, as in the cross-examination above. We have impeached from the outside. We have prodded and even tormented in a kindly way, but we have not gotten into the cage with the expert, and we remain safe and our client's case remains unharmed.

Cross-examining the jailhouse snitch. The jailhouse snitch is often the prosecution's key witness. Too frequently the cops put a willing snitch in the prison cell with the client. At the time of the trial the snitch is called upon to tell the jury what confessions the defendant has supposedly made to the snitch. The deal, of course, is that the prosecutor has agreed to help the snitch, to get his sentence reduced, or to provide some other sort of assistance to the witness. In the final argument the prosecutor will excuse what the state has done with something that sounds like this: "We can't go out and find our witnesses in the Women's Junior League, or from the choir of the Baptist Church. We have to take our witnesses where we find them. They are not always pretty and they are not always as antiseptic as we might want them. But they have taken an oath and they have testified here and Mr. Spence has been given the opportunity to cross-examine them so that there is little doubt that these witnesses had the opportunity to obtain the evidence they have given, and they have given it to you as best they can," which is to say that the poor snitch should be believed, even though we all know he is a lying son-of-a-carnivorous parrot, the likes of whom align the walls of hell.

But for a full minute get into the skin of a snitch. You are the snitch. You are this miserable human being trapped in the hands of the law. You face twenty years or more in the pen on a pending charge. The pen is not just a word. It is hell on earth. It is another society, one of vicious, angry men who will hurt you. The guards and the warden have been so long in the company of the inmates that they have become less human than the murderer you will bunk with. You are a number, not a person, an animal in a cage who must be fed with the other animals, an animal that is seen as dangerous and worthless.

Inside the pen you, of course, have lost your freedom. And you have gained entrance into a satanic society in which mostly men with broken souls are its members. No women, no mothers, no little children, not even a dog or a canary. Nothing lives. The bullies who reigned supreme in the outside world, the rich, the corporate masters, the police—well, the bullies who dominate within this new society are just as powerful and as heartless. Some will want sexual favors for small favors—like protection from physical harm. A penitentiary is the most vicious oligarchy on the face of the earth.

As the snitch awaiting trial, you have not seen your wife in a long while. You have had no person to gently touch you, to care about you, to ask how your day was. You have not seen your children. They will grow up without you, ashamed of you, not mentioning your name, trying to forget who you are. You will be in this hellhole for the next twenty years, never seeing the first blooms of spring or hearing a single song of a bird. You will eat, sleep, and live in putrid concrete. And now the prosecutor is here and says he is willing to make a deal—some deal that will get you free in a year or two. All you have to do is to remember what happened, what you heard, what was said by the defendant who has become your bunk mate. Will you make up a story against him? Will you lie about him? He is probably guilty anyway. In this world, this jungle, one has to survive. You are in a trap. Someone has offered to release you from it. Will you turn it down?

Now the snitch, let's call him Arnold McGinnis, has taken the stand in the case against us. He has testified in detail about the crime our client allegedly confessed to him while they were in the same cell as cell mates. Our cross could be the usual angry cross of the defense attorney who attacks:

"You made a deal with the prosecutor, didn't you?"

"No."

"He said he would help you, didn't he?"

"No."

"You're in the pen for fraud, I see here" (looking at the rap sheet).

"Yes."

"You claim you are honest?"

"Yeah."

"Can an honest man commit a fraud?"

"It was a phony, put-up deal."

"Can an honest man commit a fraud?"

"I didn't do it."

"You know how to lie, don't you?"

"I'm not lying."

"You've lied before, haven't you?"

"No."

"Tell the jury what a lie is."

"They know what a lie is."

"No, I want you to tell them."

"It's when you are not telling the truth."

"You're a professional liar, aren't you? That's why you're in the pen today, isn't that true?"

"I'm not lying."

"You can answer my question: You are a professional liar. That's why you are in the pen today, isn't that true?"

"I'm not a professional liar."

"When did you meet with the prosecutor?"

"I don't know."

"You don't even know that?"

"No."

"You were in his office?"

"No. He come to see me."

"A couple of cops were with him, right?"

"Just one."

"And he told you what he wanted you to testify to, didn't he?"

"I told him."

"You say you didn't make any deal. But you expected to get something in return for your cooperation, didn't you?"

"No."

"You are lying now, aren't you?"

"No."

"Is there some way we can tell when you are lying and when you are not? I mean, do you hold your mouth in a certain way when you are telling the truth or what?"

This brand of questioning can go on endlessly in this hostile manner. The penitentiaries are filled with inmates whose lawyers have cross-examined in this strident, hostile fashion, their teeth bared, the sound of their words laced with enmity, their body language revealing a cross-examiner but a hair's breadth from launching a physical attack.

We must remember: Jurors are humans, the same as we. They have their own pent-up feelings against liars and cheats. But don't forget, when we become the bully, beating up on the witness who is trapped on the witness stand, the dynamic can gradually change so that, although the witness may not be believed, the lawyer himself may have fallen from grace.

No matter how lowly we are, how deprived, how hated, how worthless we feel, how twisted our psyches, how lost we are, we long for a higher state of being. A compassionate cross of the snitch, one which will be more effective, might sound like this:

"Mr. McGinnis, you must find yourself in a very difficult position."

He looks blankly back.

"I mean, you are facing twenty years in the penitentiary yourself."

He shrugs his shoulders.

"I don't mean to embarrass you, but you've been in the penitentiary before, haven't you?"

"Yes."

"It is not a very pleasant place to be, is it?"

"It could be worse."

"What's it like to be in the penitentiary?" (Here we use the open-ended question. His answer cannot hurt us, but his refusal to be completely candid will reflect on the witness as someone holding back.)

"What do you mean?"

"Well, as you say, Mr. McGinnis, you are facing twenty years in the pen. Could you help the jury understand what a day in the pen is like?"

"I don't know."

"You've spent many days in the pen, haven't you?"

"Yeah."

"What is a day like?" (An interested sound in our voice.)

"Like any other day."

Here we can lead him from the moment he arises from his steel bunk, a bed without covers, it's cold and the place is noisy with the sound of steel on steel as the doors open and close. The men are noisy and vulgar, the place is never dark, not even at night—the lights on, so that one cannot tell if it is day or night, the lineup, the breakfast of cold, pasty cooked cereal, the long hours of nothing, of loneliness, the hours dragging, the brief time in the exercise yard, and on and on.

"A day in the pen is a day in hell, isn't it?"

"You get used to it."

"And you are looking at seventy-three hundred of those days unless you can do something to shorten the time, isn't that true?"

"They gimme twenty years."

"You're married?"

"Yeah."

"Arnold, how long has it been since you've seen your wife?"

"She comes once in a while."

"How long has it been since you just held her hand?"

"I don't know."

"Been over a year, hasn't it?"

"I suppose. Never kept track of it."

"You love your wife?"

"Sure."

"She love you?"

"Yeah. I guess."

"She was good to you?"

"Yeah."

"There's no one in the pen who cares about you, isn't that true?"

"I got friends."

"Tender, loving people like your wife?"

He doesn't answer.

"And you have children, I understand?"

"Yeah."

"You're proud of them."

"Yeah, sure."

"How long has it been since you've seen your children?"

"I don't know."

"Do they come to see you?"

"No."

"You miss them?"

"Yeah."

"And you know they are growing up without a father."

"Yeah."

"It must be a very frightening and lonely life you live in the pen."

He says nothing. Looks down at his hands.

The examination goes on covering the facts we have learned by simply reversing roles with the witness. At last the hell of living in the pen becomes very real to anyone who listens, and the jurors are listening. Perhaps the final questions might be:

"I guess, Arnold, that you would do or say about anything to get out of this hell?"

"No."

"Would it make you feel any better if we told you that we understand how you can lie against an innocent man?"

Objected to and the objection is sustained.

"Arnold, it's all right. My client, Joe Low, understands."

The open-ended question in cross-examination. The home of the leading question is, of course, cross-examination. We all know the old saw: Never ask a question on cross-examination to which you don't know the answer. Insulate yourself from disaster by always leading. But if we pause to reflect we will soon recognize many a place where the open-ended question is called for.

I want an expert witness to explain the meaning of technical terms. "Doctor, when you speak of the heart's right atrium, what do you mean?" On cross-examination I will require him to show us that those intimidating, technical words are just big words that usually mean simple things that ordinary people can understand. When the expert talks of atherosclerosis we ask him to tell us what that means in ordinary language. It means, simply, that a deposit called plaque builds up on the inner wall of the coronary arteries, which supply the blood to the heart, and gradually narrow the arteries which, in turn, restricts the flow of blood, which, in turn, can lead to a heart attack.

I will ask the witness to describe a location, a person, to set the scene, to give us a history. Often the direct question provides a fertile field for a cross-examination that will follow. And often direct questions will give us better details from a witness who is supposedly impartial. For instance, we want to know the details of an accident in which our client's child was killed. If we have the officer on the stand who was the first to arrive at the scene we might say:

"Tell us, Officer King, exactly what things were in the car when you arrived at the scene of the accident?"

"There was an empty beer bottle. Two of them, to be exact."

"Did you see the Bible?"

"No."

"You didn't see the Bible?"

"I saw it later."

"Did you see the little girl's car seat?"

"Yes."

"What was on it?"

"What do you mean?"

"Did you examine it?"

"Yes."

"What did you see on it?"

"Blood."

"Whose blood was it?"

"Hers, I suppose."

"Who sat in the car seat at the time of the accident?"

"The little girl."

"What was her name?"

"Betty Lou Jergonson."

"How old was she?"

"Three."

"Did you see her at the scene of the accident?"

"Yes."

"Describe her as you saw her."

"She was bleeding around the head."

"What was she saying?"

"She was unconscious."

"What did you notice about the injuries to her head?"

"She had a deep cut over her right eye."

"What else?"

"Her right eye was protruding."

"What do you mean?"

"It was hanging partially out of the socket."

"Did you notice anything else concerning her head injuries?"

"Yes. Her mouth was smashed in and her front teeth were gone."

"What did you do with the seat she was sitting in?"

"I took it to the station."

"Where is it now?"

"I don't know."

"Who did you give it to?"

"I don't recall. I think Mr. Fortune."

"Do you mean the attorney representing the driver of the other car?"

"Yes."

We can immediately see that these open-ended questions may force the witness to tell more than the witness wants to. If we are dealing with a witness who claims to be impartial, the open-ended question may often provide a better story for us than if he were crossed. Every witness that the adversary may call is not necessarily hostile merely because he has been called by the other side.

Cross-examinations that keep our witness off the stand. I remember in the defense of Randy Weaver of Ruby Ridge the prosecutor called a witness to testify who had not been previously identified as a government witness. Moreover, he had failed to give us the twenty-four-hour notice, as was the court's rule in the case. I, of course, objected.

"We were not given notice that this witness would be called, Your Honor," I pleaded at the bench. "I ask the court to order the witness to stand down."

The prosecutor offered a lame excuse.

The judge gave me that sly old fox look, one that said, "Come on, Mr. Spence, you don't need my help." What he did say on the record was, "Mr. Spence, the government has called forty-two witnesses to date. They have all testified for you. I will permit this witness under the circumstances."

What the judge was saying was that my cross-examination was making my defense. He'd seen that I was able to cross-examine and that his granting this one exception to the prosecutor would not create sufficient error in the record for a reversal in the event the defendant was convicted—a matter of little solace to me. I did, in fact, examine the witness to our benefit, and when the state had concluded its case after scores of witnesses had testified and had been cross-examined by me, it seemed to me that we should rest without putting on any evidence. After twenty-three days of deliberation, a time that left us hanging over a bubbling caldron of torture for what seemed like an eternity, the jury acquitted Randy Weaver.

As I have said many times, most often we can tell the accused's story better than he. He is seen by everyone in the courtroom as the villain who will lie to save himself. The only defendant in a criminal case who can testify with ease and effectively is a sociopath who is probably guilty of the crime charged. Innocent defendants are most often helpless to defend themselves—their fear, their anger at being charged with a crime they did not commit, their inability to match wits with a seasoned prosecutor makes it almost impossible for the defendant to take the stand and convince the jury of his innocence. As a consequence, I rarely call the defendant to testify unless the defendant insists and I am unable to convince him otherwise, or unless the prosecution has gotten evidence before the jury that is fatal to our case, and the only witness who can dispute it is the defendant himself. As a consequence, I attempt to get my entire case on display in my cross-examination of the state's witnesses.

Credibility again becomes an issue here—a strategically imperative one. In the criminal case where the burden of proof is on the state we have shown that the prosecutor has not been completely candid with us. He has told the jury about his case in the opening statement. But at the earliest opportunity we have shown in our cross that he has not told the *full* story. He has only told his side of a many-sided story. His witnesses have not been up front and completely honest. They have not been the most reliable kinds of good citizens.

The cops have not acted competently. There are huge holes in the state's case. Moreover we, the cross-examiners, seem fair and decent. We have shown the jury that there is much doubt in the state's case. In fact, we have earned the jury's respect. The jury seems to trust us.

But now we who were once the trusted cross-examiner put our case on. Suddenly, through the cross-examination by the prosecutor, the jurors see that our case, too, has holes in it. They see that our witnesses are just like the state's—sometimes not fully candid. Then we, who were once trusted by the jury, call the accused to the stand. After the prosecution gets through cross-examining him and displaying all his contradictions, the implausible facts he has testified to, and considering his poor deportment on the stand, his anger, and his evasive answers, it now seems probable that the accused is lying (even though he may have been telling the truth). The jury concludes that we have been presenting false colors. The jury feels betrayed and they find for the state.

No matter how open and honest we are, and we must be, the effect of permitting the prosecutor to cross-examine our witnesses is dangerous. And the risk of letting our client take the stand is an overt invitation to disaster. I recognize the exceptions. I have put my clients on the stand when I had no other choice. We can and must be the most reliable persons in the courtroom. But in the eyes of the jurors we lawyers will take the blame for each witness we put on the stand who cannot survive a daunting cross-examination. When we put an honest witness on and the prosecutor cuts him up we are the ones who take the blame. The witness did not hold up as we claimed he would. The witness does not turn out to be as pretty and lovely of soul as we told the jury he would be. Our credibility plummets. Often at that moment our case is lost.

In the end it is most often better to do without critical witnesses than to put them on and have them fail to live up to their billing. When we disappoint the jurors, when they suddenly see us as attorneys who have failed to keep the faith, often nothing will suffice to restore their confidence, their faith. So it is, also, with jurors who have trusted us when we put on our case and it fails in one way or another. Since many witnesses can be shaken on cross, and since our client, the accused, has a nearly insurmountable task in convincing the jury of his innocence when a well-prepared prosecutor confronts him skillfully, I have long ago concluded that calling any witnesses in the defense of one's case is not a good global strategy, especially if one has become skilled in the art of cross-examination so that it may become unnecessary to call any witnesses at all.

Cross-examining the fragile, the timid, the diminutive, and the grieving. One fact we must always remember: If the jurors can identify with the witness, we must be extremely considerate to that witness, because there is a part of the witness in the jurors, and when we attack the witness we are attacking the juror. I am thinking of a grieving mother whose son was killed and our client is charged with the crime. I am thinking of a widow whose husband was the driver of the car who injured our client and we are seeking damages from his estate. Often the veteran lawyer will ask no questions at all, rather than have the jury rise up and throw their protective arms around the witness.

But people are all the same. As with us, the grieving mother has her own defense mechanisms to protect her. While the cross-examiner cannot lunge headlong into a confronting cross-examination, still he ought not be intimidated by taking on this sympathetic witness. Instead, we should approach the witness with caring, but with solid, relevant questions. Moreover, in fairness, the other side has put this witness on the stand. We didn't. And it would be unfair for us to be deprived of our right of cross-examination, simply because our opposition has decided to put on this sympathetic witness. A sort of putative necessity exists, demanding that we rise to this difficult occasion.

"Mrs. Allison, I understand the pain you are experiencing here today. This must be very hard for you."

"Yes, sir."

"You understand that we have not caused you this pain by calling you as a witness?"

"Yes."

"You were asked to come here by the prosecutor—not by us."

"Yes."

"I have to ask you some questions about this case. Do I have your permission to ask you these questions?"

"I guess so."

"Thank you, Mrs. Allison."

At this point we have begun to cut through the shield of sympathy that our opponent enjoys with this witness. Our questioning will start with open-ended questions.

"I want to take you back in time to the night in question. I am so sorry I have to do this, but could you tell us where your husband was?"

"He was at work. He worked the shift from twelve midnight until eight in the morning."

"Were you left alone in the house?"

"No, my son was asleep in his room."

"Could you tell us something about your home? Could you take us there and show us how the house looked at two o'clock on that morning?"

"Well it was just a two-bedroom house. There's the front door, the living room, and then the kitchen. Two bedrooms adjoin the living room and the bath between them."

"What was the lighting like at two in the morning?"

"The lights were off, but there was light coming in the living room window from the street light outside." The witness is beginning to change a bit. Her voice is no longer wavering near tears. She is sounding quite different than when she was answering the questions for the prosecutor. She sounds almost defensive, perhaps a bit hostile.

"You were in bed in the back bedroom and your son was closest to the living room?"

"Yes, I was." She is now responding, as many witnesses do, as if we are trying to trap her. We have never changed our tone of complete courtesy—focused and factual. The change in her demeanor is actually startling. It's not that she isn't the grieving mother that she purports to be. She is. But she, like most witnesses, has begun to react defensively to the cross-examination. And the jury is seeing that the once untouchable witness is presenting herself as one who, indeed, can and should be cross-examined.

"You never saw the person enter the front door, did you?"

"How could I? I was in the back bedroom."

"Of course, not, Mrs. Allison. You are quite right." She stares at the cross-examiner as if she has just won a major point.

"And the first thing you heard was somebody hollering, 'Matt, you son of a bitch, come out here'?"

"No, the first thing I heard was the sound of a key in the door."

"You heard that from the back bedroom?"

"Well, absolutely. I heard it."

"You had been asleep?"

"That's what I testified to."

"And you were awakened all the way back in the back bedroom by the sound of a key in the front door?"

"Yes, I was." Why is she so hostile? Our questions have been simple, reasonable questions. She is losing the shroud of sympathy that once protected her.

"Did you hear the car drive up?"

"No, like I said, I did not."

"You know that the car had what the kids call 'pipes'?"

"I knew no such thing."

"You heard a key, but not the car, do I understand you correctly?"

"Yes you do."

"Thank you, Mrs. Allison. So then you heard the man yelling your son's name?"

"I heard the front door shut."

"And you say you got up?"

"Yes, I did, and I saw him standing in the living room with a gun."

"What kind of a gun was it?"

"Like that one up there." She points to the revolver that has been identified and is in evidence.

"The man was looking at you when you came out of the bedroom?"

"Yes, he was, and I saw him plainly."

"The lights were off, Mrs. Allison."

"Yes they were. But I saw this from the street lights shining through the front window."

"You were facing the front window?"

"I certainly was."

"And he was facing you?"

"Yes he was."

"His back was to the front window?"

"Yes."

"So the light in this darkened room that was coming through the front window was on his back, not his face. That's true, isn't it?"

"I could see him."

"Mrs. Allison, please help us, will you?" We wait for her to settle down a bit. "The light from the street lamp was on his back, not his face?"

"It lighted up the whole living room."

"You, of course, notice that Ted, my client, is a black man."

"Yes he is."

"He has a darker complexion than many black men?"

"I wouldn't know." The jury can see.

"And you were able to identify both Ted and the gun?"

"Yes."

"Your son Matt then came out into the living room?"

"Yes."

"And the lights were still off?"

"Yes. The light switch is over by the front door."

"And your son was standing by you and he said, 'Who is it, Mom?'"

"That's what he said."

"He could see the man standing in front of the two of you as well as you?"

"I suppose so."

"Yet he asked, 'Who is it, Mom?' He must not have recognized the person standing there."

She is silent.

"But your son knew Ted. They were longtime friends."

She is silent.

"Then the person, whoever it was, shot him." And we ask no further questions.

What we have seen here is common. The sympathetic witness, whether a grieving mother, a small, vulnerable person, a timid, even fragile child—all are still human beings who, if treated fairly but in a focused way will often shed the very demeanor that protects them the most. Even the witness who remains within the protective cover of empathy can and should be kindly cross-examined if there are important facts or admissions to be gained.

Passing the witness for cross-examination. Despite what I have said, there are those witnesses who ought not be cross-examined. Witnesses who merely establish foundation facts, witnesses who testify to matters not in dispute, who can offer nothing to otherwise support our case—these witnesses should be passed with a courteous, "No, questions, Mrs. Perkinson. Thank you for coming."

I see lawyers who believe it is their utter duty to cross-examine every witness who has ever walked into a courtroom. The examiner has reduced himself to a nitpicker—someone who soon wears out his welcome with the jury, who bores the jury with his love of all the junk in the junk pile of facts that surround every case. At his best he is seen as one who provides little more than endless piles of trivia. When it comes time for him to cross on a critical fact, the jury is likely as not to miss the point, because he's made so few along the way. When the lawyer gets up to cross-examine he should have a significant story in mind that he wants to tell with this witness. He should be prepared to make an important point. Otherwise he should remain seated and provide the jury with blessed silence.

I look for the witness I can pass with a kindly, "No questions." It adds to my own credibility, and it clearly tells the jury that if I choose to cross I have something important to provide them. They should be on the edge of their seats to find out what it is.

Before we begin the cross-examination we must ask: Who is this witness? At this point how does the jury see him? Is he seen with respect, with caring, with sympathy, or is the witness one who the jury doesn't relate to, like an emotionless cop or a long-winded expert who uses big words. Before we begin the cross we should become the juror. As a juror, how do we see this witness at this point? Do we like him? Do we trust him? Do we want to know more about him and what he is testifying to? Has the witness hurt us, or did he hurt our opponent? How we see the witness *as a juror* will tell us how we should approach the witness.

Again, the common denominator is courtesy. But whether we choose a controlled cross-examination where the witness is dangerous and hostile, or whether we use a compassionate cross, or even a cross with open-ended questions, depends on our initial assessment of the witness through the eyes of the jurors.

Then, before we begin the cross-examination, we must have in mind the story we wish to tell through this witness. We have prepared the story for each witness and we'll not muddle around asking a bunch of meaningless questions in order to hear our own melodious voices, nor will we repeat the questions we heard on direct examination, except where it is necessary as foundation for a well-prepared cross. And, at last, we ask ourselves, do we want to cross-examine this witness at all?

For the lay persons—the principles of cross-examination outside the courtroom. We can't cross-examine the boss. That's too obvious. We can't be heard to say, "So, Mr. Hemlock, you've failed to include in next year's budget the raise you promised me last year at this same time, isn't that true?" In the morning the pink slip with your name on it is nearly guaranteed. But the methods of courtroom cross-examination we have discussed have multiple applications out of the courtroom as well. We can certainly get together with friends and do a small psychodrama by which we can learn how the boss feels about any given subject, and how, therefore, we should approach him.

We can discover the facts of our case in the same way that we discover the facts preparatory to a cross-examination during a trial. We can take the position of the boss, the CEO, the administrator, the school board, or municipal board member. We can understand what their problems are, their agenda, what they are afraid of, and how we might discuss the case with them from their viewpoint, which, in the end, we must fully understand to become successful.

The problem outside the courtroom is a bit more difficult for another reason—the *power person* to whom we are making our presentation is often not only the decision maker, he is also the adverse witness. He is not only the opposing party, he is often the jury as well. Simply understanding this fact is the first step toward a successful encounter.

Let's take as an example something that has always concerned me as a photographer—the limited warranty we read on the back of every roll of film we buy. It says, in effect, if the film is defective, well, that is too damn bad. All we, the film manufacturer, will give you is the cost of the roll of film. Wonderful!

Let's look at a case—one in which a photographer has been given an important assignment. He's going on an expedition to the Antarctic to photograph the elusive but recently rediscovered albino whale—the white whale of *Moby Dick*. This mammoth creature has been merely a myth growing out of Melville's classic, but what he has recently discovered is that the whale exists! There have been two sightings, and if our photographer can photograph the whale it will be the first and only photograph known to mankind—and absolute proof that the whale exists. He has gathered up his equipment, bought the best film on the market, and has joined the expedition as its sole photographer.

219

Then one day . . . yes, there the whale is! Yes, it is sounding! Yes, it is even showing off, like the whale in the insurance company ads—its whole body is out of the water in a perfect dive, and our photographer, his telephoto lens in place and his camera fully loaded with the so-called best film in the world, snaps the photograph. He's got it! The only photograph of a white whale in all history.

But you know the story. The whale is not even discernable in the photograph, and when the negative is examined it is only too clear that the film was, indeed, defective. The justice our photographer is going to enjoy under the terms of the warranty is another roll of film—his total compensation for the loss of one of the most valuable photographs man has ever taken.

So what? The company had itself fully protected by its warranty, so that a controlled cross-examination of the photographer by the company lawyer, in or out of court, might sound like this:

"You have used our film for many years, isn't that true?"

"Well, yes."

"And you know that we can't guarantee our film, because things happen. It happens to everyone."

"Well, it sure happened to me."

"And when you bought our film you knew what the warranty was—it is written plainly on the back of the box. Let me read it to you:

WARRANTY

The Manufacturer's sole liability, and the exclusive remedy, for any acknowledged defect(s) shall be replacement of the film. The Manufacturer shall not be liable under any circumstances for any indirect, incidental, or consequential damages.

"So we are very sorry, but you knew this was the extent of our liability when you purchased our film, isn't that true?"

The film-manufacturing company employs a sales representative who does a lot of business with the company that hired our photographer. The purchasing agent for the company who sent our Moby Dick photographer to the Antarctic has some clout with the film manufacturer because of the volume of its film purchases. The purchasing agent asks the film manufacturer's rep to meet with the photographer for lunch, to see what can be done. In preparation for that lunch we can anticipate the psychodrama that might take place between the film manufacturer's rep, let's call him Robert, and one of his colleagues who will take the part of the photographer, whom we will call Ivan.

Robert the rep knows that the "warranty" fully protects his company. But does it? What happens if the photographer goes to the media with a story about his trip to the Antarctic, explaining that he took the most valuable picture in the history of wildlife and it was lost because of a batch defect in the film? His problem becomes the problem of the manufacturer, warranty or no warranty. The photographer lost a historical, priceless photograph. But the film company's reputation may be challenged outside of court. The warranty protects the manufacturer from a court action, but it does not protect the company from hundreds of thousands, maybe millions of dollars in lost revenue if the photographer goes public and the public decides they should buy a different film.

To discover how this can all play out, Robert, the rep, immediately reverses roles with Ivan, the stand-in for the photographer. "I'm sorry about what happened to your whale picture," the stand-in playing Robert says.

"It wasn't just a whale picture. It was the single most awesome photo of a *white* whale that could be imagined. The photo was worth millions, and you want to give me a new roll of film. Big deal!"

Again Robert reverses roles and becomes the film company's rep. Thinking as a compassionate cross-examiner might, he says, "You must be devastated, Ivan. This must be the worst thing that could happen to you. You were brought from the heights of success to the depths of despair, and it is all on account of a defective roll of film. What could we do for you?"

Ivan says, "I don't know."

"What about a nationwide promotion of your photography? We could put you in every photo magazine across the country, turn you into the star photographer that you deserve to be." The conversation goes on from there, and the best resolution that the circumstances can provide is achieved.

The ultimate power of cross-examination. If truth exists, and if it can be discovered, it will best be exposed in a well conceived cross-examination. Facts are more than mere words. They are imbedded with the demeanor of the speaker—his conviction, his forthrightness, his interest in the outcome of the case, his honor, his humanness, and his credibility. Although I have written about it here at length, cross-examination is just another form of storytelling, and, of course, listening with our third ear. If there be an art to it, it is the art of preparing, of listening, and, finally, of being a human being ourselves.

15. CLOSING THE DEAL—THE FINAL ARGUMENT

THE FINAL ARGUMENT: THE HAPPY ENDING. So the day of the final argument is here. Now it's time to close the deal with the jury. It's time for the salesman to push the order pad over for his customer's signature. The final pitch is about to be made to the committee. Our story has been told. But the story's ending will be written by others, by the *power persons*.

This is our last chance. If we haven't made the sale to the jury, the customer, or the council by this time, if the boss hasn't been convinced by our presentation, is it too late? If our story in the opening wasn't compelling, if the jury, customer, or the council weren't made to care, if our opening statement was proven false in substantial ways, if we held back the truth and now, after all of the evidence is in, the jury has discovered that we have betrayed them, we can do little to save our case.

If on the other hand we have been genuinely who we are, if we have been connected to our case, cared about it, cared about our clients and ourselves, if we have laid it all down every day, day after day in the courtroom, and our caring has become contagious, so that the jury cares as well, we are ready, indeed. We have earned the right to make our closing argument. But haven't we already won the case?

I have said that the *power persons* will write the ending to our story. Our story can end as a tragedy. Or it can end in joy, in fulfillment, in justice. But how the story ends will depend on how we have told it. The only cases that can be won in the final argument are those that have not been previously lost. On the other hand a good case can be lost in those fatal, final moments.

What is the final argument? The morning news of the world's turmoil fades into insignificance, compared to our concern for our client who sits next to us. We can hear him breathing. We see his face, drawn and pale. He has visited hell. His eyes are blank. He doesn't speak, the words stuck somewhere in the unyielding pain of fear. We reach over and touch his hand. His life is in our hands. The final argument, our last chance at justice, is on us. The judge nods in our direction, indicating it is our turn to speak to the jury. Will they reject us, turn their heads from us, shut their hearts against us? Our minds are blank, white. No thoughts can penetrate the wall of fear that surrounds us. We walk toward the jury. Our feet feel heavy. We know the jurors' eyes are peering, the jurors waiting, waiting. Yet we cannot see them. They are blurred objects sitting in chairs in front of us. They stare. We try to smile, but the smile will not come. If only we could run. But it would be more painful, more frightening to run than to stand and fight.

The final argument is a fight. It's more. It's the climax of the war in which we've been engaged. We have asked the jury to trust us. But we must also trust ourselves. We stare down at the floor, at our feet. We turn inward for our power. Is it there? Has it forsaken us? Will the words come? We feel a sense of helplessness. We try to locate the fear. Where is it? Yes, there it is—around the ribs, under the ribs, its center where the ribs converge. It has taken but a moment, this centering, this becoming the self. At the moment we are nothing but a bundle of fear tied up neatly, our guts around it. We take a deep breath and look up at the jury. Then we hear our own voice:

"Ladies and gentlemen of the jury." There is a long pause as we look at each juror in their eyes. Each of them, juror by juror, and thereby acknowledge them, confirm for them that they are individuals who count. Our eyes say it as they linger on theirs, linger a millisecond longer, long enough that our eyes say we see you, you have trusted us and we trust you also. No one on the jury has been by-passed. No one forgotten.

Then we hear the first words of our argument slipping out. The words are the truth.

"I'm still afraid."

I think about what I have just said. It is the truth. Then I say my thoughts. "It is the truth. If it were otherwise it would mean I don't care.

"Why am I afraid?" Why? "This is the most important time of the trial. Your decision will be the story's ending. And I pray for a happy ending. I wonder if I have done my job well enough. It is too late to turn back. I've made mistakes that I wish I could correct. If I had it to do over again, I would be more kind to Mr. Henderson (the opposing counsel), who I know is only doing his job. I would have listened more closely to his honor who was only attempting to see that the parties have a fair trial. If I had it to do over again I would have done a better job in presenting our case. There were many questions I failed to ask. And I am afraid that I have not done a good enough job. When I think of it I feel panic rising up. Yet, that is in the past, and we can't go back.

"On the other hand, I am eager to talk to you, for this special time with you. I have been waiting for over two years for someone to hear this case. Mr. Henderson would not hear me. He only filed motions to keep me from getting here. His clients would not listen to me. They turned a deaf ear to George (our client). No one has listened, except, thank God, you have listened. George and I have waited these long years to be heard, and here we finally are, and I am eager to make these last statements to you, because you are the only persons in the world who will hear us and who can finally give us justice."

Suddenly, I have the sense that the door to my final argument has been opened, and out of it, as if by magic, my argument begins to unfold. It begins to present itself. It will be a symphony, again a presentation essentially in three movements, the beginning, the middle, and the end. Like the music of the symphony itself, it will have harmony, rhythm, and texture. It will rise to a crescendo and fall to a whisper. It will not be contrived. It will be the product of unleashed, genuine feelings. It will not be feigned. No room exists for artifice. Rhetoric is out, there is no room for it. The heart cannot get itself around pretense. It is too taken up with the real.

Every space in the heart where the argument is stored has been marinated with urgent feelings. We stand on these two solid feet and decry the wrongs that have been forced upon our client. What is the final argument? *It is the time when, with a sense of ethical anger, with a justified righteous indignation, we ask the jury for justice.*

The guide through the forest. I have spoken of the guide—the concept applies to all salespersons, to trial lawyers and laypersons alike. We are all salespersons and, as such, we are also guides. I compare our role to that of Kit Carson or Daniel Boone—someone who knows the territory, and whom the jury trusts. That they trust you! What a responsibility! That they will follow you! What an honor! How humbling must that be! There was another guide they could have followed. There's somebody over there who is called the prosecutor in a criminal case, and the defense attorney in a civil case. Each wants to be the guide. But we are the guide they have chosen. They've chosen us not because we are big or beautiful or strong or articulate. They don't choose guides based upon the sound of their voices. They choose a guide they trust.

The jury's guide comes in every size and kind. If we can dig deep into the mother lode of who we are, then deeper still, if we can become even more real, if we can shed all of the masks, if we can always be painfully honest we will become the guide the jury follows.

Preparing the final argument. The final argument, as with every element of the trial, will be fully prepared. As always, we are filling our computer brain with the materials and their organization. The argument has become a part of us. Indeed, *we are the argument.*

We began to understand the theory of our case as we prepared our opening statement. We developed a theme. We have lived the case. We have wrestled with the demons that visit us as we sleep, and have made our argument a hundred times.

I begin to prepare the final argument the day I get the case. Many a time I've found myself sitting up in bed at night before I turn off the lights. I am making notes of ideas, of phrases that come to me. I write out whole paragraphs I think will someday be said to the jury. I keep a file by the bed that I have labeled, "Final Argument." Sometimes I am visited by a powerful metaphor, or a compelling phrase will come to mind that awakens me—usually in that faint unconscious zone between sleep and waking, in the early morning—and I will write the epiphany down before it escapes.

Recently I was asked to consider the defense of a young man who was charged with the murder of his mother and of a child who was his niece. Days before the murder this young man had displayed irrefutable evidence of psychosis, was delusional, and obviously medically insane. His mother had him hospitalized, and he was examined for a few days. The doctors and other attendants recorded his mental aberrations that clearly showed he was suffering from a severe psychosis. But the hospital personnel released him (he had no insurance), and within hours he returned to his home and bludgeoned his mother and his niece to death. He was committed to a state hospital because he was unable to aid in his own defense. He was there for many months, and finally, on medication, returned to jail to await trial. The state had asked for his life.

As I heard the facts of this case I immediately began creating the final argument. I had a paper napkin in front of me and began jotting notes: Here the villain will be the state itself. The question is, should the state be permitted to cover its own wrongdoing, its criminal release of this man, by now killing him? Should the state be permitted to kill to cover its own mistakes? How can the state seek death, when the state itself caused it?

Under any theory of justice the state should be charged. But because the state cannot be dragged into the criminal court and charged with murder, should it be allowed to kill the victim, the young man who, insane, was knowingly turned loose on the people and converted into a murderer? The state is the villain. The young man is the victim. The heroes in this case will be the jurors who will surely see the injustice of the state's demand for the life of this man. Surely the jury will see that he should be treated for his illness and confined for life in a state hospital. But from the state's perspective, so long as he remains alive he is a living reminder, year after year, of the state's failure to protect its citizens.

The point I hope to make is that when I first hear of a case the facts immediately begin to form the final argument—what is the justice in the case? Who is the villain? The hero? How can the facts be argued so as to reach those psychic places that lie tender and waiting in all of us, that, when touched, respond in our own sense of justice?

I make the final argument in the shower in the morning. While I drive across the land on business I will find myself addressing an imagined jury.

During the trial the final argument file is with me at council table. I will slip in notes as the inspiration comes while I listen to a witness, a statement made by opposing counsel, or a comment by the judge.

The organization of the final argument is made many weeks before the trial. It will be edited and altered and added to, to be sure. But its basic form will have developed as a part of the overall preparation of the case. When I walk into the courtroom, on the first day of trial, I could make my final argument then and there. Between the beginning of the trial and the moment the judge nods to me to begin my final argument, all of the ideas and thoughts that will end up in my argument will have been gathered in my final argument file.

In the same way that I write out my opening, I also write every word of my closing. The argument has become fully embedded in me. Although I will take the notes to the podium, I will rarely refer to them. I have not memorized the argument. Instead, the argument has taken on a life of its own. It will direct me once I begin to speak. I will find myself giving arguments with words and supporting metaphors that I had never thought of—not until the very moment they are delivered to the jury. The argument, if it is unleashed, if it is trusted, will create itself. But it has been built and nourished over many months. It has become like a living creature. Preparation gave it life. Once it has been formed it moves on its own, creates on its own, and finally comes to its own climax and asks for justice with an indomitable power.

Approaching the final argument. The final argument is not a rehashing of evidence. It is not a summary, witness by witness, recounting what each witness has said. True, we will talk about the testimony of some witnesses, both theirs and ours, but what a witness may have said or what an exhibit may have proved are but threads woven into the final argument.

The argument *is* an argument, the reasoning that supports justice, the creation of the whole aura of rightness that shines down on our case. But there can be no demand for justice until we ourselves feel the ethical anger, the pain, the loss, the righteous indignation.

If we do not know how it is to be Bill Day, a crippled man, a once healthy, happy worker who is now confined to a wheelchair, who cannot feed himself or go to the bathroom or even brush his teeth, we cannot make a final argument. If we do not know what it is to be June Bailey, the mother of a tiny girl, little Sharon, who was burned severely over most of her tender body as a result of the explosion of a pipeline and then died of her injuries, we can never make a final argument. If we have never been to the prison in which the state wishes to cage our client, never seen how it is to lie down to sleep in a six-foot concrete cell where our head nearly touches the toilet stool, we can never make a final argument. The approach to the final argument is to become the victim, to be the accused, to understand the human issues that demand justice.

We remember: *Justice is a feeling.* It is born of a need for retribution that comes bursting out of the deepest recesses of the human condition, pain that has been fueled by loss, or fear, or depravation, and that is responded to within the limits of our meager ability to provide it. No amount of money damages can bring back the health of Bill Day. A steamship full of money can never stand for the loss of little Sharon. We can never restore the dignity, the lost peace of mind, and the permanently damaged psyche that those wrongfully charged with crimes experience. We who are charged with the impossible task of obtaining justice do the best we can with limited tools—a money judgment for those who have been injured, a march to freedom out the courtroom door for those who have been wrongfully accused. But this is not complete justice. Complete justice could be realized only if we had the power to take our clients back in time before the injury occurred, if we could erase the mutilation, the psychic damage, and put death aside.

Thoughts behind our arguments for justice. As we know, *justice is a myth.* It cannot be defined. It most often cannot be delivered. What is justice for one can be injustice for another. Justice is the gift of the most compassionate and wise. Yet it always falls short. The victim's family, whose member has been murdered, cannot experience justice when the guilty is executed. The involuntary eternal sleep the murderer is provided when he experiences the executioner's needle cannot assuage the grief of those who have lost their loved ones to the murderer. The state's murdering the murderer in the false name of justice will likely only intensify their injury.

How do those who have lost their life's savings at the hands of a corporate thief experience justice when the prosecutors make their plea bargains with the thief—all of which will be of little comfort to the penniless in their old age? The state cannot provide justice to victims.

Most often those who commit crimes are the product of the state's failure, the sad offspring of poverty and prejudice. How does the state dare attempt to deliver justice for the crimes of a person who, from the moment he was born, was himself unjustly punished? As a child he was as innocent as our own. Yet his very birth was a punishment. His life has been a punishment, because the child was deprived of the simplest human rights—the right to be respected, to be loved, to be protected, the right even to experience minimum shelter and nourishment.

I think of two bassinets side by side in the hospital nursery. Two babies have been born on the same day. One goes home to a family such as ours, one in which he will receive all the love and attention and every advantage we can bestow. He is sent to the best schools and plays all the sports, the doting father at Little League, and all the rest. He engages in all the activities we believe precious children should experience to become healthy, useful citizens.

The other child goes home to a three-story walk-up filled with filth, a half-dozen other dirty children, and a drugged-out mother. He is neglected and often goes hungry, is left alone, and is injured and rejected. He soon learns the worthlessness of human life, and his only visions of success are the drug dealers on the corner. He was born as innocent as our own children. Our children are rewarded in their innocence with the best we could provide. He was punished in his with the worst that could be laid on him. Man commits no worse crime than punishing the innocent.

Let me have my arguments: How dare the state punish those who are the products of the state's own neglect, its own failures? The state can build more prisons, but it cannot provide decent schools and nurturing, protective environments for its innocent children. Most of the criminals who line the walls of our prisons are the product of a failed system, a system that has cared more about war and profit and the domination of the world than about its innocent babes. But it is the same state that points its long, white, accusatory finger at this once-innocent child, now grown up as the criminal defendant, and demands that he be further punished for his crimes, when the original crime was the state's. It is difficult to understand the concept of justice when it is injustice that causes too many crimes in the first place, the victims of which now petition the same state to deliver them justice.

But at last we understand. The state is not actually interested in preventing crime, otherwise the state, being fully capable, would take such steps as are necessary to reduce crime by fighting the virulent diseases that cause it—such as poverty and lack of opportunity. We know that the state cannot deliver justice, no matter how many of its miscreant citizens it executes or imprisons. The state punishes the crimes of its people in order to retain an orderly society. An orderly society is necessary for those in power to retain power. If crime is rampant, if the streets are not safe, if those who are the victims of crime personally undertake to avenge the crime, the resulting chaos would threaten those in power to hold on to their power. The United States houses more of its citizens in prison than any other nation in the world. We have more African-American men in prison than in our universities. Can we do better?

I am not in favor of anarchy, nor do I believe that we ought not have a system governed by a rule of law. I believe in the elusive goal of justice and hope for its rendition, as inadequate as it is. But the notion of justice is complex. It demands that we consider it beyond the simplistic idea that Joe shot Harold, and therefore Joe should be locked into the gas chamber and the nozzle turned on. Those who suffer from a disease are not taken out and shot—not in this society. But in a rich society such as ours, much of our crime is a disease, the base cause of which is the simple need of its citizens—nourishment, shelter, education, and an equality of respect and justice.

Seven steps for winning the final argument. I have never been one to rigorously follow rules. I think, instead, that we have a duty to break rules whenever possible without injury to others, because rules most often become a substitute for creativity. Rules are like the paint-by-numbers paintings that were so popular years ago. If people can be taught to follow rules, they need not explore their own unique and perfect potential.

But the expectation of a how-to book is to tell folks how to do it—often step by step. So I wondered as I began to write this chapter, how do I organize the final argument? I proceed, usually in an unconscious way born of many years of experience. Now I've tried to bring those steps to the surface of my own consciousness, to consider them step by step, with the hope that they will help you with an approach of your own on how to put together your final argument.

Step 1: Identify the hero and the villain. As we have seen, in every novel and movie, indeed, in every trial the story centers around the conflict between the villain and the hero. In the courtroom we need to identify who occupies these roles. Our client, yes, we, are the good guys and our opponents the scoundrels. Successful lawyers are usually subliminally aware of this dynamic, and both sides instinctively vie for the position of hero. Whoever emerges as the hero will likely be the victor. We do not side with villains. In our final argument, then, we want to cast ourselves in the role of the hero, the humble hero to be sure, the kindly hero who smiles through his tears, who has been courageous, steadfast, and true, and at the same time to cast the other side as the uncaring, greedy, insensitive villain who exercises his power over the weak and the helpless for profit. In the criminal case we are the wrongfully accused, or the grossly misunderstood. We have become a victim ourselves, and the prosecution is callous, cruel, and vindictive.

The jurors may be the heroes. In every case we empower the jurors as heroes and cast them in the role of rescuing champions who refuse to deliver the helpless defendant to the state to imprison or to kill, or who deliver a money-verdict justice to the injured plaintiff against the will of the wrongdoer.

Revisiting the voir dire and opening statement. By now we begin to realize how important the first two segments of the trial are—the *voir dire* and the opening statement. Justice to a poor family who has been evicted from their home by the bank may be quite different than justice to the banker whose loan to the poor family remains delinquent. As we choose jurors in the *voir dire,* and later tell our story in the opening, it becomes apparent how critical the selection of jurors can be. We search for persons who will identify their heroes according to the same values we cherish and for persons who define justice as do we. To the banker, justice is the timely payment of the loan he made in good faith. To the poor family, justice is some magical legal reprieve from being cast into homelessness. To jurors sympathetic with the tenets of sound business, justice is the enforcement of a promise, the consequences of which, although sad, were the risks accepted by the borrower at the time of the loan. To jurors who have lain awake at night worrying how they were going to manage their indebtedness, any rationalization to prevent the bank's foreclosure will serve justice. As we have seen, that which is justice to one is often injustice to another.

We do not attach ourselves to heroes we do not trust. Oftentimes one of the lawyers becomes the hero—the other lawyer the villain. I have discussed the notion that jurors tend to identify one of the lawyers as their guide through the forest of litigation. And as the trial proceeds, the parties themselves often re-cede into the background and the attorneys become the focus. We see this when a corporation is represented in the courtroom. The lawyer tends to be-come the corporate entity. He speaks saying, "*We* are so sorry for the injuries the plaintiff has suffered" (though the corporation cannot feel), and he goes on speaking in the first person plural, to the end that the jurors, even the judge, begin to see the corporation as Mr. Heartfelt, the corporate lawyer.

In both civil and criminal cases the parties in the trial begin to fade away, because for days only the lawyers may be heard from, while their clients for the most part remain silent. Day after day, as the lawyers argue and question the witnesses, the lawyers gradually become the litigants, so that, as I have so often emphasized, the credibility of the lawyer is all he has—and, at last, all the client will also have. In the courtroom we may encounter the most honest client who ever drew breath, but if his lawyer has lost his credibility, so, too, the client will be seen as a bird of the same feather.

In sum, before we can make the final argument we must identify the par-ties, the heroes, the villain—there may be more than one of each. But there will always be the star, and there will likely be the one who is principally re-sponsible for the injuries or the failure of justice—the villain.

Step 2: Become the victim. We know we cannot make the final argument without having become the victim. It's only when we've felt the injuries and the pain of the injured that we can begin to understand the stakes. Often the victim may be more than one person. In a civil case for personal injuries, the victim may not only be the child who has been injured at birth by a careless doctor, but the parents of the child are victims as well. Their burden will be to care for the child for the rest of their lives.

The victims in a wrongful-death case are not only the deceased but the sur-viving heirs, the husband or wife, the orphaned children, or the parents who have lost their child. In the criminal case the victims may occupy both sides of the case. In a murder case the victims include both the murdered as well as his family. But what about the family of an accused who will be put to death or imprisoned for long periods of time? The murderer's family is often as inno-cent as the heirs of the person he killed.

What justice for the victim? To understand the life of the victim, we must understand what justice is available to the victim. In judgments against the negligent corporation that bestows death or injury on innocent citizens, that corporation will only be made to pay money out of its coffers. In the criminal case punishment is often seen as justice. Punishment, of course, implies that the person punished will be taught something. We justly punish a child for his wrongdoing, hoping that the child will reform. We dock a worker his pay for his misadventures on the job, hoping that he will not repeat them. But I have never been able to understand how we can teach a corporation much, unless, of course, it is required to give enough of its green blood to cause its management (the members of which are usually immune from punishment) to take notice of its diminishing bottom line. And how, pray tell, do we teach the murderer not to murder by murdering him ourselves through the executioner's needle?

In the civil case justice will be the money it takes to provide the necessities the victim will require, and to pay in dollars for the pain and suffering he has endured. Still, the equation is never balanced. Would we rather be a man sitting for the rest of his life in a wheelchair with ten million dollars in the bank for his loss of enjoyment of life, or a healthy man who is so poor he must sleep under the bridge? Justice always comes up short. And no matter how many murderers we kill, we know that their moldering in the prison cemetery will not bring back the victim's loved one. Yet victims are entitled to the best justice that the system can offer. When the system falls short, not only does it fail its citizens, it also exposes itself to its eventual demise.

What about the injured person, say, the mother, whose child was killed by a negligent driver who was insured and is now being defended by the insurance company? Call the driver Blatty. Preparatory for our final argument let us walk in the mother's shoes. We have done a psychodrama and we have become the mother. As someone said, the longest journey we will ever take is from the mind to the heart.

To this mother, this strange process called a trial is like walking into a bad dream where the people in the room speak a foreign language, where they seem oblivious to her, this person who quietly sits at counsel table slowly disintegrating internally.

She has been admonished by her lawyers to say nothing and never to cry out. She struggles with a nightmarish potpourri of grief and anger and a sense of helplessness. The attorneys are arguing over things that make no sense to her, about other cases, rules, and evidence. And some of the witnesses are lying. Her own lawyer seems unconcerned about her misery and the insanity of the whole draconian drama unfolding in front of her. People are screaming and pointing their fingers at her and each other, the judge is pounding his gavel, and all she wants to do is to run out of the place. This is justice? No. It is a trial.

This mother, this plaintiff, as she is called, senses that she is being used. Without her there could be no trial. Without her, her lawyer could make no fee. Without her, the defense attorneys would likely be in ragged suits bulging at the knees, instead of their sleek, well-pressed designer clothes that cost more than the old jalopy she was driving when the drunk, Blatty, ran across the road and killed her daughter. What is there to argue about? Yes, she is being used. They do not care about her—not deeply. They care about the money, about their reputations, about winning. They have their personal agendas. They seem barely aware that she is in the courtroom.

No one has spoken to her for most of the day. The judge has never looked at her. The witnesses do not talk to her but to the lawyers. The jurors look at her from time to time with dark, skeptical faces, as if they believe she is there only to enrich herself. She is embarrassed when they look at her. They must think she is an evil hussy who wants money for a dead daughter. They are right. How can she ask for money for her dead child? It denigrates her child and reduces her to a money-grubbing bitch who would turn her dead child into dollars.

But she had gone this far. She couldn't let Blatty get away with killing Polly and pay nothing. She wanted him to pay, to go to jail, to suffer as she has suffered, but her lawyer said that the guy was insured by a national insurance company and that he would never have to pay a penny of his own money. Somehow the cops forgot to take a blood-alcohol. The driver claimed he had drifted off to sleep momentarily. Swore he wasn't drunk. And her own lawyer said the defendant would never be charged with anything worse than negligent homicide.

She wept for months. Once she beat at the walls in frustration. Her husband felt grief too, but not like hers. No, he was tough and he tried to comfort her, but no one knows what it's like to be a mother who has lost her child, except a mother who has lost her child.

They sent her to grief counseling, and she learned it was all right to have her feelings, to be angry and hurt, and to experience those feelings of help-lessness. For months she was unable to sleep. She lost her appetite. Her hus-band said she was wasting away and that she had to straighten up and face the loss. In the meantime she was told that her neighbor recently saw the guy who killed her daughter, that Blatty, at the bowling alley drinking beer and having a good time.

She and her lawyer were in and out of court for nearly two years with all the experts' depositions and the motions filed by the insurance company. The insurance company lawyer tried to beat her lawyer with a bunch of technical garbage that made no sense to her. The insurance company attorney, a smiling prig, asked her a lot of questions when he took her deposition. He made her cry and then pretended he was sorry. He wanted to know how much money she wanted for her dead Polly and her lawyer told her not to answer. She felt like some sort of money-sucking Dracula, and his questions weren't fair. He tried to make her look like she didn't remember, or that she was on his client's side of the road, or that she could have avoided the accident—that it was her fault! Her fault that little Polly was dead! He tried to make her feel guilty.

Her lawyer said she hadn't handled it very well in her deposition. She knew she didn't. She cried, and then she hollered at the insurance company lawyer—said he was trying to make a liar out of her. She was ashamed of her-self afterward. Her lawyer said that if she did that on the stand in the trial she would lose the case for them.

As she sat in the courtroom she was afraid. What if she couldn't control her anger? What if she broke down crying in a public courtroom? Blatty was star-ing at her. She couldn't bear to look at him. She couldn't look at the jury. She didn't know how to look. Pretty soon her lawyer would be calling her to the stand and she would be required to testify about the accident, and about little Polly. She wished her husband were there, but he had to work. They had bills. Funeral bills. Hospital bills for her and Polly before she died. And since the accident—it wasn't an accident, but everybody called it an accident, even her own lawyer—since the accident she had been unable to work and had quit her job. They needed the money.

Yes, just before trial the insurance company offered them a settlement—her lawyer said a hundred thousand dollars. Then the judge ordered that everyone get together in a mediation and try to work it out. She had gone, and the defendant was there along with that smiley insurance company lawyer, and all that happened was that the company offered another hundred thousand dollars, total of two, which just made her own lawyer mad. He said it was pathetic—that they were trying to get away with another murder. They had already killed little Polly, he said, and now they wanted to sneak out of the case for a measly couple hundred thousand, when the case was worth a couple of million. He pointed out to her all of the cases around the country where little girls were bringing two million and over. They were trying to cheapen Polly.

She went home and talked about it with her husband and he said they should leave it to their lawyer to decide. He knew more about this than they did. She cried a lot more and couldn't sleep, she kept hearing her lawyer say that little girls were worth a couple of million—like the price of a racehorse or something, as if her little Polly was a thing that could be bought and sold on the auction block. She wanted justice. She wanted Blatty to pay. She wanted someone to feel like she felt, lost, drowning in grief, helpless, lost. She felt like her life was over, and that the only justice she would ever get would be the insults they were throwing at her in court, the lies in that awful place, the coldness of an impersonal law that never knew her, never knew her husband, never knew little Polly, and never had the slightest desire to do so.

Not once had the judge even smiled at her. The court officials, the clerk, the court reporter, and the bailiff never spoke to her. The jurors passed her in the hallway and never even nodded in her direction, never looked at her.

Now she was called to the witness stand. She had worn her black dress, the one she wore to bury her mother, and then little Polly. She put on no makeup because her lawyer said she shouldn't look too pretty, even if she was pretty. She never believed him when he said that. She hadn't been pretty a day since Polly died. She walked to the stand on her low-heeled black shoes and tried to settle into the chair and look right and proper. People were staring at her, she knew that. They were going to judge her now, to come to a conclusion as to what kind of a woman she is, what kind of a mother she'd been, whether she lied, whether she had caused Polly's death, whether she was just trying to take advantage of a tragic situation for a bunch of rotten money. But her lawyer told her that money was all the justice she could get. Just cold, dead money, she thought, for a cold, dead child—that's all the law provided.

And she knew the lawyer was going to ask her a lot of questions about little Polly, what she did, how they laughed with each other and played together— actually played together like little children. She would have to share the most intimate things with this jury, with utter strangers, about their relationship, the prayers they said at night, the things little Polly wanted to be when she grew up, the secret ambitions she had for her child—maybe to be a great scientist or a doctor, or someone who could make the world better—a teacher maybe. Yes, maybe a teacher.

Little Polly was bright as new pennies. The teachers said she was a very smart and lovely child. And she thought about God. If there was a God, a loving God, why had the child been taken from her? What sins had she committed, what wrong so terrible that she should suffer this loss? At times she had wanted to die, when she had thought about taking all of the pills the doctor had given her. What was the use? She had been put on this earth as a mother. Her child had been taken from her. Perhaps, in God's eyes she didn't deserve to live. Perhaps if she died she could be with little Polly again and they would be happy forever. She mentioned that once to her husband and the next thing she knew her lawyer and her husband had her in the office of a shrink who thought he knew all about what she was going through.

Now, on the stand, her lawyer would drag her through the whole horror again. Yes, she had to tell the jury. She was the only one who could. She had to tell them how it happened. She had to do it for Polly. And worse, she had to tell them what she saw when the crash was over—how she saw the blood covering the child's face and her long blonde locks soaked in it. She had tried to get the child out of the car, but her own leg was broken and her ribs as well. She reached over for the child and all she could do was scream. She couldn't move and her baby was breathing mouthfuls of blood that came out in terrible bubbles. Then she passed out and didn't remember anything after that until she came to in the hospital. Her husband was there, and the first thing she asked was how is little Polly, and her husband just looked down at his hands and didn't answer her.

She also doesn't remember much about what she said on the witness stand. It was as if she were a talking mannequin and that what she said was in a foreign language that no one understood. She remembered the insurance lawyer, still smiling, asking her questions. She answered them as truthfully as she could. She was crying sometimes. She was unable to understand what the catch was in some of his questions, little nuances that she knew must be there but that she couldn't decipher under the pressure. She never looked at the jury. She couldn't. Her husband would never cry like this.

Then she had to listen to the lies of the so-called experts for the insurance company who tried to make it look like she was on the wrong side of the road. Then Blatty got up and lied, and she saw one of the jurors nodding as if he believed him. The next day the judge read a bunch of legal stuff to the jury, and after that the lawyers got up and argued the case. Her lawyer was first.

Before we can argue effectively we must become the mother, to join her at the heart level. It takes skill and caring to get there. How must it be to lose the child, to have people blame you, to have people suggest there is shame in suing for money for a dead baby, to have to relive the horror of your child's violent, bloody death? This is the stuff the jury must hear from the mother's lawyer who has tried to live this case with her. And the jury will also hear the lawyer's own frustration—that the law of mere mortals can do nothing more than award money to these grieving parents. That's all the justice there is.

In a way, it has become an unholy war between devastated parents and the insurance company. A fund exists. The insurance company calls it "a reserve" set aside for this case. The fund is supposed to represent Polly's life, the reserve the insurance company clings to so desperately as if its own nonlife depended on it. If Polly's parents decide not to go to court the insurance company would simply keep its profit—profit over the death of their child.

In the courtroom the parents' lawyer will never be permitted to mention that the defendant was insured. The jury may believe Blatty is represented by the lawyer he hired out of his own pocket and that he is only a working stiff, as are most of the members of the jury. It's the unfortunate law in every state in the union that insurance can never be mentioned—a lie the law foists on the jury. The insurance companies enjoy better laws than the people. But that's another issue.

By employing the methods we have taught here we have become the mother, the victim. We have felt how it must feel to be the victim. And that experience becomes a part of our final argument. Perhaps some of it will be delivered in the first person, as if the lawyer is little Polly's mother. I can hear that part of the argument as it begins:

"Ladies and gentlemen: This is a mother who has lost her child. (The lawyer stands behind the seated mother with his hands on her shoulders.) What is that loss? Is it money? It is a search for justice, for all of the justice the law can give. How does it feel to be seated here, your child in the grave, the jurors looking at you, the smiling Mr. Heartfelt questioning you, suggesting you caused your own daughter's death, when you and everyone, even Mr. Heartfelt, know that that is a lie, a horrible lie? If this mother could speak her feelings at this moment we would hear her say, 'I have had to relive the hell of this case all over again. I had to see little Polly's happy face turn to blood. I have had to relive being trapped in that automobile. I am there right now. I am screaming, trying to get the door open. . . . ' " And the rest of her story, as we have experienced it together, will come out in the final argument in the first person so that the jury, too, will relive it.

In the criminal case. Let us remember: The human emotions that are felt by the victims in a criminal case, say, the feelings of a mother whose child has been abducted and murdered, or the feelings of a woman who has been assaulted and raped, are not substantially different from those felt by Polly's mother. The need for vengeance, for retribution, for justice are part of the human composition. But we are defending the alleged criminal—that is to say, we are there to see that the defendant gets a fair trial and that his rights are preserved. Why do we want to know anything about the victim in the criminal case?

Each of the jurors has likely been a victim of some crime—a break-in, a theft, an assault. Jurors are afraid of criminals, and the most expeditious way of protecting themselves as potential victims is to do away with the accused, guilty or innocent, by seeing him to the gates of the penitentiary as quickly as possible. So we must become the jurors, the surrogate victims in any criminal case.

Employing the methods we have learned here by reversing roles with the victims, our argument to the jurors on behalf of an innocent client might sound like this:

"I cannot tell you, nor can we ever fully feel the pain of having a loved one

240

murdered. It leaves a scar so deep and so intractable that it will never heal, not if Mr. and Mrs. Schoolcroft live a hundred years. The horror of having a loved one taken from us by the hands of a fiend is something we cannot understand. There is no pure time to grieve, because our grief is overlaid with shock and anger and a need for justice. A part of us wants to kill back. But we cannot. And we would not.

"We cannot sleep without seeing the face of our murdered child asking why this has happened to her. We cannot go about our business, because everything we see or touch reminds us of her. We cannot turn on the television, because our case is being discussed publicly as if it is some kind of spectacle to entertain the viewers. We are ripped apart with our emotions. There is no place to go, to hide, to relieve ourselves of the sight, the horror.

"But there is another victim here, and that's Jimmy, the defendant. He is charged with this horrible crime. It is a crime that the evidence shows he did not commit. We have all been made victims here, you, the jurors, who have been victimized by the state's false charges against Jimmy, the Schoolcrofts by the horrible loss of their beloved child, and Jimmy by being charged with a crime he did not commit because the state failed to do its job honestly, fully, and competently. The state wants to solve this case and to close its files as do we. But we cannot let them do so by victimizing all of us, including the Schoolcrofts who would be the first to object with all of their hearts if they knew that the state's files should be closed by the persecution of an innocent man."

This argument might continue with living a day in the life of Jimmy, who has been confined in jail for seventeen months awaiting trial. It will recount his own horror (that can be fairly inferred from the facts) at being charged with a crime he did not commit. The argument will discuss his terror at being confined for the rest of his life, or even executed, when he is innocent, and his sense of helplessness. (Many states do not permit lawyers to argue the punishment that awaits a person found guilty of the charge brought against him. But jurors know, and the issue can be approached in a general way so that the specifics of the punishment are not set out.) We have tried to live the client's case, to understand his fear. And part of the argument in that regard might sound like this:

"How would it be to go to sleep at night on a dirty, hard mattress in a steel

241

box called a cell and dream of the executioner's needle and to awaken in a cold sweat knowing that it is not just a dream, that it is the reality awaiting him if he is not able to convince a jury of his innocence?" Perhaps there will be objections here. Strangely, in many states the law does not want jurors to consider the consequences of their decision. The same law demands that we fully consider the consequences of our acts, failing which we may be held responsible by the law.

Step 3: Feel the righteous indignation, the ethical anger that motivates us. We have traveled to a painful place, to the heart place of our clients. How we got there may depend on who we are and what resources we have. Perhaps we have arrived there through days of attending to our client, from hours of listening. Out of our listening skill we will be able to hear not only what little Polly's mother has said, but what she has not said, what she is afraid to say, what she has blocked from her mind in order to simply survive another day. We have reversed roles with her. By these methods we have grown to understand her, and she us. We have said to the mother, "Let me be you for a moment. I see Blatty's car coming at me. What do I feel? What do I say? What do I hear?"

If we are the Schoolcrofts, the victims in the criminal case, we feel the same, a grief that is also stained blood red with anger. If we are Jimmy and we are innocent, we feel fear first, and then anger and frustration that we cannot escape from this trap. A fog of justice denied, of righteous indignation covers all of our feelings. It is an ethical anger. And our anger is the fuel of our passion for justice that moves the final argument, that forms the tone of the argument, that touches and energizes us in our delivery. We can be gentle, if it is appropriate. But let us think of this energy as *the empowering anger of justice.* We will not lose our sense of reason, but justice, at last, demands retribution. Our need for justice will become the theme of the argument and will set its tone; and having felt it, it will erupt in an argument that will connect to the jurors' native need for justice as well.

Step 4: Determine the justice you want. In little Polly's case the final argument might sound as follows.

"We know we cannot get justice. The only justice the law offers for little Polly's parents is a fund of money. It sits over there on the desk of Mr. Heartfelt. Imagine it as a large box. (I might pick up a cardboard box and take it over to the defense table and set it there.) Imagine that this box is filled with bills of a large denomination. In the law it is the fund that represents the life of Polly. How much is in the box? You will have to tell us. I would suppose the box contains five million dollars. Perhaps more. Perhaps ten. You will decide. This is how I imagine the justice in this case—sadly, the only justice there is. But Mr. Heartfelt's clients want to keep all that's in the box.

"What are little Polly's parents to do here? Their child has been killed by Mr. Blatty over there, this child who was suddenly smashed so that what seconds before was a beautiful, happy child is converted into blood and horror and death. Mr. Blatty was drunk. The evidence is clear on that. He doesn't even try to deny it because he can't—he's a drunk driver who ran his car onto the wrong side of the road and killed a little girl. Had he done it with a club, we would call it murder. But he has done it with something thousands of times more deadly than a club—a car that weighs more than a ton and becomes a steel club traveling at eighty miles an hour, the force of which is nearly incalculable. He was the killer. His car was the weapon. Yet the only justice we can ask for here is what's in the box. No one goes to jail in this case. Why? Well, his honor says we cannot go into that.

"The law is so helpless. It cannot bring little Polly back, not even for five minutes. If it could, her parents would say to the defense, "Keep the box. Keep all of the money in the box. Keep it all! Just give us back little Polly for five more minutes! One smile from her, the feel of her arms around the neck of her daddy, her cheek against her mother for five minutes—but the law is helpless to provide little Polly for even five minutes. It can only give money.

"So what are Polly's parents to do? Should they say, well, Mr. Blatty, since the law cannot give us back little Polly, not even for five minutes—since there is no adequate justice here, well, just keep the box. Keep the money that stands for Polly. You want it so badly. Well keep it. Should they say that? Should they permit Mr. Blatty to not only kill their daughter but to be enriched by keeping the fund that is in the box? Are they not entitled to receive the best justice the law can provide, even if it so piteously inadequate?

"And the guilt here! Ah, yes, the guilt! How can parents take money for a dead child? That is the guilt that is laid on Polly's parents. You'll not hear Mr. Heartfelt say so in so many words, but he will likely remind you that these parents are here to get money, as if what they are about is shameful. But he will not say that it is wrong for the defense, for Mr. Blatty's side of the case, to keep that money. How do parents feel who have lost their child, to take money in place of their child when there is no other justice but a fund of money? They feel guilty. But should they?

"I have not heard Mr. Blatty even say he was sorry. Not a single whispered word. Not a bowed head. Not a tear of remorse in his eye. Just the smirk, the arrogant swagger. This man has done nothing but desperately clutch onto that box of money by launching the defense he has in this case—a false defense that he knows is false.

"I feel sorry for him. He must hurt terribly inside, the killer of an innocent child. It must be hard for him to face it. It must be hard for him to look over at Polly's parents and to say what he has said. He must be a very miserable man, to have first killed and then tried to cover it up with his denials and with the expert he has hired in this case to undermine the testimony of the patrolman. I am sorry for you, Mr. Blatty, and I have no hatred against you. Only sadness that you could not walk into this courtroom and admit what you did. Perhaps you cannot bear to face the truth. I can understand that. The burden of guilt you must bear must be horrible. Yet, in the end, your denial of the facts, yes, even your attempt to cover the facts with the testimony of your expert, Dr. Fix, can be no substitute for the truth, and, in the end, cannot assuage your guilt.

"The defense in this case has not tried to make life better for little Polly's parents. Instead they have tried to transfer their own guilt for Polly's death onto her mother, who was driving the family car. The defense has hired an expert here to come into this court, an expert who took an oath, and who tried to show that the patrolman was wrong when he fixed the point of impact clearly in the lane of Polly's mother. It is one thing for a drunk driver to kill a little girl. But what are decent people to do when the drunk hires the likes of Dr. Fix to come in here and tell you that Polly's mother lies, that the patrolman lies, that the experts we called are all wrong, and that the truth in this case is the story Dr. Fix, this so-called reconstruction expert, has concocted?

"Justice has many facets. It is not just money. Justice will also be a verdict that tells Polly's parents that the suffering, the grief, the pain, the inexorable ripping of their very hearts and minds has been understood by this jury. You can turn them out if you want. You have the power. You can say with your verdict, we do not know, nor do we care how it has been to sit in this courtroom and hear the evil mendacities that have been hurled at these parents—the unspeakable transfer of guilt. You can say that you do not care to concern yourself with the pain that comes from seeing one's child killed in front of one's eyes, the shock, the horror of it and then have the drunk over there blame the mother for her own child's death. That is the most despicable assault that one human being can make on another.

"Justice speaks in many ways, and although the verdict here can only be in money, your verdict can say that these parents were heard, that there were other human beings on this jury who understood.

"We are not here asking for sympathy. No one wants sympathy. We want only understanding. We want to know that somewhere out there on the face of this earth are humans who understand the pain, the helplessness, yes, the anger that these parents have endured, endured as decent law-abiding citizens, endured silently, endured without aggression toward the man who killed their child, that they have instead expected the law to do its duty, and that you, as jurors, the spokespersons for the law, will do yours and return the full justice that the law allows."

We can immediately see that the specific facts of the case have not been repeated. They have been used as reference points in the argument. There may be further facts that should be argued that show that the defendant's reconstruction expert is wrong, that he is a hired charlatan—whatever the evidence may be in that regard, but always, the facts are but ammunition for the argument and are never to be recounted in the form of witness summaries. But throughout the argument the tone will reflect our sense of ethical anger, and honestly delivered, our argument will infect the jury and create in its members a powerful need to provide justice.

Step 5: Ask the jury to give you the justice you want. We know the old biblical admonition: "Ask, and it shall be given to you." Whether we are talking about a jury verdict, a sale, or a proposition we present before a board or commission, we must ask for exactly what we want. Remember, when we ask for justice, it transfers the ball into the *power persons'* court, in this case, the jury, who must agree to the request, modify it, or deny it. Those who leave justice to the *power persons'* whim, who are afraid to ask, have already been defeated. If we do not ask, we will likely not receive. If we are too timid to lay out our prayer for justice, why should the jurors do it for us? Being candid about our expectation of justice is merely a continuation of the policy of honesty we have learned to adopt in our presentation. Lawyers ask me, "How do you get those big verdicts?" I reply, "I ask for the money. I simply ask for it."

In this case I might say to the jurors, "How much money is enough, here? We can load a freight train full of money and never get little Polly back. The defense knows that. And they will agree wholeheartedly with the argument that since money can do no justice, well, why give any? Yes, sometimes I feel that way too. What is the use? Wouldn't we all be better off just to let drunks kill our little children than to try to get the only justice that is available to us?

"I think about that a lot. But money speaks. I do not want to bargain for Polly as if she were a car sitting on a cheap used-car lot. I have said the fund in this case is at least five million. It's in the box over there. I don't want just a part of little Polly. You could give me half a million for an arm. Another half a million for her smile and her loving eyes. I don't want justice that stands for just part of her. I want it all. All of the money that stands for her.

"Sometimes I think I have asked for too little. I am afraid and I wish I weren't so afraid. But I am afraid that people will think that I am taking advantage of a horrible situation here, that people might say, 'Look at that man, Spence, asking for five million dollars for a dead child. That is vulgar.'

"But the killing, was that vulgar? The most disrespect that can be given to the human race is to kill an innocent child and then claim it is vulgar to seek full damages.

"I think of the world's most valuable painting, the Mona Lisa by Leonardo da Vinci. Its value is hundreds of millions of dollars. But it is merely a painting created by a man on canvas with paint. If some villain came into the Louvre, the museum that houses this painting, and slashed it beyond the ability of anyone to repair it, if they killed the painting so to speak, no one would argue that its full value shouldn't be recovered from the culprit. But what if someone destroys the perfect work of our creator? Was not Polly the perfect work of God? Should I be embarrassed, yes, even afraid, to ask for a sum that stands reasonably in this society for her? I ask you not for part of Polly. Don't cut her in half for me. I want all of her. All of her."

In the criminal case we might argue:

"What do we want here? We want out of this horrible concrete and steel trap where nothing but hatred and vileness grows, where the sound of birds is replaced by the raging of criminals, and the sound of the voices of little children is drowned out by the laughter of the insane and the clanging of steel on steel as the prison doors are slammed shut. We want freedom. We are not interested in part freedom. There is no such thing. A person is either free or not. We do not want part justice. People who get part justice are caged along with the guilty. We do not want to bargain. Jimmy is either innocent or not. We do not want injustice. Injustice will be leaving the smear and the stink of guilt on Jimmy that can only be washed away by your verdict of not guilty."

Step 6. Create a vision of a better person creating a better tomorrow. By the time we have lived but a few decades we soon realize this is not a perfect world. People cheat. Corporations and politicians, their lackeys, are powerful and in control. People are careless. Government is filled with bureaucrats who exercise their power wrongfully. Prosecutors want power and sometimes persecute the innocent. Greed and profit trump caring. It's dangerous out there. People's rights are in jeopardy. Things are not fair. Injustice is rife like the weeds in the lawn. And because we are who we are, most of us suffer a quixotic fixation of doing good and righting wrongs. Were it not so, I should not have written this book and perhaps you would not have read it.

Every case is more than a case. Most judges and jurors are at least subliminally aware of their need to make things better. Most judges will confess that they believed when they took on their robes that they could make their community better by ascending the bench.

It is we who provide the vision of a better tomorrow. It is we who empower the jury and the judge. The sixth step in the final argument is to create a vision of a better tomorrow. Martin Luther King Jr. had his dream. Christ made his promises of a place beyond that he would prepare for his followers. Our founders had their visions of freedom. Today, both Republicans and Democrats have theirs. The talent of a true leader is to create the visions that empower us. Their dreams, their visions of a better time to come become ours. Without such visions the history of the human race would be locked in stagnation. So we must provide a vision for the jury.

But there is perhaps an even more compelling need that hunts us down like hounds on a hare. We have that bothersome need for ourselves to become worthy, to feel the joy and the pride of having done right. Ebenezer Scrooge ultimately listened to his noisy inner voice that also commanded charity. The human race engages in the most abominable of atrocities. It conducts wars against the innocent and destroys the earth for profit, but all of our cruelty and viciousness is for the announced goal of doing good. In the courtroom we will create a vision that will empower the jury to do right, not only for those who follow, but in the fulfillment of the juror's own need to become worthy. In little Polly's case we might hear ourselves arguing:

"Factually, little Polly's case is simple—a drunk runs onto the wrong side of the road, smashes into an oncoming car, and kills an innocent little girl. What do we, as jurors, want to say about this? We have the power. Justice is in our hands—today, and yes, tomorrow in countless other cases of innocent mothers and fathers and children being killed. Do we recognize our power? Do we understand that in a nation whose laws are based on precedent that there will be an endless line of innocent children, yes, innocent people who will look back on this case for guidance? Do we realize that jurors in the future will need the courage that you can provide by your verdict here to bring uncompromised justice to many other innocent little Pollys? Do we understand that our verdict today may save some children in the future by making the killing of innocent human beings so expensive that society itself will take more urgent steps to prevent the placing of such a deadly weapon as an automobile into the hands of a drunk?

"Most of us do not understand our power. We live so vividly in the present we have little understanding as to what the consequences of our acts will be in the future. I think of the founders of our Constitution, who, by their vision, are responsible for our being together today. But for them there would be no jury, no trial of the kind we have experienced. But for them there would not be twelve ordinary citizens deciding what is right and what is wrong. As they met on that hot Philadelphia summer, to sweat and argue in a poorly ventilated place we now call Constitution Hall, do we think that they foresaw us gathered here today? Did they have full understanding of the consequences of their labor, their love for freedom, their passion for justice? It was probably more likely business at hand—the need to act wisely and decisively to establish a new nation. I doubt that they could have understood that a jury would be evaluating the life of little Polly here today.

"So it is with us. We have the power to do right. We have the power to do what is just. We have the power to tell the world that drunks cannot kill our children without paying every uncompromised penny that that child stands for. It is your power. It is a power that will extend into the future to protect the innocent. Rarely do we have the opportunity in our lives to bring about important change and, by doing so, to fulfill our own destinies. Most of us are never given a chance to exercise the God-given power that is vested in each of us. It ought not be wasted. These are such rare opportunities that fate provides the chosen few."

In the criminal case the vision is of an innocent man walking out of the courtroom free. The argument could be:

"A great American said, 'I have a dream.' I have one as well. As the clerk reads your verdict, our hearts will be wildly pounding in our chests and we will be barely able to breathe.

"I dream that after your verdict has been read a great joy will erupt in this courtroom. I have a dream that when your verdict is read an indescribable, nearly godly relief will come over Jimmy and over us. He is free. And in my dream I see us all walking out of this courtroom together as free persons— you, as jurors who have done your duty, who will go home to your families knowing that you have done the right thing, and Jimmy who will walk out of this courtroom with you, also a free man, a man who can go home to his wife and his family, a man who has learned that there is still love in this world— even for a simple man such as Jimmy—and that the greatest proof of such love are two simple words, 'Not guilty.'

"I have a dream that this great American system of justice still works, and that even the humblest of us, the poorest, those of us who were forgotten both by man and by the law, can achieve justice here within these hallowed walls."

Step 7. An ending transferring the lawyer's responsibility for the client to the jury. So you are a juror, and you have heard the final arguments from the plaintiff in the civil case or the defendant in the criminal case. In both the civil and the criminal case there must be a truthful but dramatic ending, one that transfers the responsibility for our client from the lawyer to the jury. This is a story I have told many jurors in both civil and criminal cases as a way of transferring responsibility for justice from me to the jurors.

"Soon you will march out of here and into the jury room where your decision of justice will be made. Perhaps you have looked forward to this moment. Perhaps you have dreaded it—this moment when you will be called upon to pass judgment on another human being. It is a frightening time for me. In a few moments I must give up my client to you. In a few minutes I must entrust this case into your hands. I do not want to let go. I am afraid.

"What if I have not done my job well enough? What if I have failed in creating the same level of caring for little Polly and her parents (in the criminal case, Jimmy) as I care for them (him)? Yet, in the end, I trust you. But this is a hard time for me.

"Before I leave you I want to share with you a story I tell in nearly every case. It's about transferring the responsibility of the case from us, on behalf of little Polly and her parents, to you, the jury (or on behalf of Jimmy to you, the jury).

"It's a story of a wise old man and a smart-aleck boy who wanted to show up the wise old man as a fool.

"One day this boy caught a small bird in the forest. The boy had a plan. He brought the bird, cupped between his hands, to the old man. His plan was to say, 'Old man, what do I have in my hands?' to which the old man would answer, 'You have a bird, my son.' Then the boy would say, 'Old man, is the bird alive or is it dead?' If the old man said the bird was dead, the boy would open his hands and the bird would fly freely back to the forest. But if the old man said the bird was alive, then the boy would crush the little bird, and crush it, and crush it until it was dead.

"So the smart-aleck boy sauntered up to the old man and said, 'Old man, what do I have in my hands?' And the old man said, 'You have a bird, my son.' Then the boy said with a malevolent grin, 'Old man, is the bird alive or is it dead?'

"And the old man, with sad eyes, said, 'The bird is in your hands, my son.'

"And so, ladies and gentlemen of the jury, the case of little Polly (or the life of Jimmy) is in yours."

In the civil case, preparing the rebuttal first. As a young lawyer I lost an important case because I hadn't prepared a rebuttal. The purpose of rebuttal in a civil case is to show that the defense's argument is wrong, or incomplete, or not relevant. I thought, how could I prepare my rebuttal argument until I had first heard what my opponent argued?

So I was listening hard, furiously making notes. I was not only listening to his argument, but at the same time I was trying to come up with an argument to rebut it. I was attempting to make notes on both what he said and what I would say back. I began to panic. "Oh my God. I can't remember what he just said because I'm writing what he said before, and now I've got to hear the next thing that he's saying and make a note as to what my response will be," and suddenly I was lost. His argument was overwhelming me, and when I got up I was not only frightened but confused as to how to organize my last words to the jury.

If during the planning stage of our final argument we reverse roles with our opponent, as we have so often in this book, we will have anticipated nearly everything that our opponent is going to argue. If we have taken time to prepare our rebuttal argument in the quiet, it will be simply brilliant. The few points that we need to add we can add with ease. The few points we may overlook will not be important. We have been in control of our rebuttal, not our opponent, and we will win.

Listening to the opponent's argument. Over many years I have learned that the sound of the opponent's voice will tell me if he is saying something important—at least to him, and if it's not important to him it will not be important to the jury. I simply close my eyes and listen to the sound of his voice. Often his argument will be mumbled, spoken fast, delivered in technical, dull language or otherwise dumped on the jury with little or nothing to cause one to take notice. Why should we answer those arguments? By rebutting them, we call the jury's attention—probably better than our opponent has—to issues or facts the jury likely paid little heed to. Only when I hear the excitement in his voice, a vibrancy that stirs me, do I choose that point as one to be answered.

Other arguments in the criminal case. In the criminal case we are fighting for freedom. The life of our client, and, indeed, our own, is at stake. When the jury brings in its verdict, it is as if our necks are stretched out on the chopping block as we await the fall of the ax, or mercifully the ax will be withheld when the clerk reads the magical words of life, "Not guilty."

Of course we will argue the facts as they show innocence or as they (more often) show the failure of the state to make its case. We will remember with the jury the flaws we encountered in the state's case, the lack of proper investigative procedures, the carelessness of the officers, the fact that others could have committed the crime, the unreliability of eyewitness identification, the motivation of snitches to lie, the infamous characters that surround the prosecution as witnesses, the need of the prosecutors to convict at any price, the suggestion of behind-the-scenes shenanigans, the failure of scientific evidence, the tests that were not made, the state's experts who were mere lackeys, whatever unfair tactics were put into play by the prosecutor during the trial, the witnesses that should have been called but were not, the evidence that should have been preserved and presented and was not, the failure of the state to prosecute the big shots instead of the easy mark—the powerless defendant, the absense of the proof on each element of the crime, including the failure to prove a criminal intent, the interest of others in using the criminal processes against the defendant for their personal gain, and whatever other facts and issues exist that should be argued. All of these questions point to the defendant's innocence, the lack of sufficient evidence to prove his guilt beyond a reasonable doubt, or, indeed, the injustice of finding the defendant guilty under the circumstances of the case—something called jury nullification, which we shall consider in a moment.

Arguing reasonable doubt and the presumption of innocence. All of us are presumed innocent, or so the old saw goes. But once the charges have been leveled and made public we are *presumed guilty*. The human brain is incapable of graciously bestowing on the accused the presumption of innocence. We have been fooled too often. Corruption among the most respected members of our community is rife. Poor people rob as well, but not as efficiently. Crime on and off the streets is rampant. You can't tell the innocent from the guilty by looking at them. They can all look innocent. Then the realization begins to sink in: They look innocent, act innocent, are presumed innocent, but they are guilty. If they weren't guilty, why would the prosecutor charge them? Where there's smoke there must be fire. So much for the presumption of innocence!

But if at the beginning of the trial the jury sees Jimmy as probably guilty, the presumption of innocence becomes merely a meaningless technicality, leaving Jimmy with the burden of proving his innocence or going to prison (or perhaps the death house).

Yet under our law the defendant is not required to prove anything. The total burden of proving him guilty rests with the state. So what do we do when we know that the jurors do not, cannot and will not see our client as innocent from the start? I often discuss this phenomenon with the jurors during *voir dire*. The discussion might go like this:

"Do we really believe that Jimmy is innocent?" I wait for an answer. Not one of the prospective jurors raises a hand. I might then turn to one of the jurors. "Mr. Abernathy, do you believe Jimmy is innocent?"

"I don't know."

"Of course, you are right. You don't know. But the law says that Jimmy is presumed innocent. What does that mean to you?"

"It means that we should see him as innocent."

"But in our hearts we think he is probably guilty, don't we? I mean, that's what I thought when his file was handed to me, and I was assigned his defense. This man is just another one of those criminals who now wants us to think he is innocent."

"I don't know."

"When we are told to presume Jimmy innocent, we are simply being told by the judge that his being charged here with these crimes means nothing about whether he is guilty or innocent. It means that the prosecutor has to *prove* his guilt because he is presumed innocent. How will we remember that during the trial?"

"We'll just have to remind ourselves, I guess."

"Yes. Thank you, Mr. Abernathy. And I will try to remind us as well."

Simple visual aids are often more effective in making a point than a wheelbarrow full of words dumped on the jurors. In the final argument I may go to the blackboard or flip chart and draw a line: Then on the line I may insert a middle point on the line. I say to the jury, "This is where the trial begins. No evidence had been given to you at this point. Now, this is where the prosecution must go to prove Jimmy guilty beyond a reasonable doubt." (I then mark the far right end of the line labeled GUILTY BEYOND A REASONABLE DOUBT.) "And this is where Jimmy is throughout the trial—even to the moment you go into the jury room to deliberate." (I mark the far left end of the line labeled PRESUMED INNOCENT.)

Presumed Innocent   Trial Begins   Guilty Beyond a Reasonable Doubt

"Now, folks, the prosecutor's proof must be so clear, so convincing, that his proof has caused each of us to move the place where Jimmy is, presumed innocent, from the far left of this line to the far right of this line. Even now Jimmy still sits here presumed innocent. The evidence of the prosecution has come and gone. It has been examined and cross-examined. And after these many days of your patient listening and consideration, nothing has budged Jimmy from the safe place where the law places him and each of us who may be charged with a crime—that is, he was presumed innocent to begin with, and he is still presumed innocent because the prosecution's evidence has failed." At this point I may begin my dissection of the state's case.

And this business of reasonable doubt—the defendant says the state must prove every element of the crime charged beyond a reasonable doubt. But what is reasonable doubt?

That which is reasonable doubt to the accused is just so much lawyer talk to the prosecution. The prosecution sees reasonable doubt as a stew of unreasonable arguments meant to mislead the jury from its bounded duty to convict. To the defense, reasonable doubt is the safeguard provided every citizen to protect against the conviction of the innocent. Jurors may have their doubts, all right. There may be those arguments revealing that every crack in the case has not been sealed shut. But what if the juror embraces a reasonable doubt argument and a guilty man is freed to commit a similar crime again? What if a serial killer has been created by the juror's vote for acquittal based on reasonable doubt?

The defense of reasonable doubt is more readily accepted by the jury when the crime is one of passion, where the likelihood of a repeat performance is not real, where there is sympathy for the accused, where the alleged crime was morally justifiable or humanly understandable—the wife, for instance, who is charged with murdering an abusive husband; the husband who is charged with having beaten up a person who has intruded into the sanctity of his marriage; the accused who is charged with murdering someone who was morally depraved. But beware the argument of reasonable doubt where the accused may be a vicious murderer.

Jurors will not chance their own potential guilt for turning a killer or a rapist loose. There may have been reasonable doubt, all right, but under those circumstances reasonable doubt is merely an argument. And like all arguments, it can be rationalized into oblivion.

In such cases, perhaps the argument of reasonable doubt would sound like this:

"I wonder why our founders protected us with reasonable doubt? Why isn't it enough that we should trust the prosecutors who sit so comfortably over there? They are honorable men and women. Why should we demand that they prove this case beyond a reasonable doubt?

"I suppose lawyers in the days when our Constitution was formed were as zealous as we lawyers are today. Prosecutors have their jobs. And they have their personal agendas. They want to win, as do we. But winning for them is quite different than for us. Winning for them is just another victory in long careers of countless victories. If they win they can go home tonight to the comfort of their family and their home and the security of the law protecting them. But if we lose, Jimmy goes back to a lonely concrete wall where his companion is his terror of what will become of him, of his family, and his very life. He will go back to steel bars and foul food and evil men for company. And we, his lawyers, will go home to our own nightmares and our sense of guilt that we did not do enough to save Jimmy.

"But our founders knew from their own unhappy experience that prosecutors have all the power and that an innocent accused can never prove the negative. Few of us can ever prove our innocence. How many of you have watched the prosecutor in this case take innocent acts and turn them into evil acts? Jimmy changed clothes, not because we all change clothes for whatever reason, but, as the prosecutor insists, because he wanted to hide his identity. He didn't come home as he usually did. Sometimes we vary from our habits. But the prosecutor argues that he must have dreaded seeing the body where he left it in the middle of the living room floor. He had life insurance on his wife, as do twenty million other Americans. But in this case the prosecution will argue that Jimmy had life insurance because he wanted to profit from the murder. He sold the house. Who wants to live in a house with such horrid, bloody memories? But he sold it, according to the prosecution, because he knew he killed his wife there. No innocent act, no innocent statement, is immune from an evil connotation attributed to it by this prosecutor.

"The accused can tip his hat and say good morning to the neighbor lady and the prosecution would claim he was trying to act normal and cover up his guilt. The accused can say, 'What a beautiful day,' and the prosecutor will claim he made that remark to his secretary at the office in order to cover up

his state of mind, a guilty mind that was contemplating murder. The most innocent of acts are all subject to an evil interpretation by the prosecutorial
mind.

"But the way the prosecutor sees things tells us more about the prosecutor
than the defendant. And our founders knew this. As a consequence, proof beyond a reasonable doubt became a part of our system of justice. The Constitution says prove your case, Mr. Prosecutor. Do not make those clever
arguments by which you turn innocent conduct into premeditated malicious-
ness. Prove your case by hard, irrefutable facts. And prove not just one fact or
a dozen. Prove all of the facts, so no reasonable doubt remains.

"The right that is bestowed upon us, that protects us from the clever and
persuasive arguments of the prosecutor—that the state must prove its case beyond a reasonable doubt—was given to each of us. This is a right that belongs
in the family safe, if we had a safe and could put it there. It is the most precious right of all. If it is swept over lightly, if it is ignored even in part, if every
element of this case is not proven beyond a reasonable doubt, we have opened
up the family safe of each of us, yours, your children's, and their children's to
come, and it is not all right to ignore reasonable doubt—not even a little bit.
When we do that, the right is stolen, and case by case it becomes less and less
able to protect us, until we give it only lip service and innocent people are sent
to prison.

"The problem we face is an insidious one. None of us believe that we or
any of our loved ones will ever have to call upon reasonable doubt to protect
us, because none of us or our loved ones will ever be in such a situation as
Jimmy is today. We do not believe we will ever get cancer or we will ever have
a heart attack; in fact, some of us believe we will never die. If we lived every
day in fear of death to the same extent that we may fear it when faced with a
terminal illness, we could not live our lives. We are constituted as human beings to believe that the bad luck, the tragedies always happen to someone
other than ourselves. So we will never be charged with a major crime. It will
only happen to the Jimmys of this world. Not us. And we are not so careful in
protecting the sacred right of proof beyond a reasonable doubt. But remember: When we do not afford its protection to the likes of Jimmy, to the poor
and the helpless, we will find one day that that right is no longer available in its

full and beautiful power to protect *us*. When you protect Jimmy with reasonable doubt, you protect us all.

"Simply put, we cannot *guess* Jimmy into the penitentiary."

Often the defense of reasonable doubt is interpreted by the jury to mean, "Well, the prosecutor proved the bastard was guilty, all right, but the defense is saying he didn't prove it enough." But a case well proved by the prosecution can be thrown out on reasonable doubt if the jurors have prejudices or experiences of their own that mitigate against the conviction of the accused. I think of the O. J. Simpson case. To many, the case was a slam-dunk for the prosecution. Simpson was guilty of the murder of two people: his wife and the unfortunate, attending male acquaintance. But who were the *power persons* in the case—who were the jurors? They were ordinary people, mostly black, who had their own experiences with the police and the law. No doubt their experience taught them that the police do lie, that they do plant evidence, that they often can't be trusted. They saw Mark Fuhrman claim that he never said the *n* word, and likely disbelieved him as they disbelieved much of the state's case. And the prosecutors? What about them? Did they think that Marsha Clark was the kind of guide the jurors would feel comfortable with, one who would lead them through the forest of evidence and law, one they could trust? And Chris Darden—what about him? Did they see him as the token black man who was thrust into the case to appease a predominantly black jury? Possibly these issues would not have persisted with an all-white jury. But most white jurors have not experienced the police and the law in the same way that black people in Los Angeles have. Reasonable doubt, like beauty, is in the eyes of the beholder. What is reasonable doubt to some is only a specious argument to others.

The role of reasonable doubt in protecting the jurors. Jurors have rights too. We often forget that jurors want to do the just thing. Suppose a juror has to go home wondering if he or she was right in voting for conviction. The juror realizes that he or she has the power to stop the conviction, because the verdict had to be unanimous. What if the juror tosses and turns in the night, not quite sure of the evidence, not quite sure that the defendant is guilty. The juror lies there staring at the ceiling thinking, "I could have stopped this. Maybe I should have. What if the state was just too powerful? What if Jimmy didn't have a good enough lawyer and he failed to bring out the facts surrounding the lineup identification? What if the witness the state failed to call would have told the truth and Jimmy wasn't even there?"

One might argue to the jury, "The protection of reasonable doubt is not just a protection for Jimmy. It protects each of you. You are men and women with good souls and clear consciences. But what if you were pressured by the prosecution's arguments to convict Jimmy, and when you got home you began to worry about what you had done, lying awake at night concerned about your decision, your worry that you may have convicted an innocent man?

"The rule of reasonable doubt is to protect you. You have a right not to be concerned about your decision. It must be clear to you so that all worry about whether you were right has been removed by the evidence. That is why we have reasonable doubt—not only to protect the accused, but to protect you as well."

Exposing the motivations of the police and the prosecutor. As we have seen, every participant in the case possesses a need that must be filled. The judge has his needs—to be seen as fair but tough on crime, and never as one who lets a vicious criminal escape through some legal loophole. The judge has a need to satisfy his constituency. If the judge is on the federal bench he has a reputation to maintain. He has to face the criticism of the media as well as that of his friends and colleagues. And perhaps he wants to be elevated to a higher court.

The prosecutor has his needs. He wants to become governor, or a judge, or he wants to become the chief prosecutor, or he is simply a competitive person and wants to win.

The defense counsel has his reputation to protect. He can't afford many losses at the hands of a jury, or he'll never get the big case. And when he's representing an innocent accused, he must somehow save him. In any case, he must show himself to be competent, so that if his client is convicted another lawyer asking for a new trial at the time of the appeal can't claim in the public record that the defendant had incompetent counsel.

The jurors want to make certain that they have done justice, that they have not turned a guilty man loose, that they can go home and face their friends, neighbors, and fellow workers and not be embarrassed by their verdict—that some smart defense attorney hasn't pulled the wool over their eyes.

That which is left after all of the participants have fulfilled their personal needs is what remains for the defendant. The defendant wants his freedom, but he can't have it until everyone else has first satisfied their needs. That's why we see so many plea agreements. The prosecutor overcharges in nearly every case. The defendant may be facing, say, fifty years in prison. The prosecutor offers to accept a plea to a lesser crime that carries ten. This was probably the crime the prosecutor should have charged in the first place. The defendant is afraid. If his lawyer (often an overworked public defender) can't win before a jury, the defendant will go to prison for the rest of his natural life. If he accepts the plea, maybe he can get out in five to seven years. His lawyer is afraid as well. If his client will accept a plea agreement, then he doesn't have to risk the total loss of the case. The prosecutor is satisfied because he has another conviction. The judge is satisfied because the prosecutor is happy and will not use his office to criticize the judge. What's left is what the defendant gets—and most often it's not justice.

I remember a case I defended in which the young man accused of murder was a pitiful-looking smallish kid who wore thick glasses and whose eyes were as large as half dollars. He was charged with having stabbed a pretty female worker to death. But there were other legitimate suspects for the crime. The prosecutor was a tall, skinny man who displayed a protuberant hawklike nose. In my final argument to the jury I referred to my client, the boy, as the sparrow. I walked back from the jurors to where the boy was seated and looked at my helpless-looking client. "The hawk wants the sparrow!" I said. "The hawk is hungry for him, yearns for him, has spent these many weeks trying to sink his talons into him. Well, the time has come." I walked over to the prosecutor's table and took him in with a gesture. "Let the hawk have the sparrow!" I shouted. I saw some of the jurors shake their heads, no. I went on to say that the police had to solve the case. It was easier for the police to charge this little sparrow than for them to do a thorough investigation and come up with the guilty party. The heroes would be the jurors who were empowered to save the boy. And they did.

In my defense of Randy Weaver at Ruby Ridge, the interest of the government was to cover up its own crimes, the crime of murdering an innocent boy, his dog, and his mother, who was standing at the door with her baby in her arms when she was shot by a government sniper. The FBI and the federal marshals were out of control. They abused their power, and again the jurors would be the heroes who would save an innocent man, but only after the venal conduct of the government had become the centerpiece of the defense.

The question is always, why did the state or the federal government choose this person to charge with these crimes? The answer is often vested in the needs of the prosecutor or the law enforcement agency. In my defense of Imelda Marcos, the former first lady of the Philippines, the need of the government was very clear. The District Attorney in New York, the now-famous Rudolph Giuliani, had written a letter to the State Department guaranteeing the conviction of Mrs. Marcos. Her husband was dead, and the new regime in the Philippines would not permit Mrs. Marcos to return her husband's body to his homeland. The case was about international politics—the need of the United States to foster a favorable relationship with a country where we maintained an important military base. She had been charged with scores of crimes that she had not committed. Out of the many witnesses who testified over the months-long trial, not one could claim they had ever seen her commit a single wrong. But when the jury understood the reason she had been selected for these charges the jury forthwith acquitted her. (Who else was there to charge? Her husband was dead and obviously couldn't be brought to trial.)

Sometimes the motivation of the prosecutors is to quell public outcry when, indeed, to do so against a particular defendant may be unjust. But if we are representing an innocent defendant we need to discover why the prosecution is trying to convict an innocent accused.

In Chicago I represented a black man who, along with two other black men, was charged with the rape of a young woman and the murder of both her and her boyfriend. All three men were convicted and my client received the death penalty and languished on death row for eighteen years, an innocent man. I got into the case after he had been released from prison and absolved of the murders through DNA. I sued Cook County for this young man's wrongful imprisonment, and the county, on the edge of trial, settled the case for a very substantial sum.

In the murder trial the evidence against these men had been thin and perjured. I believed the police knew all along that the case was wrong, and the prosecutors must have known it as well. There seemed to be an attitude prevalent in those days among the police—maybe we did get the wrong kids, maybe they were innocent. But what difference did it make? If they weren't guilty of this crime, they were guilty of other crimes that they got away with, or crimes that they would surely commit in the future. It was just one more black kid off the streets. So, what was all the crying about? In that case, the murder and rape of the white girl, and the murder of her white boyfriend had caused a furor in the city. The cops had to find an answer, and quickly. They did, with the testimony of a young black woman whom they forced to give perjured testimony against the young men the state had fingered.

Even when the accused may have committed the murder, the question is, why does the state seek the death penalty? If the public were against the death penalty the prosecutors, also astute politicians, would not seek it. Why are some low-level corporate renegades charged with crimes while the top dogs go free? Why does the prosecution choose this defendant, but fail to charge others who are guilty of even worse crimes? The motivation for the prosecution's decisions in any given case needs to be carefully examined and, if appropriate, fully revealed.

Shotgun charges. Rarely do we see cases today in which the indictment is but a single charge. In the case of money crimes, each alleged embezzlement or each fraud is alleged as a separate crime. We see cases that include scores of charges, each of which carry many years of penitentiary time, so that if the accused were convicted of each and were required to serve the time for each he would be as old as Methuselah by the time he became eligible for parole.

The prosecutor knows that his proof may fail on one charge, but maybe he'll get the accused on another. He also knows that the accused faces the almost impossible task of defending himself not just in one case, but in many cases which are combined for a single trial. Facing such an overwhelming challenge is like being shot at with a shotgun loaded with buckshot. If the shooter doesn't get you with one of the buckshots, he'll get you with another. And any one of the pellets can kill you. Facing this nearly impossible challenge to survive, many an innocent person has pled guilty to one charge, in order to be saved from a conviction of many—better that an innocent man spend, say, five years in the pen than a lifetime.

I see prosecutors and defense attorneys trading on the lives of the human beings who are dragged before them as if they were commodities. Many are guilty of crimes, yes. But these citizens were guaranteed the right of due process under our Constitution. The trick of prosecutors has been to find lawful ways to deprive the defendant of his right to a fair trial. The method is overcharging, either by charging a defendant with a crime more serious than the one he has committed, such as charging him with an assault with a deadly weapon (the deadly weapon being the boxer's fist as an example), rather than a simple assault and battery, murder instead of manslaughter, or charging the defendant with many crimes that stem from a set of single misdeeds. A defendant has a right to a trial by jury on, say, a charge of manslaughter, something that might carry ten to twenty years. But he is deprived of that right, forced by his fear of a conviction of the more serious charge of murder, which could land him in the penitentiary for life, so he pleads guilty to manslaughter. The prosecutor wins another, without even a trial. The defendant is deprived of his right to be tried on the only just charge that could have been brought against him. This injustice is a standard, daily occurrence in every community in America.

Suppose that the defendant is a brave person, one braver than most of us. Suppose he believes he is not guilty of the crime and that he'd rather spend long years in prison, yes, even the rest of his life, than to plead guilty to a crime he did not commit. The final argument might sound like this:

"I think of Jimmy who sits here silent, afraid, his life out there as a target. The prosecutor has leveled his shotgun at him. The prosecutor's gun is loaded with buckshot. He doesn't have to be a very good shot to hit Jimmy with a shotgun. Anybody can hit you with at least one deadly pellet of buckshot from a shotgun. One pellet can kill you as easily as a dozen, yes, one charge can convict Jimmy as easily as the twenty charges that the prosecutor has leveled here. The prosecutor knows what he's doing. He understands that he has a weak case. That's why he's shooting at Jimmy with a shotgun loaded with buckshot.

"What is the strategy of the prosecutor? He knows that jurors are reasonable people. He knows that a juror will say, 'Well, yes, it's obvious that Jimmy hasn't committed every crime with which he has been charged, but he must be guilty of something.' The prosecutor knows that some of you will say this is a totally unjust case—that it should never have been brought. He had the same facts and evidence that you as jurors have. But the prosecutor also knows that there may be some jurors who will argue that out of the twenty charges he must be guilty of at least one. Maybe more. And he knows that in the jury room you as reasonable people may argue and argue until, at last, as reasonable people, someone will say, 'Let's compromise. Let's find him guilty of one and let the rest go.' Then everyone will be happy. Everyone except an innocent man who will be as dead with that one pellet that he's been hit with as if he'd been hit with all of them.

"That is the insidious dynamic of this case. The prosecutor knows that reasonable people like to compromise. We have been taught to compromise from our earliest years. Do not fight. Don't be so stubborn. Listen to the other side and compromise. This is what we do. And Mr. Prosecutor knows that. He goes home tonight while you deliberate, and he relaxes in front of his fireplace and has a nice dinner with his wife and family, and he's not worried about the outcome of this case, because he knows that you, the jury, reasonable people, will compromise, that you will allow at least one pellet from his shotgun charge to strike Jimmy, that you'll find him guilty of at least one charge, and that will satisfy Mr. Prosecutor, because he has convicted Jimmy and made a criminal of him forever, and Mr. Prosecutor has won yet another case—another notch on his gun.

"In the meantime Jimmy will be a criminal and he will always be a criminal. He will always be smeared with the taint and stink of being a felon. His wife will always be living with a criminal, should he ever get out of prison, and his children will always have a criminal for a father."

Arguing punishment. As we've already seen, in all but a death penalty case, the law in most states prohibits a defense attorney from mentioning the punishment the defendant will face. Obviously, the law is attempting to hide from the jury the consequences of its acts. People who are called upon to make decisions that will affect the life of another forever ought to be fully informed as to the consequences of their decisions. Don't we put people in prison who have failed to consider the consequences of *their* acts?

We might try to let the jury in on the secret—what will happen to the defendant if he is found guilty. Objections to our attempt will likely be sustained, but it seems to be a morally proper argument and unless we try we have already given the opponent that victory. The attempt is a no-lose proposition— if we try to make the argument and are prevented from doing so, we are just where we would be if we hadn't tried in the first place. On the other hand, we just might be successful.

I attempt to discuss punishment not directly, not saying, "The defendant will go to the pen for twenty years if he is found guilty," but discussing the matter in a more oblique way. If my effort is wrong, the prosecutor can object and the judge can rule so as to prevent a further discussion of penalty. Perhaps this is what I will say:

"I can see Jimmy now. The case is over and the sheriff puts the shackles around his legs and the cuffs on his hands and he is dragged back to his cell, a convicted criminal. One word has changed his life. One word! The word is 'guilty.' I go to him in his cell. He can hardly speak. I can hear him say, 'Well, Mr. Spence, you did pretty good for me. You saved me from all but that one charge. You won nineteen but you lost just one. That's pretty good.' But what he hasn't said is, 'I will suffer as much from one guilty charge as from twenty. I will be away from my family as long with one guilty charge as with twenty. Why didn't you tell the jury that?' And so I have told you that. One buckshot kills as surely as twenty.

"What are the consequences of finding him guilty of a single charge? I am not permitted to tell you the years he will rot in the penitentiary. The law does not permit me to do so. But I can tell you that Jimmy will never take his boy fishing. Perhaps not even a grandchild. He will never celebrate his twentieth wedding anniversary with his wife. Will she be there when he gets out? I would bet on it, but both she and their little boy are innocent of any crime, as is Jimmy. And this good woman and their child will be punished as surely as if they had been a part of this alleged scheme—for twenty years or more."

Vouching for our client's innocence. Many courts do not permit the defense attorney to argue that in the attorney's opinion his client is innocent. It is a prohibition against *vouching* for the innocence of one's client. Here again, one wonders why? If his client is innocent, why can't the defense attorney give his opinion on the matter by saying, "I believe my client is innocent" as well as the prosecutor who says, "I believe the defendant is guilty?"

But we can argue that "the evidence establishes that this defendant is innocent." That is argument, not vouching. A closer issue is when we say "the defendant is innocent," or we speak of "an innocent client," which can be interpreted as merely implying that the evidence establishes that the defendant is innocent. Such statements fall just short of vouching, but when we represent an innocent client we need to get as close to the truth of our case as we can.

The power of a single juror. We must not forget that a jury is composed of individuals. In any group there will be leaders and there will be followers. If we have not been elegantly successful in our jury selection, there may be a juror or two who will lead the rest over the cliff. Each of us, jurors or not, must learn to appreciate our own power. No one has power over us. The jailer may hold the key, our employer our opportunity to advance, the police on the street the power to direct us where we travel, but the ultimate power over each of us is the power we wield over ourselves. A juror's vote is his power. It belongs to him or her exclusively. In a criminal case perhaps that is the most important power in the courtroom. But jurors need to understand their power before they can use it. Let me explain as I might to the jury.

"I hear all the time that I am only one person. I don't have any power. How can I change anything? We have grown up believing that the power over our lives is vested in others, in our parents, our teachers, the boss, the politicians—everyone has power, but we do not. It is a sort of insidious robbery of our personhood, because each of us has great power, not only over our own lives, but over the lives of others. And I can think of no better example of the power of the individual in America than one who serves on a jury.

"The verdict here must be unanimous. Each of you must agree to send Jimmy away. That is a huge power vested in each of you—each of you—because when any one of you say, no, I do not agree to send Jimmy away, then that will stop it. Any one of you can stop it. To put it another way, what happens to Jimmy is your *personal* responsibility—not the jury's responsibility as a whole, but the responsibility of each of you, individually, as jurors.

"I know we work in groups. We do not want to stand alone. We do not want to be the odd person, the troublemaker, the one who does not follow. On the other hand, each of us has our own individual power. It is for us to decide how to use it. Of course, it is your duty, as the court will instruct you, to listen to the position of your fellow jurors, but you are not required under the law to relinquish your honest conviction. It is yours. Your power, your right, your duty to determine this case for yourself. Each of you can stand alone if you believe you are right. And if you do it is your duty to do so.

"You have told me you would do so when you were chosen as jurors. Each of you told me that if you believed Jimmy was innocent, or that the proof of the state fell short, you had the courage to stand alone. I asked you that during jury selection because it is the most important power any citizen in America has, to determine the fate of another's life.

"It is for this reason that Jimmy is in your hands—not in the hands of all of you, but in the hands of *each* of you. He is yours to do with as justice demands of you. You have the power, each of you, a power separate from anyone else's power. Each of you have more power than the prosecutor. Yes, each of you have even more power than the judge. The judge cannot dispose of Jimmy or free him until each of you decides first. Jimmy is the one who is powerless. He is in your hands, each of your hands."

The jurors' promise not to pressure each other. I am always afraid of the browbeating juror who forces one of lesser strength to submit to his position. So, we might say to the jury:

"One of the beautiful things about the American jury system is that it honors each of you as individuals. Although you are a member of a group, you are each respected individually. Some of you may be more outspoken, more assertive, even more argumentative than others. We would expect that, would we not? But the mere fact that some may be more expressive does not mean that they have more power. For each of you has the same power, the power to save Jimmy.

"Because the law respects each of you as individuals, I know that each of you will respect the right of your fellow jurors to their opinion. It is alright to present your ideas. You should. But it is not alright to put undue pressure on your fellow jurors to agree with you. You have told me when you were chosen that as a juror you will respect the opinions of other jurors, even if they do not comport with your own, and more important, that you will protect the right of any juror to disagree with the majority. And we are grateful to you for doing just that."

The defendant has failed to take the stand. I have said I rarely put the defendant on the stand in the criminal case. And I will tell the jury why.

"Folks, we know that Jimmy is not required under the law to take the stand and to testify on his own behalf. And we know the reason. The Constitution of the United States protects those who have been charged with a crime from having to testify. The law further says the fact that Jimmy has not testified will not be considered by you in any way, that you will not take that into account in determining Jimmy's guilt or innocence.

"Why did our founders give us that protection? Why shouldn't a person who is charged with a crime, and who is innocent, not want to take the stand and testify? I would want to. Perhaps you would too. But our founders knew that something happens to a person who is charged with a crime. It is a horror, a living horror to be charged and to be innocent. He cannot defend himself. He must cry out his innocence. But if he protests too much he will be seen as guilty. If he gets angry he may be seen as guilty. If he forgets a fact under the heat of this trial he may be seen as guilty. People often do not believe the accused who testifies. They think he may not only be guilty as charged, but a liar as well—someone who will take an oath and perjure himself to escape conviction. Nothing that he says on this witness stand can ever acquit him, and our founders knew this.

"Moreover, the defendant is but a lay person. He is not skilled in dealing with the likes of Mr. Prosecutor over there, who would love to bombard him with those clever questions that can confuse and confound and make the most innocent person look guilty. How could Jimmy, with an eighth-grade education, ever compete with this prosecutor who is skilled in this business of cross-examination? It's for these reasons that our founders have protected us. I have decided as his lawyer that it is best for Jimmy to let me speak for him as best I can. At least the contest will then be fair."

And I might add in the appropriate case: "And in any event, why should Jimmy testify when the state has failed so miserably to prove its case? What is there for him to rebut? One cannot rebut the state's guesses and its assumptions that are based solely on circumstances. No one could. And Mr. Prosecutor sits over there, eager as a cat on a mouse to get Jimmy on the stand so that when Jimmy gets confused, or forgets, or gets angry at his harassment you will believe Jimmy is guilty. I am not going to give Mr. Prosecutor the opportunity to try to make a case out of Jimmy when he has none."

Jury nullification. We often hear people wonder about jury nullification, that is, the power of the jury to nullify the law and to return a verdict that is just, despite the law. Jury nullification was a part of our system until judges began to realize that jurors too often for the judges' liking returned verdicts in favor of defendants who were charged with crimes under unfair laws. Today the courts or legislatures in nearly every state have nullified jury nullification, despite the constitutions of many states that provide for it. How do we talk about jury nullification when that right has been stripped from juries? One might discuss the issue in the following way:

"The purpose of the law is to do justice. The laws of this country are supposedly designed to provide justice to the people. But what if the law, as applied, does not do justice? What then do we do? What do we do in such a case?

"Jurors are judges. You judge the facts, the judge judges the law. But facts are meaningless if the law is unjust. The law was not intended to punish innocent people. Sometimes the law does not fit the facts. Sometimes the law, if applied, will result in a terrible injustice. You cannot change the law. You will be instructed by his honor that you must follow the law. Yet, in the end it is in your power, and yours alone, to do justice."

This is our last chance to speak to you. In all but a few jurisdictions in this country the prosecution has the right to close—the right to the last argument. Here is what we might say to the jury about that:

"When I sit down, Mr. Prosecutor has the right to the last argument. I must remain silent. You will hear nothing from me again on this case. My lips will be sealed by the law. The logic of the law, if it is logical, is that, since the burden of proof rests with the prosecution, the prosecution should be give the last opportunity to convince you, to rebut what we have said in our defense, and leave you, the jury, with the words of the prosecutor ringing in your ears.

"That is the law. We cannot change it. As the prosecutor argues, I must remain silent and you will see me squirm. I will not be squirming because of what he says, but because I cannot get up and point out the fallacy of what he says. I have only one comfort, and that is your good, sound, honest memory of what took place here. And I know you will be fair. So here is what I ask of you: When you hear the prosecutor's close, know that I could answer every point he raises. Every one. But instead of me answering, you can answer for me when you go into the jury room. With the belief that you will do just that, I will feel more comfortable remaining silent as Mr. Prosecutor hurls his last word."

Charisma and other considerations. We do not speak to each other in the same way that we speak to the jury. An effective closing argument can be made in a conversational tone, but the excitement of the case, the justice that begs for attention, the emotional need for retribution and vindication call upon us to speak with all of the genuine power we can muster. The final argument should not be seen as a performance. Yet it becomes a performance, and, as such, it is rooted in truth and sincerity. Indeed we must perform.

Charisma is the controlled transfer of raw emotion. It is getting in touch with one's own molten center and permitting it to come forth in a controlled eruption that touches the listener and passes on its inimitable heat.

One cannot speak in any convincing way about falling in love without first having experienced it. Two people in love cannot experience it without the transfer of the emotion between them. So it is with the performance on the stage or in the courtroom, before the jury or in the boardroom. Nothing happens until the raw emotion is somehow first listened to and felt by the speaker, and thereafter transferred to the listeners.

The performance of the final argument permits us to tap into an area of creativity that is not available to us when we speak one-on-one to our friends or to our wives and children at the dinner table. We do not perform for them. The dramatic is not the tone people adopt in speaking to each other. The dramatic is acceptable on the stage, but it is not appreciated in everyday conversation. In the courtroom the theatrics must be real. The presentation must be honest. But it will not flow over a cup of coffee. At last, this business of effective oration is in part the product of charisma.

First, let us again remember that our heads have been put into strenuous training from almost the moment we could say our first words. Think of it this way: Suppose that at about the age of two our parents put us into rigorous, continuous body-building workouts. By the time we get to kindergarten we could press fifty pounds, and the training goes on for year after strenuous year, until, by the time we get out of college, we could lift nearly a thousand pounds. But we couldn't run even a block. We couldn't dance. We couldn't even skip and hop. About all we could do is to trudge along carrying a monstrous body, flex our muscles, and lift those prodigious weights.

So our minds likewise have been put into training from the time we were old enough to begin counting. The focus of our training has been mental exercise. We learn that logic, reasoning, and thinking, always thinking, are the keys to success. We are told not to engage in that "touchy-feely stuff." We believe that those who are sensitive, creative—those who are spiritual—are somehow acceptable misfits. We endure them but we do not deeply respect them. Most often they do not make large sums of money. They are not a part of a thinking, intellectual society. We most respect those who have a powerful, measurable intellect.

No college offers courses on how to feel. Academia is chiefly brain muscle. To weep or to explode in joy are not the end result of a college education. We build the muscles of the mind so powerfully that there is no room for the tiny, atrophied creative and emotional spaces in our makeup. We cannot sing. We cannot paint a picture. We cannot write a poem. We cannot hear the early morning song of a bird and recognize its attachment to heaven. We are crippled by the muscles of the mind.

But as we have learned, justice cannot be defined. It is not the product of a mathematical formula. When we have experienced justice we feel it. When it has been taken from us we also feel it—deeply. Justice may not be understood as a conventional feeling such as pain, or fear, or joy, or sorrow, but justice can be understood only on a feeling level. If we have received it we may experience peace or a sense of satisfaction. If we have not, we may feel anger or pain. We can argue all day about what is or is not justice. We can exercise the muscles of the mind until they collapse. We can cite the law, or old, moldy precedent, and drown ourselves in the intellectual marathons of scholars, but, at last, justice is nothing more than a feeling. That being so, how can we argue for justice without having a deep, soul-deep, understanding of how it feels to be deprived of it?

Charisma is the transference of the passion we feel to those with whom we communicate. We can exhibit no charisma if our communication is anchored in the intellect where it becomes frozen and shriveled like a pansy in a snowstorm. Charisma does not emerge from the mind. It rises up out of our passion. Passion is not a mental exercise. Passion is an unleashing from the emotional core. And it is difficult for us to experience passion when our emotional core is buried beneath the rock-hard iceberg of the disciplined mind.

I am not arguing that we ought not use our minds or that we ought to scoff at intelligence. I am saying that to be real, to be whole, to become a person, we must be open to the heart as well as the mind. To many, especially lawyers, any dealing with heart stuff is frightening. Where might it lead one? One might care or love, and that leads only to hurt. One might weep, and that leads only to shame. One might show anger appropriately, and that leads only to rejection. Emotions, we have been taught, get in the way of reason. But as we have seen, reason is the slave of emotion. We make our decisions on an emotional basis of one kind or another and end up supporting the decision with reason. Although we have been trained otherwise, every decision we make is first made in the gut and then shored up with reason.

I have said that charisma is derived from passion. Without passion we are shooting blanks, as it were. Our passion comes from outrage, outrage that our client has been injured, killed, improperly charged, or deprived of human respect. Charisma can also come out of love and understanding, out of caring, and out of the faint joy of hope. It can be spiritual, but it is always directly connected to the emotional core.

Unless we have a passion for justice there can be no justice. Unleashing our passion is the power we call charisma, a power that is contagious, that has moved us first and that surges on to move an audience, a jury, a customer, or a friend. I see charisma as being located within my heart area, as if it is contained within a large internal bowl. When I speak out of my passion I sense that I have inserted a tube into the heart's bowl, and that the passion I feel is transferred through the tube, up into the throat. The throat opens, and the power escapes through my lips and at last begins to fill the emotional container of my audience. That transference is the dynamic of charisma. But it starts with us. Without our own bowl filled with passion, our own caring and outrage, indeed, our love and understanding, there can be no charisma, for there is nothing to transfer.

Eye contact. So we are about to make our final argument to the jury. To whom do we make this argument? We refer to those twelve people as "the jury." But, remember again, they are individuals. Each has an immense power. Each can vote against us. Each can become our ally in the jury room. Each can save us. And none must be passed over or ignored.

On any jury there will be those individuals with whom we feel most comfortable and those with whom we feel more distant. So it is in every group of people. You can be sure that the mirror is at work here. If we feel distant to Mrs. Smith on the jury, it is very likely that she has the same feeling toward us. And we can very easily alienate her, because we are not going to speak as readily to her as to the other jurors who have shown their openness toward us.

271

But if we do not talk specifically to each juror, the juror who has been by-passed will feel left out. And that juror will resent us. We must spend equal time talking directly to each juror, not in the order of their seating, but randomly. Eye contact is the way we talk to the juror personally. I see lawyers skimming the jury panel with their eyes as they talk. That lawyer has, in fact, refused to become personal with anyone. And the jury will refuse to be very open to him. We must speak to each juror. Generally I speak to a juror until I feel it is time to move on. Sometimes my discussion with the juror will last as long as thirty seconds, before I decide to speak to the next juror. Absent such eye contact that is combined with the completion of a thought (or at least a sentence) we will have missed one of the most important opportunities to convince our jury, because no juror is likely to be convinced by the lawyer who doesn't care enough about the juror to spend some personal time with him or her.

What shall we wear? Everything we wear makes a statement. I know lawyers who wear the finest suits, the most expensive shirts, with those embroidered initials on their cuffs and diamond-studded cuff links. I see them parade in front of the jury in alligator shoes and pretty silk handkerchiefs in their suit pockets that match their ties. The statement is that I am fancy. I am wealthy. I am a dandy.

I see lawyers who come into court with their shoes scuffed, their shirt collar curled up on the ends, and their pants puffed out at the knees. And the statement is that I am careless and have little responsibility—at least for myself—and if I have none for myself, how can I be trusted to have any for anyone else?

I have often been seen on television in a fringed buckskin jacket. But the courtroom is a different arena. One should wear clothes that call as little attention as possible to the wearer. We are not models. Our garb should be plain, simple, neat, and inconspicuous. I usually wear a dark jacket, perhaps navy blue, and gray trousers. My only variance from my rule of dress is that I wear plain black boots because they are historically a part of me, and it would be uncomfortable for me to wear any other footwear.

I am not a fashion expert by any means. For women, their dress should be simple, with little or no jewelry, the skirts should not be tight fitting or short. A lot of leg and belly may be in style on the street and in the cocktail lounge, but it creates problems in the courtroom. Any attention that is contrary to the business at hand, a statement that says, "Look how sexy I am," instead of "Look how professional I am, how reliable, how trustworthy," will send the wrong message.

Some years ago I was trying a case in New Mexico for the family of a young man who died on the operating table as the result of the negligence of the anesthesiologist. I thought I had tried a compelling case and that my final argument had been powerful. I expected the jury to return a sizable verdict for my clients in short order. But the jury was out for many hours. The jurors did, in fact, return a record verdict. But I wondered why it had taken them so long.

I had the opportunity to talk to one of the jurors later. He said, "Well, Mr. Spence, one of the jurors noticed your Rolex watch." So what? I thought. Like many tourists who have been in Hong Kong, I bought a Rolex, but the model I chose was an unpretentious sports model in stainless steel. "Why would that make any difference to the juror?" I asked. "Well, because," the juror said, "you present yourself as a simple country lawyer. You drive to court in an old pickup truck. And here you are wearing an expensive Rolex watch. The juror wanted to know, who is this guy anyway? Is he real? Is he to be trusted? Things don't match up here." That was a lesson to me. We ought to be consistent in who we are. A guy who drives an old pickup truck and wears plain clothes in the courtroom ought not be wearing a Rolex. And I haven't since then. Credibility is often founded or lost on small things.

The sex thing. I am not against sex or being sexy. Its energy is the stuff of life, and life without it would be like biscuits without gravy, or pop without fizz, or something like that. But in the courtroom the sex thing has to go. I admit that as a younger lawyer I often tried to seat a handsome-looking woman on the jury, with the rationalization that, since I had to talk to a jury for many days, I might as well have the pleasure of looking at some comely lass. But the rest of the jurors are quite aware of what's going on. That an attorney might give more attention in the direction of the pretty one, that, indeed, he might forget himself and be guilty of showing off a bit, like a puffing sage grouse strutting his stuff in rutting season, is a matter that is not missed by the other jurors. Their resentment sets in immediately. And it can be costly.

Once, as a younger lawyer at the peak of my superciliousness, I decided to try my case to an all-woman jury. In one way or another I was able to get all of the men off the jury except one. I found out later that in the jury room the contest became one between me and the one man on the jury, a sort of revisit to the primeval. I suspect, without knowing, that that contest cost my client many thousands. The fight was not with the opposing counsel, but with that one male juror—a contest for dominance over the eleven females. The center of the conflict should have been with my opponent and his unjust case. The sex thing in the courtroom hurls us back into primal places that are usually at odds with justice.

The nonlawyer in the boardroom, the sales room, the boss's office—closing the deal. It's time to close the deal. We've prepared and presented our case and supported it with facts and data. We've faced the opposition bravely and intelligently. We've listened and we've been heard and the time is at hand. It's now or never. Although the decision on the part of the *power person* will likely have been made even before our final pitch, we have this one last chance to prevail.

Creating the vision. At the close our attitude is one of confidence, but it is laced with a kind of joy. I feel it all the time when a salesperson is painting his vision for me. He seems happy. He sees the beauty of the automobile he wants to sell. He touches it fondly, lets a certain joy escape that seeps out as a smile on his face. He loves his product and his love for it is contagious. I begin to love it as well, more than before. I see me driving down the street in this beautiful machine. It makes a statement about me. I can smell its newness. I feel its soft leather caressing me. I sense a sort of happiness derived not from the car itself, but from the vision I have of driving the car, of becoming its owner, all of which is buttressed by this salesperson who continues to smile and speak on and on about the virtues of my pending decision.

My wife, Imaging, is talking about remodeling the house. There will be a cozy room where we can sit down in the evening alone and read or watch a movie. Her vision of the room is transferred to me, and I feel the joy of it, the closeness we will share. I think of it as the love room, and the first nail in the new room has not yet been driven.

Creating the vision is the ultimate calling of any who wish to close a deal, to sell the boss on a new idea, to convince a council to adopt a better approach. Whatever we want, whatever our agenda, the closing pitch is our final argument. As we have seen, we all yearn to be worthy. The vision we offer a committee is its opportunity to do good, to be remembered, to be lauded. The vision may simply be their roles as heroes of a kind, those who face the adversity of a hostile majority and nevertheless do the right thing. The vision we create for the boss may simply be seeing himself as a fair and successful businessman.

As we have seen, in business trials exist as well. When there's trouble in the business, responsibility for the trouble is unloaded on someone. The person who is the target will occupy the same position as the accused in a criminal trial, except the constitutional safeguards that protect us from the state are not usually available to the poor devil who stands to answer for some corporate failure.

As we have seen, trials in business are conducted in meetings and presentations that are sometimes stacked against the accused. The presentations are rigorously prepared. A judge presides, often the reigning officer, or a jury, sometimes a committee of vice presidents or department heads. The stakes are high. The winner may save his job, the loser may be gored with a pink slip. Fairness is not the issue. Profit is the issue. Power is the issue. The personal agendas of the company officers are the issue—securing their position up the company totem pole is the issue. Fear is the prevalent emotion, fear that is often exchanged for anger.

The agenda may deal with what the business world thinks of the corporation, the value of its stock, and the integrity and competence of its officers. Appearance may become more important than substance. Truth may become lost in deluding company smoke. In the end, the meeting, the trial and its conclusion in the corporate setting has most of the elements of a final argument. We will hear from both sides, who will make their pitches. A judgment will be made. Heads may roll.

Some last thoughts about the final argument. The final argument is not a plea for sympathy. We get sympathy from our loved ones, the priest, our friends, and a paid-for sympathy from our psychologists. The final argument is about justice. It reaches into places where we store our ethical anger. It focuses on our righteous indignation, but the argument can be delivered with compassion, with love, but always with a demand for justice.

The final argument is not only about justice, it's about those who are called upon to deliver justice. We define ourselves by the decisions we make. When a plea for justice is delivered to us as the decision maker, we either stand by our own sense of justice or we join those whose injustice brought the matter before us in the first place. We are given choices—we can seek a kinder world, a better place in which to work, a better corporate community, a society that refuses to condone profit over human life, a civilization that puts human life above all else, or we can join the unenlightened who have preceded us at the expense of justice. The final argument will at last define both those who seek justice and those who provide it.

My final argument to you. The human race from the beginning has been engaged in a terrible cosmic struggle from out of the darkness into the light. We are an infinitesimal part of it. Still, each of us, no matter how humble, no matter how lowly and seemingly powerless, has a critical part to play. We must only recognize our role. And take it on.

I've been around a long time and I've made many mistakes, both in and out of the courtroom, some of which I deeply regret. Yet without our mistakes and the pain we've suffered on their account we would have lost the opportunity to grow. So, at last, we must embrace our mistakes.

I often think of my life as a flower. One of my favorite flowers of spring is the alpine buttercup that follows the melting snow into the sunshine. In the early spring it fights its way up through the cold, hard earth. If we could reverse roles with a buttercup as we have reversed roles so often during this adventure, what might we discover? We become this tender, whitish-yellow shoot. It hasn't touched the sun yet. The green is yet to come. The tender shoot pushes up through this cold, hard earth and—behold!—this year's plant is born. But, from the moment it first peeps above the surface of the ground it is subject to all the dangers and injury that can befall anything alive and growing.

The old elk comes wandering along and steps on the tender shoot and smashes it down. Yet the shoot pushes back up. The hungry chipmunk discovers it and bites off its tender delicacy. Still out of its reservoir of power the buttercup once again pushes up. There seems to be a magical energy in its roots that causes it to struggle toward the sun despite the adversities that attack it. Then one day it bursts into a tight, light yellow bud. Perhaps we understand the buttercup. Are we not budded up as tightly when we emerge from our schools and take our places in this unyielding, rigid society? Do we not complain that we can't bloom in the face of the soul cramp and heart trap we experience in this money society? Then something happens that permits us to either bloom and burst out into all of our pure golden glory or, sadly, we wither while we're still in the bud.

In these chapters I have hoped to provide for people's lawyers, as well as for people themselves, a vision of how they may more effectively present their case and win in and out of court, a vision that will permit you to launch into blooming.

I have gone through the process of blooming. But is it not the obligation of plant and man to spread its seed? That, in part, is what I have been about in these pages.

I have said that justice in America is a myth. Much too often justice is not delivered to the deserving. Much too often it is a dream, a hope, an ideal from which we are rudely awakened when our time comes to seek it. What we see is not the blindfolded Justice holding her scales, awaiting the time when right outbalances wrong, but, instead, a vision of the same woman with her back turned to us.

The failure of justice in America lies at the feet of those who are responsible to deliver it, from the politicians, the judges and lawyers, to the corporate overlords and their minions who exercise power over the daily lives of their workers. But the burden belongs to each of us as well—to the teacher who creates visions for our young and to the cop on the beat who sets an example of fairness and justice on the street. Indeed, it belongs to parents whose cautious and caring exercise of power in the family instills a respect for authority and a love of justice in their children. At last, the responsibility to seek justice also belongs to those who suffer its failure.

Many a decent citizen struggles daily before boards and commissions and in the workplace toward a betterment of their lives and those of their neighbors and fellow workers. And whenever our rights are trampled by power there will always be those who courageously step forward to fight for justice, lawyers for the people and, yes, the people themselves. Yet their goals are often stymied by their inability to communicate effectively and to present their cases in a winning way.

I join the masses of citizens of this world whose goal is to make their contribution, as trivial and parochial as it may seem, so that the space we occupy on the earth has not been wasted. It's my hope that I have provided some insights here that will touch each of you in a way special to you, guidance that will help make more of your life's struggles, from bud to bloom, winning ones, ones, in the end, that will empower you, as well as me, to spread our seeds.

Acknowledgments

I HAVE LEARNED AS MUCH about trying cases in the course of living as in the throes of courtroom wars. Among my greatest teachers is my darling, Imaging, who by her example proves that love, at last, is the most powerful energy of all.

For their gifts as teachers and friends at Trial Lawyer's College, whose contagious spirit has nourished me, I thank Joane Garcia-Colson, our visionary executive director; and our skilled psychodramatists, Don Clarkson, Katlin Larimer, John Nolte, and Kathie St. Clair, all of whom teach us to reverse roles with the world. I thank Josh Karton, our amazing drama guru, who infuses us with useful joy and passion, and the many members of our loyal and dedicated staff for their insights into the art of trials that is, at last, the art of living.

My agent, Peter Lampack, believed in this book and has engaged in his own winning wars to see it to publication and marketing, for which I am deeply grateful.

I thank John Sargent for seeing that the teachings of this book might be made available to an audience beyond the profession, to the lay public, who yearn to win the wars in their own lives. His friendship and belief in me over the years have permitted me to freely share my passions, knowledge, and ideas beyond my own parochial boundaries. I also thank George Witte for his vision for this book.

ACKNOWLEDGMENTS

I thank Mendel Peterson Jr., my dear brother, for his friendship, for his love, and for his many insights into the corporate culture.

At last I remember those great lawyers who have fought shoulder to shoulder with me in many a trial, especially my partner, Edward Moriarity, and my opponents who, because of our struggles together, have made us all better lawyers and, hopefully, better persons.

Index

About the Author

Gerry Spence has spent a lifetime representing the lost, the poor, the powerless, the voiceless, and the damned. He has tried and won many high-profile cases, including the Karen Silkwood radiation poisoning case, the defense of Randy Weaver at Ruby Ridge, the defense of Imelda Marcos, and the case brought against *Penthouse* magazine by Miss Wyoming. He has never lost a criminal case and has not lost a civil case since 1969. Spence is the founder of the nonprofit Trial Lawyer's College and is a well-known national commentator on the justice system. He is the author of fourteen previous books and is a noted photographer. He lives in Jackson Hole, Wyoming.